Discourses on the Beautiful Game

Discourses on the Beautiful Game

Leon Grunberg
&
Sunil Kukreja

Ashwin-Anoka Press
New Delhi / Kuala Lumpur

First Published - 2007

ISBN: 978-81-904750-0-6

Published by
ASHWIN-ANOKA PRESS
New Delhi / Kuala Lumpur

Branch Office
4830/24, Ansari Road, Darya Ganj
New Delhi-110002, (India)

CONTENTS

ACKNOWLEDGEMENT

The chapters in this volume, which appeared in the autumn 2006 special issue of the *International Review of Modern Sociology*, are published as part of a new collaborative effort between International Journals, Serials Publications, and Ashwin-Anoka Press. Pele is often credited for referring to football as 'the beautiful game.' This reference to football was further popularized in the musical by Andrew Lloyd Webber and Ben Elton as well as by various other publications on football. As evident by the title of this volume, we quite share Pele's sentiment about football.

We thank Emma Grunberg for her editorial assistance on earlier versions of some of the chapters in this volume, and Reggie Tison for her administrative assistance. We are also grateful to Rowman and Littlefield for permission to excerpt and reprint the chapter "The Beautiful Game and the American Exception," by Michael Veseth from his book, *Globaloney: Unraveling the Myths of Globalization* (2005). We appreciate all the support we have received in making this volume a reality.

INTRODUCTION

Leon Grunberg

1

Millions of fans around the world watch, play, and obsess about football (or soccer in the USA). For some, football is a source of enjoyment, an integral part of their leisure time. For others, it is a consuming passion that dominates their thoughts and emotions. Into this vast and some would say fertile terrain sociologists and political economists have entered and begun to dissect, analyze and interpret this global phenomenon. It is understandable for those who love the beautiful game to worry that rigorous academic research on football might lead to a disenchantment with the game; that probing too far beyond the spectacle fans see on the pitch will somehow remove the magic and mystery of the game and eliminate another way for people to escape from the humdrum travails of their 'normal' lives. I must admit to sharing some of these fears and to resisting well-meaning advice from colleagues that I begin to study the things, such as football, that give me pleasure.

Yet there is no denying the considerable developments over recent years surrounding the beautiful game. The sport has had to confront racial controversies, hooliganism, fan violence, and sectarianism. Celebrities and legends within the game have not only reshaped the image of football and footballers, they have crossed over into popular culture influencing it in multiple and unprecedented ways. At the international level, football has provided a unique window into relations between nations and various manifestations of nationalism. These and other changes associated with the world of football continue to draw the attention of social scientists.

Included in this volume are the works of scholars who, I suspect, are for the most part devotees of the game, but who also believe that football is important enough to be worthy of academic study. As readers of this book will see, the authors of the ensuing chapters address several key issues in current public and academic discourse related to football. Mellor, Crabbe and Brown examine the changing nature of fan communities as geographically local fan bases give way to global, virtual communities following particular clubs. Millward looks at how the owners and directors of elite superclubs, who share economic interests, are also furthering globalization as they deepen their links across Europe. Veseth, while acknowledging the global popularity of football, explores the exceptionalism of the USA as it continues to resist the lure of the game. And Amara demonstrates how a "friendly" football game between France and Algeria becomes an occasion for "French-Algerians" and Algerian journalists to re-assess past colonial relationships and identities. The tensions between local and national realities and global forces are well-represented in these articles. The other five chapters show that football is also afflicted by the social problems that can be found throughout our societies. Violence or "hooliganism" (Moorehouse), drug use (Malcolm and Waddington), racism (Crabbe), "bad" management practices (Bloyce and Murphy) and the obsession with celebrity (Bairner) are each examined systematically and with insight.

So does the academic study of football (and sport more generally) squeeze the joy out of the game? I don't think it does, because the experience of playing and watching tends to immerse one completely in the moment with little thought about the larger import about what one is doing. But in our more dispassionate moments it is wise to remember that football has become a multi-million dollar, global enterprise, one that can affect lives and politics as well as commerce. And making sense of such phenomena is something that social scientists do very well. I believe the contributors to this volume not only provide fascinating analyses of some of the complex realities associated with football, they also demonstrate the many creative and multifaceted ways by which social scientists shed light on our social world.

ENGLISH PROFESSIONAL FOOTBALL AND ITS COMMUNITIES

Adam Brown, Tim Crabbe and Gavin Mellor

During the past 15 years, there has been something of a love affair with professional football in England. This is manifest in the blanket media coverage which seemingly accompanies every aspect of the elite levels of the game, the increased attendances which have been enjoyed by most clubs, and the ritualised identifications with football which have come to permeate wider contemporary social formations. English professional football clubs have been regarded as sites for the expression of common identity for much of the game's history, and it could be argued that recent developments in and around the game have seen this process emphasised with renewed vigour. Football clubs now, as much as ever, embody many of the collective symbols, identifications and processes of connectivity which have long been associated with the notion of 'community'.

At the same time that 'community' connections and identities are being expressed strongly through football, the very term 'community' has itself become the focus of renewed interest within popular discourse and amongst academics, politicians and policy makers. It has become something of a 'buzz' word, wheeled out as both a lament to more certain times and as an appeal to a better future: a term which is imbued with all the richness associated with human interaction. Indeed, a 'crisis of community' has emerged in the UK and elsewhere in recent years in which policy makers have sought to blame crime and 'anti-social' behaviour, health problems, poor educational standards, and a variety of other 'social issues' on the decline of community and civic culture more generally. In this regard, the very notion of 'community' is increasingly open to debate as people reflect on what it is to be a member of a community, and what reciprocal responsibilities come with such formations. It is in this context that we have conducted a major research project entitled 'Football and its Communities' (Brown, Crabbe, Mellor, Blackshaw and Stone, 2003, 2004a, 2004b, 2006).[1] Funded by the English Football Foundation,[2] the project had a broad range of interests including: the responsibilities that football clubs have for 'fan,' 'neighbourhood' and other types of 'communities;' the impact that new football stadia have on economic and social regeneration; and the role that professional football clubs have in providing or supporting 'community services' such as health, education and community sport development. However, the project's central theoretical aim was to lead the debate over the use of the term 'community' in the context of English football. We wanted to clarify and better understand who 'football's communities' might be, and analyse how these groups can be said to constitute distinct and observable community formations.

The aim of this paper is to outline the research team's thoughts around the 'problem' of theorising football clubs' communities. In the first section, we analyse the historiography of writings on football and community to outline the traditional predominance of geographical conceptualisations of 'community' in writings on the English game. Secondly, we investigate the notions of a split between football clubs and 'their communities' in England from the 1970s, and discuss how clubs emerged with specific 'community programmes' as a result. This section also analyses the co-option of these football and community schemes by the British Government and other agencies as part of the communitarian project. Thirdly, we outline our thoughts on the contribution that mainstream contemporary social theory can make to debates around football supporter communities. Finally, the paper concludes by outlining a new analytical framework for considering the relationship between football clubs and a variety of community formations.

THE HISTORY OF FOOTBALL AND COMMUNITY

It is today seen as axiomatic that English professional football clubs have deep roots in 'their communities.' Many of today's most successful English clubs have their origins in 'community organisations' such as churches, social clubs or work's teams, and as English football clubs underwent professionalisation in the late nineteenth and early twentieth centuries, strong links between football clubs and local populations appear to have developed (see Russell, 1997). The vast majority of football clubs emerged from their formative years with names shared with towns, cities or areas of cities, and as such came to fulfil something of a representational role for large numbers of citizens from England's urban neighbourhoods.

The development of English football clubs along these lines has meant that social historians and sociologists of sport have frequently written about the historical emergence of relationships between football clubs and communities in relation to the social identity-building properties of football spectating. The eminent labour and sports historian Tony Mason, for instance, has written that football 'often contributes to an individual's sense of identity with or belonging to a group or collectivity. It can be district, village, town, city or county. It can be class, colour or country' (1988: 118). Similarly, sports historian Richard Holt (1989, 1996, 1997) has written that football clubs are historically one of the principal agents through which collective social identities are created and reinforced. He claims that football clubs are sites of representation through which people (usually men) are taught norms of behaviour, and that football teams and football 'heroes' have historically acted as exemplars of spirit and behaviour for the communities they represent. He suggests that football clubs enable communities to 'know themselves,' and in doing so help signify what differentiates one town, city, region, county, or nation from another.

To explain why football clubs emerged as sites for community representation, Holt (1989) notes that professional football developed in England at a time of rapid urbanisation and provided opportunities for expressions of common identity during a period when it was becoming more difficult to feel a sense of belonging to amorphous, ever-expanding towns and cities. In noting that of the twelve teams that formed the first English Football League in 1888 all came from towns with populations over 80,000, except for Accrington and Burnley, Holt states:

> *The massive expansion in the scale and size of urban communities in the second half of the nineteenth century created new problems of identity for their inhabitants ... In essence, football clubs provided a new focus for collective urban leisure in industrial towns and cities that were no longer integrated communities gathered around a handful of mines or mills ... These inhabitants of big cities needed a cultural expression of their urbanism which went beyond the immediate ties of kin and locality. A need for rootedness as well as excitement is what seems most evident in the behaviour of football crowds (1989: 167).*

Holt is not alone in adopting this essentially functionalist reading of the development of links between football clubs and communities. Richard Giulianotti, following Durkheim (1893), has stated that early football clubs can be understood as creating 'organic solidarity' and 'collective consciousness' within the potentially atomised urban environments that were common in England and other places by the beginning of the twentieth century (1999: 14-15). He notes the arguments of those who suggest that modernity destroyed traditional communities through industrialisation, urbanisation and rapid social/geographical mobility, and asserts that sports such as football 'may [have] repair[ed] much of this social damage by enhancing the cultural bonding and integration of disparate individuals within modern societies' (1999: 14). However, Giulianotti ultimately rejects this position and suggests that early football clubs actually had strong connections to pre-modern, 'mechanistic' types of bonding. He notes that football clubs were (usually) named after places, and produced 'the kind of affective tie to a specific locality that one finds in more traditional and localist societies' (Giulianotti, 1999: 15). According to this line of thinking, football clubs developed links with communities because they helped to sustain the close face-to-face, geographic, affective communities that were under threat during modernity. To put it another way, they helped to preserve a version of Tönnies' (1974) pre-modern *Gemeinschaft* emotional community bonds amongst people who otherwise only encountered modern *Gesellschaft* type connections.

The apparent identification of the social and emotional duties that football clubs performed for new urban communities in the late nineteenth and early twentieth centuries means that much contemporary writing on football and community is based on a fairly commonsense notion of which people actually constitute football clubs' communities. By associating the emergence of professional football with the (re)creation of geographical community ties when they were under threat from modernity, many popular and academic writers now adopt the position that football clubs' communities are principally their immediate 'geographical communities' from which they draw the majority of their support. This has led to a situation in which few distinctions have traditionally been drawn between 'geographical' and 'supporter' communities around football clubs, particularly in writings on the pre-1990s game. As sociologists and social historians worked from the assumption that football clubs' emerged functionally to satisfy geographical communities' needs for new or traditional forms of social and emotional bonding, so it followed *ipso facto* that football clubs' supporters must also be their geographical neighbours (or at least it was assumed that supporters lived in relative geographical proximity to their club). Indeed, in some historical work the impression (whether deliberate or not) is given that everybody identified with their local team, regardless of whether they were a regular, attending 'supporter' or not (see, for instance, Hill, 1996). This means that little historical (or indeed contemporary) work has been conducted on the specific types of communities that football supporters have constituted. It has simply been assumed that supporter communities have been synonymous with geographical communities in the context of football for much of the game's history, and that supporters' relations with football clubs have historically been based on a need to maintain and/or recreate existing geographical, face-to-face social relations.

In more contemporary writings on sport and community, some appreciation of the distinctions between geographical communities and supporter communities has begun to emerge. Andrews' (1998, 1999) work on community formations around the Australian Football League is rare in the sociology of sport in that it engages in a prolonged discussion of different conceptualisations of community, including comments on community as a geographical locale, community as a social system, community as a sense of identity/belonging, and community as an ideology. However, this study is, to some degree, still locked into a belief that the 'natural' or 'purest' form of community around a sports club is a geographical community. Similar sentiments can be found in the work of Fawbert (2004) and others who have studied the globalisation of English football, and the subsequent emergence of dispersed or overseas fans of English clubs. Again, in these studies the presumption is often that the natural historical community of a football club is its geographical community, and that relations between geographical communities and football clubs have been disrupted by *recent* social and cultural change, or, more perniciously, the commercialisation of the game. Unsurprisingly, this approach to understanding football supporter communities is also very powerful amongst English supporters themselves, especially at clubs such as Manchester United that have developed large 'out of town' followings (see Brown, 2004).

There is much to be drawn from the work of Andrews, Fawbert and others. They are at least cognisant of the fact that relationships between football clubs and communities are not straightforward, and that the very concept of 'community' is contested. However, they are not particularly historically sensitive and, therefore, tend to overestimate the recentness of the disruption of 'traditional' geographical football communities. From at least the 1930s, and almost certainly before, football supporter communities in England (particularly at successful clubs with large geographical hinterlands) were not drawn exclusively from the immediate neighbourhoods of football clubs (Mellor, 1999: 29-34). They were made up of people from relatively wide geographical areas and, therefore, can be said to be specific, relatively autonomous communities that were based around *a choice* to engage in a single cultural/sporting interest. The constitution of football supporter communities along these non-geographic lines became even more dramatic in the post-war period. From the late 1950s, a serious bifurcation can be said to have occurred between many English football clubs and their local, geographical neighbourhoods and this has created sources of tension between neighbourhood and supporter communities (although these groups are clearly not always mutually exclusive). This was the consequence of a number of social changes common to post-war England including: 'slum-clearance' programmes in major cities; the changing ethnic profile of certain neighbourhoods within English cities brought about by immigration from the Indian subcontinent and the Caribbean from the late 1940s; the exclusion of new 'ethnic communities' from football because of cultures of racism both within and without the game (see Back, Crabbe and Solomos, 2001); football clubs being increasingly regarded as 'nuisances' from the late 1950s because of hooliganism and associated problems; and the growth of 'out of town' supporters at successful football clubs who did not live in the city (or even the region) of the clubs they supported. This final change was underpinned by the increasing availability and ownership of motor cars and televisions, both of which made it easier for people to support teams to which they had no obvious historical, geographical or familial connections (Mellor, 2000: 158-161). These changes resulted, to a greater or lesser degree, in developments that made communities around football clubs *even more* specific to their particular cultural contexts. There was little sense in which football communities were geographical inevitabilities in the post-war period as some people (although by no means all) increasingly chose 'their clubs' (or rejected them) on grounds other than geographical heritage.

The key point to draw from this debate is that the theorisation of community around English football (and sports in other geographical contexts) has largely started from the assumption that professional sports clubs emerged to satisfy a functional need for social bonding for their supporters: a need that was created by industrialisation and associated phenomena such as urbanisation. However, very little detailed empirical work has been produced in association with this assumption. Few oral history studies, for instance, have been conducted on the types of bonding that people created by attending football matches in different historical periods, and few questions have been asked about whether these forms of sociation were approximate to 'traditional', geographical and emotional ties (for an introduction to this see Mellor, 2002: 166-172). This has resulted in a lack of debate about the various types of community that have developed around football and other sports clubs, and has stopped sociologists of sport from accessing and reflecting on recent developments in community theory.

OFFICIAL FOOTBALL AND COMMUNITY SCHEMES, COMMUNITIES OF DISADVANTAGE AND POLITICAL USES OF THE GAME

Whilst academic studies of English football clubs' communities have not been particularly cognisant of the 'split' between supporter identifications and geographical neighbourhoods, or of the theoretical and practical consequences that this might create, the increasingly non-geographic nature of football support was ironically identified relatively early by the English football industry. Indeed, in Sir Norman Chester's report on the football industry for the Department of Education and Science in 1968, it was reported that a 'standardisation of national life' had occurred in England that had seen local identities, and institutions associated with the expression of community identity (such as football clubs), fall into decline (Department of Education and Science, 1968: 14). The report stated that this large-scale social change had occurred because of improvements in national communications, and concluded that it had resulted in significant declines in attendance at all but the most successful English football clubs. By the 1970s, this problem, coupled with the ever-rising profile of football hooliganism, had for many commentators fundamentally undermined the links between football clubs and local communities. Whereas the links between 'football and community' had once been taken for granted, in the 1970s 'community' became something much more problematic for football, mirroring concerns in the wider sociological literature at the time which we discuss below. Supporter communities that continued to operate around football were increasingly viewed as illegitimate (the 'wrong type of communities') because of the continuing construction of football supporters as 'hooligans' (Armstrong, 1998; Dunning et al., 1988). For football to maintain its 'pretence' of being a geographically representative community sport, the game perceived a need to place the relationship between clubs and geographical communities on a formal footing for the first time.

In the context of the 'loss of community' for football in the 1970s, 'community' came to be something that needed support. In an attempt to recreate the close relationships that football clubs supposedly had with their local neighbourhoods in the past, most English football clubs became involved in formal 'football and community' initiatives from the late 1970s onwards, and particularly from the mid-to-late 1980s with the introduction of the national Football in the Community (FiTC) programme.[3] These programmes have had different sponsors and aims in different periods. However, until recently they have focused, rhetorically at least, on industry-specific problems such as football hooliganism, racism in the game, poor attendances at matches, clubs' financial problems, and most notably the split between clubs and local communities. In reality, however, most schemes have been predominantly focused on the provision of football coaching courses, and have not engaged with the full range of aims and objectives set out by the national FiTC programme (see Watson, 2000).

Since the 1990s, the perceived role of football clubs in promoting sporting and social change for 'good' through their community schemes has grown exponentially. This has occurred for two principal reasons. Firstly, football clubs have a history of being called upon to engage with social problems, most notably hooliganism and racism, which have long been associated with the national game. Secondly, the commercial success of a number of football clubs in the 1990s led commentators to question the extent to which clubs were meeting their social responsibilities for supporters and neighbourhood communities. The Football Task Force's *Investing in the Community* report which was submitted to the UK Minister for Sport in 1999 dealt directly with this issue when it noted 'football's commercial development has brought great benefits but also created unease in some quarters about the direction the game is taking. It is argued by some that work in the community is being sidelined as commercial considerations take priority' (Football Task Force, 1999: 1). These concerns led to a crystallisation of thinking about the 'good' that football clubs could perform in their communities, and how they could help to address important issues of the day.

By identifying the potential that football clubs and other sports institutions have for promoting social change, the British Government, the Football Association, the Football Foundation, the FA Premier League and various other bodies are currently advocating the use of sport in general, and football in particular, in a wider range of 'community' policy contexts than ever before. Indeed, many football clubs' community departments (which still usually operate under the national FiTC framework) have recently widened their remit to tackle 'social problems' within 'their communities' such as social exclusion of various types, health problems, and poor educational achievement among adults and children (see McGuire and Fenoglio, 2004). In the context of these programmes, 'community' has come to represent something different in the English football industry. Football clubs' communities are less and less spoken of as the supporters of the game or the general geographical areas in which clubs reside. Football communities are now more frequently the agency-defined 'communities of disadvantage' or 'social problem communities' that may or may not be in close proximity to football stadiums.

As football clubs have become members of the 'social problems industry' (Pitter and Andrews, 1997), the discourse of 'community' in the football industry has coalesced around a number of specific themes underpinned by a belief in the 'power' of football to contribute to different social agendas. The British government has identified football clubs as 'political technologies,' in Foucault's (1977) sense, which can tackle health issues through the promotion of physical activity and health promotion messages; low educational achievement through the delivery of football-themed educational curricula; crime and 'anti-social' behaviour through the promotion of diversionary activities; and community cohesion problems through citizenship programmes, volunteering and by providing a focus for community identification. Whilst the cultural appeal of football clubs to young people may make them excellent institutions for delivering much of this work, it is in the area of clubs providing a focus for community identification that the football industry seems to have suffered a form of historical amnesia. In documentation that accompanies industry and government statements on the power of football clubs to contribute to the creation of social capital, citizenship and, more explicitly, community building, the bifurcation between football clubs and geographical communities in the twentieth century seems to have been forgotten. The specific configurations of football supporter communities are totally ignored as the civic-pride-producing properties of football clubs are casually equated with maintaining or building social ties between people in specific geographical locales. In their development strategy for the period 2001-2006, the English Football Association writes unproblematically of the 'sense of community' that football clubs create, and of the game's capacity for generating a 'sense of community empowerment amongst those groups who are typically seen as 'excluded' from mainstream society' (Football Association, 2001: 36). Similarly, proponents of major new football stadiums in England, such as the one built in Manchester for the 2002 Commonwealth Games and which was later taken over by Manchester City FC, regularly make statements on the formal and informal 'community building' properties of professional sports teams in support of their plans, despite a lack of detailed evidence to support such claims (Brown, 2003; see also Eckstein and Delaney, 2002). Indeed, the substantial public investment that went into the City of Manchester Stadium for the Commonwealth Games was partially justified by the 'legacy' that the stadium would produce, not for MCFC, but for the 'community' as a whole. In situations such as this, football clubs are presented as being able to contribute to the project of reconstituting mutual, solidarity-based geographical communities in late modernity because of the assumption that they performed this duty in early modernity.

The pressure placed on football clubs to 'build' communities should, of course, be placed into social and political context. In recent years, concern over the 'loss of community' has been far from confined to football. As Anthony Giddens points out, 'on each side of the political spectrum today we see a fear of social disintegration and a call for a revival of community' (1994: 124). In common with the long sociological tradition of seeing community as a moral force that has disintegrated during modernity, political leaders in Britain and elsewhere now regularly discuss social problems in terms of their relationship to the 'loss of community,' a lack of citizenship or similar themes. In this they draw implicitly and explicitly on a range of communitarian philosophers and thinkers. Whilst 'communitarianism' is in no way a unified school of thought, a number of disparate thinkers, including Putnam (2000), Rose (1999) and Etzioni (1995, 2001), have been highly influential in the emergence of political strategies designed to develop social justice, social networks, local communities, and a new emphasis on family, kinship and neighbourhood (Jarvie, 2003: 140). The key issue for what Delanty has called 'governmental communitarians' is to use these strategies to reject civic individualism and its consequences for modern society (2003: 87-90). Instead, they propose programmes designed to build mutual, quasi-self-governing communities that are underpinned by people's deeply held shared beliefs in 'the community' and its values. In practice in Britain, this type of thinking has seen Blair's New Labour Government engage in a number of policy initiatives which are infused with notions such as volunteering, charitable works, and organised self-care (Delanty, 2003: 88). It has also seen larger-scale policy initiatives which promote community regeneration (both social and economic), community policing, community-based justice and, of course, community sport. In the context of professional football, it has also seen the development of the Supporters Direct initiative: a Government-funded scheme proposed by the Football Task Force to help supporters build mutually-owed shareholdings in their clubs (see Hamil *et al.*, 2001).

In the wake of these developments, it is not surprising that football clubs have been designated a role in the reconstitution of (mainly) urban communities. As this paper has so far demonstrated, the belief that football clubs have acted historically to sustain community identities at times of great social change (such as the period of rapid urbanisation in the nineteenth century) is well established. The game itself has also been struggling with its own 'loss of community' since the 1970s and has produced programmes designed to turn this around. It is, therefore, understandable that politicians and football administrators are willing to promote football club's community building properties. If they are to continue to do this, however, more conceptual clarity about the types of communities produced by football clubs is required. Questions must be asked about the historical constitution of football's 'communities,' particularly in terms of how much choice was involved in becoming a 'member' of one and what types of sociation went on within them. More importantly, greater clarity is needed on what types of community formation are going on around the game today, and what this means for future policy formation in terms of the policy and practice of football and community work.

CONTEMPORARY FOOTBALL SUPPORTER COMMUNITIES

The traditional, geographically-deterministic understanding of community which has influenced most studies of English football (and other sports) appears to have blinded many sociologists of sport to wider debates about the nature of community which have been occurring in mainstream sociology for decades. In his rare analysis of community in the Australian sporting context, Andrews notes that deliberations over the meaning of 'community' have become so complex and divisive in sociology and associated fields that some authors have suggested that we should abandon the concept altogether (1998: 105). We, like Andrews, reject this suggestion and believe it is important that community continues to be wrestled with and argued over. As evidenced above, community is now, more than ever, a central theme in sporting and social policy, and as such demands critical analysis and theorising. The point is that, whether theorists find the term useful or not, 'community' continues to be an important and defining 'conceptual reality.'

In our research, we have formulated a number of ideas about the types of community and sociation that operate around English football clubs, and have related these ideas to contemporary theoretical debates about community formation. It is not possible here to outline fully how contemporary football communities can be understood according to every competing theoretical conception: there are simply too many positions to be considered. We will, therefore, restrict our debate here to outlining how 'symbolic' and 'post-modern' conceptions of community are contributing to a new framework of analysis which will help us to understand different aspects of community in the context of English football supporting. We will then illustrate, in the concluding section, a new analytical framework that underpins our analysis of football and community in a wider range of contexts.

The first theoretical position to be considered is Anthony Cohen's conception of 'symbolic community' (1985). Cohen rejects all attempts to reduce communities to spatial categories (or any other forms of reductionism), and instead stresses the role of symbols in defining community boundaries. Borrowing from the work of Turner (who will be considered below), Cohen states that people enact rituals around or through symbols and thereby define their belonging to different community groups. He also notes that symbols are acted upon in relation to other symbols, and that people understand their communities always in relation to other groups (see Delanty, 2003: 46). A key point in Cohen's work is that he claims that symbols are not fixed entities that can only be interpreted in set, predetermined ways. Instead, he suggests that they are constantly being reinterpreted and re-negotiated and as such can lead to changes in the constitution of community groups.

Cohen's work is potentially important for understanding historical and contemporary supporter community formations around English football clubs. He points us towards understanding football clubs as symbols around which rituals of communality are acted out. He also provides a theory which enables us to see communal symbols (such as football clubs) as contested phenomena which can mean different things to different people in different historical periods. In this regard, Cohen's theory allows us to move beyond geographically-deterministic understandings of football supporter communities which see functional and inevitable relationships emerge between people and sports clubs in set spatial areas. Instead Cohen allows us to identify individual actors' agency in creating their community formations, and their different interpretations of them. For some people, football supporter communities may be (and may have always been) entirely geographical affairs. That is simply the way that they choose to define them. However, even these communities can be read as symbolic or 'performative' as people within them seek to 'display' *their* geography through their football support. For others, football communities may represent an entirely different type of bonding. The key point is that Cohen allows us to see football communities as fluid and always open to change.

The second position to be considered is Victor Turner's (1969) work on *communitas* and liminality. Turner's functionalist anthropological work analysed 'those 'between' moments such as carnivals, pilgrimages, rites of passage or rituals in which normality is suspended' (Delanty, 2003: 44). Centrally, Turner was interested in the role of these moments in producing 'communitas', or the symbolic renewal of collective identity for particular groups. In asserting that communitas occurs 'between' normal moments, Turner contended that it is a special 'out of time' and anti-structural type of bonding that temporarily obliterates differences between people around specific cultural practices or events (such as football matches). He claimed that this type of bonding is 'liminal' and marginal to 'real' life, although he did note that it can persist for groups in the form of 'normative communitas'.

It is interesting to note that Turner's work has recently been appropriated in the sociology of sport. In Smith and Ingham's (2003) study of sport and community in Cincinnati, they claim that sports fans in the city display communitas type bonding in their fandom rituals (2003: 259). This may indeed be the case. In our research with football supporters, we have observed many moments in which the 'out-of-time' social drama of the football match, be it watched 'live' in the stadium or in groups in a public house, produces moments of intense group bonding and feelings of associated community. Within football stadiums, it is undeniable that when goals are scored or other moments of high excitement occur, many 'normal' intra-group rivalries and differences within fan communities are obliterated as a new form of community bonding temporarily emerges (see, for instance, Crabbe and Brown, 2004). However, whilst Turner's work is valuable in providing a model of communal bonding that is non-geographic and cultural in focus, his assertion that communitas bonding can only take place in opposition to everyday, real existence is not particularly helpful in explaining some of the types of supporter communities that we have observed during our research. Being a member of a football club's supporter community is not a liminal or marginal experience for some of the supporters with which we have spent time. For them, being a supporter is a key part of their 'real' lives: a regular, *structuring* part of their existence that enables them to feel belonging in the relative disorder of contemporary social formations.

If attention is now turned to more 'post-modern' theses on community, our research is also investigating recent theoretical developments that try to explain the desire for community in contemporary society as expressed through football supporting. We have observed and encountered several types of sociation around English football, some of which could be read as solidly 'modern' or even 'pre-modern' in that they are based, to some degree, on 'thick' ties of family, kinship, friendship, neighbourhood and so on. This is potentially remarkable, as according to communitarian thinkers modern societies are exemplified by a lack of community that leads to a need for the re-creation of shared bonds. However, in the work of Zygmunt Bauman (2000, 2001), even these seemingly traditional forms of community which are created around football can be read in a different way.

Following Bauman (2000: 199-201), it could be argued that even when the existence of football clubs contributes to friendship ties and regular social contact, they are only really producing the 'cloakroom communities' or 'ad hoc communities' that are common to post- or 'liquid' modernity. In a society marked by increasing 'individualization' (Beck and Beck-Gersheim, 2002), it could be argued that football supporters are not attempting to hold on to, or recreate, the *Gemeinshaft* type communities which Tönnies described, but rather are creating 'communities without commitment' or 'thin communities' that people can dip into to satisfy their occasional needs for security without taking on the reciprocal obligations that define 'community' in the writings of communitarian thinkers. To put it another way, it could be said that supporting a football club allows supporters to indulge their search for community in liquid modernity without ever impacting upon the actual roots of their insecurity. In this regard, our supporter communities can never become 'real communities' in a traditional sense because 'traditional' community bonds are no longer possible (if they ever were). For Bauman, the very idea of community is a fiction.

The key point to take from Bauman is his cynicism about contemporary notions of community. For him, it is not possible to read football communities as grounding, structuring, deep forms of sociation that bring true meaning to people's lives. They cannot be read as functional in a true sense. His analysis of communities as cloakrooms at the theatre could equally well be applied to the communities that gather at football matches:

> *The name 'cloakroom community' grasps well some of their [contemporary communities'] characteristic traits. Visitors to a spectacle dress for the occasion, abiding by a sartorial code distinct from those codes they follow daily ... [This] makes the visitors look, for the duration of the event, much more uniform than they do in their life outside the theatre building ... During the performance all eyes are on the stage; so is everybody's attention ... After the last fall of the curtain, however, the spectators collect their belongings from the cloakroom and when putting their street clothes on once more return to their ordinary mundane and different roles, a few moments later dissolving in the variegated crowd filling the streets from which they emerged a few hours earlier (Bauman, 2000: 200).*

For Bauman, then, 'spectacles' such as football matches have become events around which people temporarily unite as communities, only to go back to their individualised lives at the end of the game. People 'perform' all the aspects of community and commonality around football for the time they are together 'as one,' but do not knit themselves into deep reciprocal relationships as a result. As with our earlier comments on Turner's theory of communitas, Bauman's theories do not fit with all the types of bonding which we have encountered through our research. We have found very deep friendship groups that were initially established through football and have persisted outside of the frameworks of the game. We have also found family units that are almost entirely maintained through the 'spectacle' of football. However, this does not mean that Bauman's work should be dismissed. It is vitally important in sensitising sociologists to the qualitative differences that exist within different types of community, and in pointing out the temporary nature of much contemporary community bonding.

Another post-modern thesis on community which is being analysed through our research is Scott Lash's (1994) work on 'reflexive communities of taste.' Lash's work (and associated writing such as those by Maffesoli (1996)) is important in that it theorises the *choices* involved in being part of contemporary communities. 'Reflexive' communities for Lash have four central aspects:

> *First one is not born or "thrown", but "throws oneself" into them; second, they may be widely stretched over "abstract" space, and also perhaps over time; third, they consciously pose themselves the problems of their own creation and constant re-invention far more than do traditional communities; fourth, their "tools" tend to be not material ones but abstract and cultural (Lash, 1994: 161, quoted in Delanty, 2003: 139).*

We would actually argue that some of the properties of reflexive communities identified by Lash are not only common to contemporary football supporter communities, but actually may have been more apparent in historical supporter communities than is usually considered to be the case. It is possible, for instance, that people exercised more choice in their belonging (or otherwise) to football communities in earlier historical periods than traditional 'football and civic pride' studies have suggested. What is certain is that Lash's work is vital for pointing out a number of key elements of football communities as identified in our research. Football supporters do 'throw themselves' into football communities, and do so with varying degrees of commitment and enthusiasm. Football communities are also generally non-spatial, or at least they are not bound by geography. People come and go from football communities all the time, and their members are continually reflexive about who makes up 'their community' and what this means for how the group is perceived by its own members and others. Finally, the community that coalesces around any football club is doing so not around a reified, solid, immovable, static entity. They are consuming and creating a 'product' which, culturally at least, 'belongs' to them.

Of course many of these theoretical developments have pertinence beyond the realm of football supporters as they have developed in relation to a critique of the broader community studies literature. As such, in the course of our own research we have sought to consider the usefulness of these fresh approaches to the task of re-conceptualising 'community' in the context of football more generally. The principal challenge associated with this project relates to the imperative of giving these theoretical trajectories some relevance in terms of contemporary policy and practice. In our concluding section we provide a tentative schematic framework for analysis that draws upon our appraisal of the literature in order to address this problem.

CONCLUSION–A NEW FRAMEWORK FOR ANALYSIS

In Table 1 (below) we outline five main 'forms of community' that have framed the 'Football and its Communities' research project. These are: football, place and space; football, belonging, family and kinship; football and the symbolic community; football, post-modernism and the virtual community; and political community–football, communitarianism and social responsibility. The table also outlines the main theoretical writings which shaped our debates around these forms of community, as well as the main research sites in which our empirical investigations were conducted. The final column of the table outlines the likely policy implications of our research, and indicates how the understandings generated by our work might be 'operationalised' by the English football industry (and others).

The different forms of community outlined in Table 1 indicate the comprehensive way in which the research project analysed questions of community around football. Despite our clear rejection of the geographical-determinism that has blighted much football and community work, we were still committed to engaging with the 'classic' issues that have occupied community-based studies through considerations of football's contemporary relationship with space and place, and through discussions of the continuing relationship between football, belonging and family/kinship. To do this, however, we established a detailed theoretical framework which precluded our analysis from slipping into generalised statements about football clubs' relationships with 'their communities.' Through an engagement with urban sociology and its analysis of the fragmentation of urban communities (Harvey, 1990), we were able to bring some conceptual clarity to debates about contemporary football supporter communities, and also generated greater insight into the issue of how football clubs' stadia, particularly in the ongoing context of redevelopment and relocation, impact upon people living and working in post-modern cities. This is especially important as more clubs are being drawn into wider city or sub-city regeneration programmes through their facility development strategies. Our consideration of football, belonging and family/kinship is also important in that it developed, through close ethnographic work, our understanding of the 'lived' experience of football and 'community' in the classic close, affective, face-to-face understanding of the term. It also enabled us to explore the 'deep' attachments that people form in football supporter communities, whilst understanding how supporter communities display 'distinctions' (Bourdieu, 1984), and can operate exclusively with specific cultural boundaries.

As shown in this paper, our considerations of football and the symbolic community and football and post-modern theories of community enabled us to better understand contemporary supporter connections with English football clubs. The notion of the symbolic community helped us to overcome the search for geographical football communities in these increasingly 'placeless' times, whilst post-modern understandings of community sensitised us to the multiple, 'light' and fluid ways in which people opt in and out of contemporary football communities. These are vital issues, not least in the context of the communitarian debate about the supposed loss of community, and football's place in recreating 'traditional' community connections. It is our position that English football clubs, the game's governing bodies and the British Government must come to terms with some of the contemporary forms of community that are being established and acted out around English football if they are to continue to promote football clubs as 'community building' institutions.

Our consideration of the communitarian project and its relationship with football is not only important in terms of debates about supporter communities. The strategic and political use of football clubs as key

Table 1
Football and Community–A Framework for Analysis

Forms of 'Community'	*Theoretical Frameworks*	*Research Sites*	*Re-Conceptualising Policy*
Football, place and space	- The Chicago School and urban sociology - Harvey (1990) commodification of space - Bale (1993) 'topophilia' and 'topophobia' - Robertson (1992) Glocalization	- Neighbourhood communities - Stadium re-location	- The need to reassess club practices in light of more fluid notions of space and place, whilst recognising the enduring importance of locally focused policies
Football, belonging, family and kinship	- Young & Wilmott (1957) family, kinship and working class community - Bourdieu (1984) 'habitus'	-'Football family' -Fan groups and friendship networks	- The need to recognise the inclusive and exclusive potential of football and 'community'
Football and the symbolic community	- Anthony Cohen (1985) 'symbolic community' - Victor Turner (1969) '*communitas*' and 'liminality'	- Fan communities - Match day gatherings - Civic community	- The need to understand clubs as symbols around which rituals of communality are acted out
Football, postmodernism and the virtual community	- Zygmunt Bauman (2001) 'cloakroom communities' - Scott Lash (1994) 'communities of taste' - Maffesoli (1996) 'neo tribes' - Wellman (1979) 'personalized networking'	- Consumerist fans - Regeneration and re-imaginings of the 'city' - Technological and dispersed communities	- The need to recognise the implications of 'ambivalence' for marketing and regeneration through the aesthetic of football-The need to understand new modes of connectivity with the game
Political comm-unity–football, communi-tarianism and social responsibility	- Puttnam (2000) 'social capital' - Etzioni (1995) 'communitarianism' - Castells (1983) 'social movements'	- Communities of disadvantage - Social interven-tions- 'Political' formations of fans	- The need to reconsider stakeholding and the third way, 'community policies' and new models of ownership and control in the context of football

agencies in the delivery of social policies has created new relationships between football clubs and 'communities' of various kinds. Football clubs' communities are today (in a formal sense at least) as likely to be the agency-defined 'communities of disadvantage' or 'social problem communities' that exist in urban centres as they are the broadly defined supporter communities that sports historians and sociologists of sport have traditionally discussed. This, and the debates outlined above, is why a thorough re-imagining of the football and community issue is now required, and why our project should prove timely both theoretically and practically.

NOTES

1. The Football and its Communities project was carried out by the authors of this paper and two other researchers: Tony Blackshaw and Chris Stone at Sheffield Hallam University. We would like to thank Tony and Chris for their contributions to this paper.
2. The Football Foundation (FF) is a charitable trust which is funded by the Football Association Premier League (FAPL) and the British Government. It funds facility development at elite and grassroots levels, and various community projects through its Community and Educational Panel. Our research for the FF ran from October 2002 to September 2005 and reported back to the Community and Education Panel.
3. The national Football in the Community scheme was established in 1986 by the Footballers' Further Education and Vocational Training Society (recently renamed the Footballers' Education Society).

REFERENCES

Andrews, I. (1998). The Transformation of 'Community, in the Australian Football League. Part One: Towards a Conceptual Framework For Community. Occasional Papers in Football Studies, 1(2): 103-114.

Andrews, I. (1999). The Transformation of 'Community' in the Australian Football League. Part Two: Redrawing 'Community Boundaries in the Post-War AFL. Football Studies, 2(2): 106-124.

Armstrong, G. (1998). Football Hooligans: Knowing the Score. Oxford: Berg.

Back, L., Crabbe, T. and Solomos, J. (2001). The Changing Face of Football: Racism, Identity and Multiculture in the English Game. Oxford: Berg.

Bale, J. (1993). Sport, Space and the City. London: Routledge.

Bauman, Z. (2000). Liquid Modernity. Cambridge: Polity Press.

Bauman, Z. (2001). *Community*: Seeking Safety in an Insecure World. Cambridge: Polity Press.

Beck, U. and Beck-Gersheim, E. (2002). Individualization. London: Sage.

Bourdieu, P. (1984). Distinction. London: Routledge.

Brown, A., Crabbe, T., Mellor, G., Blackshaw, T. and Stone, C. (2003). Football and its Communities Interim Report 1: Baseline Analysis of Case Study Football and Community Initiatives (Manchester: Manchester Metropolitan University).

Brown, A., Crabbe, T., Mellor, G., Blackshaw, T. and Stone, C. (2004a). Football and its Communities Interim Report 2: Mapping Case Study Clubs' Communities (Manchester: Manchester Metropolitan University).

Brown, A., Crabbe, T., Mellor, G., Blackshaw, T. and Stone, C. (2004b). Football and its Communities Interim Report 3: The Impacts of a Stadium Move on the Communities of a Football Club–The Example of Manchester City FC (Manchester: Manchester Metropolitan University).

Brown, A., Crabbe, T., and Mellor, G with Blackshaw, T. and Stone, C. (2006). Football and its Communities: Final Report (Manchester & London: Manchester Metropolitan University and the Football Foundation).

Brown, A. (2004). Manchester is Red? Manchester United, Fan Identity and the 'Sport City,' in Andrews, D. (ed.), Manchester United: A Thematic Study. London: Routledge.

Brown, A. (2003). Grounds for Change? Manchester City FC and the City of Manchester Stadium. Paper presented to the North American Society for the Sociology of Sport Conference, Montreal, Canada.

Crabbe, T. and Brown, A. (2004). You're Not Welcome Anymore: The Football Crowd, Class and Social Exclusion, in Wagg, S. (ed.), British Football and Social Exclusion. London: Routledge.

Castells, M. (1983). The City and the Grassroots. Berkeley: University of California Press.

Cohen, A. (1985). The Symbolic Construction of Community. London: Tavistock.

Delanty, G. (2003). Community. London: Routledge.

Department of Education and Science. (1968). Report of the Committee on Football. London: HMSO.

Dunning, E., Murphy, P. and Williams, J. (1988). The Roots of Football Hooliganism: An Historical and Sociological Study. London: Routledge.

Durkheim, E. (1984). The Division of Labour. Houndmills: The Free Press. First published 1863.

Eckstein, R and Delaney, K. (2002). New Sports Stadiums, Community Self-Esteem, and Community Collective Conscience. Journal of Sport and Social Issues, 26, 3: 235-247.

Etzioni, A. (1995). The Spirit of Community. London: Fontana Press.

Etzioni, A. (2001). The Monochrome Society. Princeton, NJ: Princeton University Press.

Fawbert, J. (2004). Football Fandom and the 'Traditional' Club: from 'Cockney Parochialism' to a European Diaspora. Paper presented at the European Football: Influence, Change, Development Conference, Preston, UK.

Football Association. (2001). The Football Development Strategy 2001-2006. London: The Football Association.

Football Task Force. (1999). Investing in the Community: A Report by the Football Task Force. London: HMSO.

Foucault, M. (1977). Discipline and Punish: The Birth of the Prison. Harmondsworth: Penguin.

Giddens, A. (1994). Beyond Left and Right. Cambridge: Polity Press.

Giulianotti, R. (1999). Football: A Sociology of the Global Game. Cambridge: Polity Press.

Hamil, S., Michie, J., Oughton, C. and Warby, S. (2001). The Changing Face of the Football Business: Supporters Direct. London: Frank Cass.

Harvey, D. (1990). The Condition of Postmodernity. Oxford. Blackwell.

Hill, J. (1996). Rite of Spring: Cup Finals and community in the North of England, in Hill, J. and Williams, J. (eds.), Sport and Identity in the North of England. Keele: Keele University Press.

Holt, R. (1989). Sport and the British: A Modern History. Oxford: Oxford University Press.

Holt, R. (1996). Heroes of the North: Sport and the Shaping of Regional Identity, in Hill, J. and Williams, J. (eds.), Sport and Identity in the North of England. Keele: Keele University Press.

Holt, R. (1997). Football and Regional Identity in the North of England: The Legend of Jackie Milburn, in Gerhrmann, S., (ed.), Football and Regional Identity in Europe. New Brunswick, N.J: Transaction Publishers.

Jarvie, G. (2003). Communitarianism, Sport and Social Capital: Neighbourly Insights into Scottish Sport. International Review for the Sociology of Sport, 38(2): 139-153.

Lash, S. (1994). Reflexivity and its Doubles, Structures, Aesthetics, Community, in Beck, U., Giddens, A. and Lash, S., Reflexive Modernization: Politics, Tradition and Aesthetics in the Modern Social Order. Cambridge: Polity Press.

Maffesoli, M. (1996). The Time of the Tribes: The Decline of Individualism in Mass Society. London: Sage.

Maguire, B. and Fenoglio, R. (2004). Football in the Community: Resources and Opportunities. Manchester: Footballers' Education Society.

Mason, T. (1988). Sport in Britain. London: Faber and Faber.

Mellor, G. (1999). The Social and Geographical Make-up of Football Crowds in the North-West of England, 1946-62: 'Super-Clubs', Local Loyalty and Regional Identities. The Sports Historian, 19(2): 25-42.

Mellor, G. (2000). The Genesis of Manchester United as a National and International 'Super-Club', 1958-68. Soccer and Society, 1(2): 151-166.

Mellor, G. (2002). Professional Football and its Supporters in Lancashire, circa 1946-89. University of Central Lancashire, PhD Thesis.

Pitter, R. and Andrews, D. L. (1997). Serving America's Underserved Youth: Reflections on Sport and Recreation in an Emerging Social Problems Industry. Quest, 49: 85-99.

Putnam, R. D. (2000). Bowling Alone: The Collapse and Revival of American Community. New York: Touchstone.

Robertson, R. (1992). *Globalization:* Social Theory and Global Culture. London: Sage.

Rose, N. (1999). Powers of Freedom. Cambridge: Cambridge University Press.

Russell, D. (1997). Football and the English: A Social History of Association Football in England, 1863-1995. Preston: Carnegie Publishing.

Smith, J. and Ingham, A. (2003). On the Waterfront: Retrospectives on the Relationship Between Sport and Communities. Sociology of Sport Journal, 20: 252-274.

Tönnies, F. (1974). Community and Association. London: Routledge.

Turner, V. (1969). The Ritual Process: Structure and Anti-Structure. London: Routledge and Kegan Paul.

Watson, N. (2000). Football in the Community: 'What's the Score.' Soccer and Society, 1(1): 114-125.

Wellman, B. (1979). The Community Question: the Intimate Networks of East Yorkers. American Journal of Sociology, 84(5): 1201-31.

Young, M. and Willmott, P. (1957). Family and Kinship in East London. London: Penguin.

THE BEAUTIFUL GAME AND THE AMERICAN EXCEPTION

3

Michael Veseth

I am struck by how much the history of the globalization of soccer mirrors the history of globalization more generally. Like globalization generally, global soccer was initially the product of imperialism, military and then economic. Soccer hegemony and economic hegemony were both centered in Great Britain during the Victorian era. When nationalistic forces swept the world in the 1930s, overcoming global market forces, FIFA and its strongly nationalistic structure became increasingly significant. The World Cup reinforced the authority of the nation state and gave tangible form to nationalistic rhetoric through international competition. And now, as economic globalization proceeds, creating global markets and weakening the nation-state, the same pattern is clear in soccer.[2] Basketball cannot compare to soccer as a metaphor for globalization's ebbs and flows.

As I look at global soccer today, I see three patterns (and certainly relationships among the patterns) that seem interesting enough to discuss here. I wonder if they are just patterns that are unique to soccer or if they reflect the world more generally? The patterns are these.

First, the global soccer player market seems to display a classic core-periphery structure, which is often association with exploitation in political economy. But, second, if we look closely at the periphery, it appears that there is something else going on besides simple exploitation. Soccer seems to be used as a tool to build local identity in resistance to globalization and exploitation. So this relationship seems complex and interesting. And, finally, there is the American exception to consider–what should we make of soccer's persistent inability, even during this era of strong market forces, to penetrate the United States as a spectator sport? The remainder of this article tries to understand the causes and consequences of these three images of globalization and soccer today.

CORE AND PERIPHERY

If you look at the top five professional soccer leagues in the world–England, Spain, Italy, Germany, and France–you will see the top players in the world at work. Not just the top English, Spanish, Italian, Germany and French players, but the top players from everywhere: Africa, Asia, North America, and South America. The top teams in the top leagues bid talent away from the countries and teams in the soccer periphery and then sell the finished products–games, shirts, images–back to them. This pattern has all of the qualities of a classic core-periphery relationship in political economy. The core of the system controls the key elements of economic power (in this case, it is the privileged position within the winner take all system) and uses its advantage to purchase cheap natural resources from the periphery, selling back finished products at advantageous prices. That is a basic core-periphery relationship, considerably over-simplified, as originally conceived by Immanuel Wallerstein (1979).

The intensity of the core-periphery relationship in soccer is quite amazing. Here is some information that I collected about some of the players from four teams from the 2002 World Cup finals.[3] I have put together some representative segments of the rosters of four teams from the economic periphery of soccer so that you can see where the members of the Cameroon, Nigeria, Argentina and Brazil teams play during the professional league seasons.

Let's begin with Cameroon. Cameroon is clearly not in the periphery in terms of soccer skills and strategy. Its team features several players of exceptional ability who play club football for elite teams, including at Real Madrid. But in economic terms its position is much different. None of the first 11 players on the roster of the national team earned his living playing for a Cameroon league club. All played abroad, nine of them for clubs in one of the five super-leagues: England, France, Spain, Germany or Italy. The story is essentially the same in the case of Nigeria. Of the first eleven players listed on the roster, all played at clubs outside of Nigeria (outside of Africa, in fact) including Arsenal, Ajax and PSG.

The power of economics in shaping the pattern of soccer imports and exports becomes even clearer when we look at Argentina and Brazil,

Table 1
Club Affiliations of Selected 2002 World Cup Players

Cameroon		*Nigeria*		*Argentina*		*Brazil*	
Player	2002 Club	Player	2002 Club	Player	2002 Club	Player	2002 Club
Boukar Alioum	Samsunspor, Turkey	Ike Shorunme	Lucerne, Switzerland	Roberto Ayala	Valencia, Spain	Dida	Corinthians, Brazil
Bill Tchato	Montpelier, France	Joseph Yobo	Olympique Marseille, France	Walter Samuel	Roma, Italy	Cafu	Roma, Italy
Pierre Wome	Bologna, Italy	Celestine Babayaro	Arsenal, England	Hernan Crespo	Lazio, Italy	Roque Junior	Milan, Italy
Rigobert Song	Cologne, Germany	Nwankwo Kanu	Arsenal, England	Javier Zanetti	Inter Milan, Italy	Edmilson	Olympique Lyonnaise, France
Raymond Kalla	Extremadura, Spain	Isaac Okoronkwo	Shakhtar Donetsk, Ukraine	Gabriel Batistuta	Roma, Italy	Roberto Carlos	Real Madrid, Spain
Pierre Njanka	Strasbourg, France	Taribo West	Kaiserslautern, Germany	Ariel Ortega	River Plate, Argentina	Ricardihno	Corinthians, Brazil
Joseph Ndo	Al Khalees, UAE	Pius Ikedia	Ajax, Netherlands	Juan Veron	Manchester United, England	Gilberto Silva	Atletico Mineiro, Brazil
Geremi	Real Madrid, Spain	Mutiu Adepoju	Salamanca, Spain	Diego Placenta	Bayer Leverkusen, Germany	Ronaldo	Inter Milan, Italy
Samuel Etoo	Real Mallorca, Spain	B. Ogbeche	Paris St. Germain, France	Diego Placenta	Bayer Leverkusen, Germany	Rivaldo	Barcelona, Spain
Patrick Mbomba	Sunderland, England	Jay Jay Okocha	Paris St. Germain, France	Pablo Aimar	Valencia, Spain	Ronaldinho	Paris St. Germain, France
Pius Ndiefe	Sedan, France	Garba Lawal	Roda Kerkrade, Netherlands	Claudio Husain	River Plate, Argentina	Denilson	Betis Seville, Spain

countries that are solidly the core in terms of soccer skills and competition, but still peripheral from a strict economic standpoint. Almost all of Argentina's best players are "guest workers" for foreign clubs. At the highest level, Argentina's national team players are much more likely to confront each other in Italian Serie A competitions or in Champions League games than they are to meet in Argentina.

Finally, consider the 2002 World Cup champions, Brazil. As of 2002, two of the players listed here came from Brazilian sides, the rest played in Europe with one of the super-teams. The number of Brazil-based players fell dramatically after the finals, of course, as the result of the international publicity they all received. Dida was transferred from Milan to Corinthians, for example, and many of the players already in Europe were transferred up the soccer food chain, to even better and more prosperous clubs. Brazilian soccer is still a joy to watch, but the very best players are seldom seen at home (except via satellite sports television).

Pelé is a great exception to the rule that the top Brazilian soccer players are always exported to Europe. Why didn't he leave Brazil during his playing days? Because it was against the law! He was declared a national treasure by the Brazilian parliament and forbidden to play for a foreign team. (Pelé did eventually play abroad–for the New York Cosmos in the U.S.–but only after he retired from the Brazilian national team).

The same winner-take-all forces that draw the best Argentina and Nigeria players to the top European teams also affect players from England, Italy, Spain, France, and Germany, of course, but the effect is different. The best English players (David Beckham aside) tend to play in England and the best Italian players in Italy. All the 2002 World Cup team members from these countries stayed at home, more or less. They played in the super-leagues, which have a relatively strong home country bias that is strongest in the richest markets, England and Italy, and weakest in France. Fans from these countries are able to see many of their countries' best players on a regular basis, either in league games or Champions League contests. Fans on soccer's periphery must maintain a long distance relationship.

To restate my point, the economic core of soccer is in Europe's super-leagues, even though the playing core is centered in South America, with emerging pockets of excellence in Africa, Turkey, and Eastern Europe. The economic forces of winner-take-all markets mean that clubs in Brazil, Argentina, Nigeria, Turkey, Croatia and other countries cannot possibly compete with the super-clubs for the services of their own players. So, to a certain degree, they assume the role of minor leagues or youth leagues. Players with outstanding potential are identified and trained and then sold to European clubs. Sales of players take the place of ticket or television rights sales in their economic structures.

In fact, it is possible that formal "major league–minor league" links between core and periphery teams may be developing, a process that could institutionalize the dependency condition we have observed. Ajax of Amsterdam, long a powerful European club, has negotiated such arrangements with at least two teams. One, now called Ajax Orlando, will use its Florida base to develop New World player prospects. "Internationally, there are good players coming from places like Iran and Egypt, and we're even starting to see it from the U.S.," according to Mark Dillon, the Ajax Orlando founder. "In some ways the U.S. is the new Africa: a lot of relatively inexpensive players" (Bell, 2004: C16).

The very best periphery teams can be remarkably successful, although not in the same way as the European super-teams. Boca Juniors of Argentina, for example, enjoys both economic and soccer success. In 2003 it won the Argentine league championship, the South American club competition, and beat European Cup champions AC Milan in Tokyo to claim the world club title. All this success on the field, with corresponding television rights earnings, meant that Boca was able to hang onto some of its best players for perhaps an extra season before selling their contracts to European clubs. But Boca Juniors is the exception. In 2003 it enjoyed its own version of the winner-take-all payoff. Boca's situation as the number one team was miles ahead of the average team in the Argentine league, which leaks money like a sieve, like most clubs in most countries.

Brazil is perhaps the world's leading exporter of soccer players. Brazilian players are said to have a particularly fluid and creative style and it seems like every team wants to have one. About 5000 Brazilians play professional soccer outside of Brazil, according to Bellos (2002: 10). He explains Brazil's position as a huge net exporter in simple demand and supply terms. Many Brazilians, inspired by the success of Pelé, Ronaldo and others want to play soccer (a predictable problem in a winner-take-all market). There are too many for Brazil to absorb, even with its 500 professional clubs employing about 23,000 players. With so many teams, the individual club economic markets are small for all but the top teams and the pay low (Bellos says that 90 percent of Brazilian players earn less than £100 per month). Poor clubs, poor pay–and a high demand abroad. No wonder Brazil exports soccer players to the world.

Argentina's situation is of particular interest because of the way soccer reflects globalization more generally. Argentina experienced a severe economic crisis in recent years–a currency crisis, a banking crisis, and an international debt crisis all in one. Deteriorating domestic economic conditions affected the country's soccer clubs, too. Ticket and television revenues dried up and even sponsorship funding fell. The two best teams, River Plate and Boca Juniors, were able to switch to international sponsors (Budweiser and Pepsi respectively) to shore up their revenue base, but most other teams did not fare so well. Desperate for funds, they flooded the world transfer market with players, pushing up supply at the same time that financial problems in Europe was cutting demand. The result: even their most valuable assets, the players themselves, could not be sold for enough money to make ends meet–Boca Juniors aside (Weil, 2003a). The plight of Argentine soccer mirrored in this case as in many others the sad economic situation of the country itself.

SOCCER AND LOCAL IDENTITY

If exploitation of the periphery were the whole story of soccer globalization it would be a sad story indeed, but it is not. Soccer is more than global capitalism acting upon countries like Argentina and Brazil, it is also a tool that people use to define themselves and, implicitly at least, to resist the forces of globalization.

The relationship between soccer and national or local identity has many layers and my brief discussion here can only scratch the surface.[4] It begins, I suppose, with styles of play. Although soccer is a simple game, there are endless variations in styles and strategies. "The Brazilians play like they dance; the Germans play like they make cars, with lots of technical efficiency and not much left to the imagination; the English run hard all the time, maybe because of the weather; the Spanish are a mosaic of regional styles, which has yet to find a national pattern," according to Jorge Valdano, a member of Argentina's 1986 World Cup champion team. "And the Italians, they are a paradox. In every other area they export style and flair to the world; but in football they've allowed the ideal of collective organization to crush individual talent."[5]

The way a player or team approaches the game makes a statement about their identity, or at least it can seem to do so.

The next layer is this: soccer can be used to establish or reinforce a national or local identity. Soccer is not unique among sports in this regard –Hitler famously tried to use the 1936 Berlin Olympics for particular nation-building purposes. FIFA's World Cup was inaugurated during an era of growing nationalism and has been used ever since as a way to reinforce national identity. Soccer is an "us versus them" game and therefore can be an especially effective way to define identity, both who we are and who and what we are not (see Giulianotti 2000). The case of the Brazilian Pelé is an especially interesting one in this regard.

Pelé was the greatest soccer player of his generation, perhaps of any generation. He was born in 1940 and played for most of his career with Santos, Sao Paulo's richest team. A personal sponsorship contract from the Brazilian Coffee Institute allowed him to resist the financial incentives to play in Europe (Murray, 1994: 134-37). Pelé was a black player at a time when Brazilian teams still discriminated against blacks. Pelé's amazing skill and creativity changed that and, to some extent, changed Brazil, too.

Brazil's government quite purposefully used Pelé to shape the country's identity and to legitimize its hold on power. When a military regime seized power in Brazil in 1964, it immediately turned its attention to the most famous Brazilian, Pelé, the man who defined Brazil to many people. "For the generals," Bill Murray writes, "Pelé became a resource to be shamelessly exploited in their own interests. He was encouraged to speak on behalf of their dictatorship, claiming that Brazil was not ready for democracy, and in a country with more soccer pitches than schools pointed to himself as an example of how the poor and blacks could do well" (Murray, 1994: 136). Race was an important issue. When Pelé married a white woman it was promoted as a symbol of racial harmony and integration. Pelé was an especially powerful symbol because he was, like Michael Jordan in the 1990s, a ubiquitous presence. Media and commercial interests made sure that his face was everywhere and his image was designed to sell more than just soccer and coffee–it was designed to sell a particular view of Brazil's government and a very particular image of Brazil itself: the harmonious multiracial land of opportunity.

We know that governments will use whatever tools they can find, soccer included, to advance their interests and shape national attitudes, but how do people themselves use soccer to create or reinforce their identities. There has been a good deal of scholarly work on how fan groups have used their association with soccer to build distinctive local identities (cf. Giulianotti, 2000). One very interesting personal account is *A Season with Verona* by the novelist (and literature professor) Tim Parks (2002). Parks is a fan of Hellas Verona, his local team, and spent one season attending every home and away Verona game in the company of a group of *ultras* or extreme fans. Parks' book obviously lacks scholarly distance and objectivity, but it does provide an interesting perspective on this identity-creation process as seen from inside. The particular case that Parks reports is also interesting because Hellas Verona fans were thought to be especially racist and for a time Verona was forced by the Italian league to play its home games on neutral grounds due to the alleged racist environment. Soccer identities can be negative as well as positive ones and Parks helps us understand that the meaning of soccer within an *ultra* group may be different than the meaning assigned by outside observers.[6]

The basic "us versus them" structure of soccer seems to enable team followers to assign many different meanings to the teams they support. We might expect national identities would be at stake (France versus Germany), but it is more complicated that this. A game between the English teams Aston Villa and Birmingham City, for example, assumes the identity of a class war. Both teams are based in Birmingham, but City's fans identify themselves as blue-collar working class–gritty and hard-working–versus the bourgeois suburban Villa fans. Marx's class war is played out in surrogate form inside the stadium (and sometimes in real form outside it) each time these teams play (Hammond, 2004).

The rivalry between Glasgow's two Scottish Premier League teams, Celtic and Rangers, is even more complicated. The identities of these two Scottish teams reflect Irish religious tensions as transferred to Glasgow through industry and immigration.[7] Rangers is the team of anti-Catholic protestants and Celtic is the pro-Catholic team. Rangers are "closely tied to the Unionist majority of Northern Ireland, whose livelihood was strongly associated with the shipyard industries of Belfast and Glasgow," according to Richard Giulianotti. "Celtic were founded in Glasgow's east end ... as a benevolent club for poor Irish Catholics immigrants. It soon became a symbol of sporting and cultural success of the disadvantaged minority" (Giulianotti, 2000: 18). If Catholic-anti-Catholic sentiments define Scottish soccer at its highest level, you need only imagine what goes on in Ireland! Fortunately, religion and soccer do not *always* mix in conflictual ways. Giulianotti also reports a belief held by some Greenland Inuit people that the "northern lights" (*aurora borealis*) appears when the spirits of the dead play soccer (2000: 19).

One of my favorite movies is all about how soccer can be used to construct an identity among oppressed peoples. It is *The Cup*, a 1999 film by Khyentse Norbu, a Bhutanese writer and director.[8] It was filmed in Nepal. All of the dialogue is in Tibetan (with sub-titles, of course). It was the first Bhutanese film ever to be nominated for an Academy Award. It is the story of Tibetan refugee children who are smuggled into a monastery in Nepal. Separated from their families and friends, some of the boys get it in their heads that they need to watch the 1998 World Cup being played in France so that they can root for the French team (lead by Zinedine Zidane). Why? Because France is the only country that recognizes Tibet as a sovereign nation. A victory by France is, in their minds, a victory of their own and validation of their identities as Tibetans. The movie is the tale of how they found a way to watch the game and what, if anything, France's actual victory meant to them.

Soccer's ability to help nations and individuals construct their own identities is a very hopeful sign. We hear constantly that globalization destroys local culture, replacing it with the meaningless consumption culture of the American suburb and if soccer is part of the globalization process, you'd expect it to do the same. But if soccer also builds distinct local identities, then it is also a force opposed to homogenization and commodification.

Thus, for example, when the great Diego Maradona left to play in Europe, one effect of his transfer was to actually strengthen the identity of the fans of his Argentine club, Boca Juniors. As far as the fans were concerned, or at least some of them, he was still their Boca player and his successes and failures were theirs as well as his. To the extent that this effect holds more generally, and I don't think that it can be as true for most exported players as it was for a famous player like Maradona, then I think the net effect of soccer globalization may be to strengthen local identity in opposition to whatever global forces may be weakening it.

That said, I also think that the relationship between global economics and local culture is a like a mousetrap, delicate and dangerous. I find it difficult to be confident about causes and effects, even when operating within a relatively simple framework such as soccer globalization. I'd like to say that global soccer strengthens local identity, but I worry that it just isn't so.

The economic tension between the professional clubs and the national teams seems to make this problem even worse. Players are paid by their clubs, of course, who are expected to release players for international competition (World Cup qualification games, for example) during league seasons. The clubs and their leagues are creatures of FIFA, the sanctioning body that organizes these competitions, so their cooperation is expected. But FIFA's interests and the interests of a club are often at odds when, say, an important league match coincides with an international game. The players are often caught in the middle between their clubs and fans in the super-leagues and their national teams and fans back home–a difficult situation either way. Some European-based players declined to join their national teams for the 2004 African Cup competition, for example, actions that caused many reactions–none of them good–in the home countries and teams (White, 2004: 3).

If you want to see the power of soccer to define local communities but also perhaps to destroy them, come to Buenos Aires. A city of 12 million, Buenos Aires is home to literally dozens of professional soccer clubs. Thirty-six clubs, each with its own stadium, are found in the city proper and the suburbs are home to another 37 clubs with 37 stadiums (Weil, 2003b: 22). Taken together, the 73 teams divide up the territory and population into large and small pockets of soccer identity. If local identity is an asset, then Buenos Aires fans are perhaps the wealthiest soccer fans on earth, wealthier even than the residents of London, who have 12 professional teams from the top three divisions to choose from, not counting teams from the outlying suburbs.

The sad fact of this is, however, that a population that could support three or four teams adequately in this winner-take-all world is spread too thin. Each club has its own stadium, so none of them are very good facilities (none of them would meet the standards for a World Cup match, for example). Many of the stadia are shoddy, some dangerous. Most of the clubs are financial basket cases, a fact partly due to their organizational structure: Argentine clubs are really clubs, which sponsor youth teams, women's teams, and teams in other sports such as basketball. Fans join and pay monthly dues, which give them the right to attend home matches for free (this practice is not uncommon in Europe, which accounts for the low gate receipts they receive).

The logical thing for the Buenos Aires clubs to do would be to consolidate, share facilities, share costs, and in this way evolve into an economically sustainable structure. But such changes–even sharing a stadium–are intolerable ideas because they challenge what it means to be a local club member. They threaten the identity that these soccer teams have helped their fans and supporters create. They would rather that the stadium be a shambles and the best players quickly sold than compromise the identity of the team.

In winner-take-all markets like soccer has become, team loyalty fragments the market and may doom the very clubs with which the fans identify. Or, if not doom them exactly, keep them firmly in the economic periphery of the game, despite their place at the core of the game of soccer itself.

THE AMERICAN EXCEPTION

Globalization is seldom really global. Africa, for the most part, was left out and left behind in the hot money investment-fueled, technology-driven rush to profit from economic globalization. It is the huge hole in the globalization ozone. If we look at globalization through soccer, however, Africa is right in there and it is growing in significance (the 2010 World Cup will be played in South Africa). But the United States is missing. It is the "Africa" of soccer globalization.

This is not a trivial fact. There is a lot of money behind professional soccer, lots of commercial interests and media stakes. In the super-leagues, soccer has been thoroughly commercialized and tailored to a high-end consumer market. All these factors are supposed to be ones that distinctly appeal to Americans–that define Americanization, in fact. So what gives? Why the American exception?[9]

Before I try to answer this question, let me remind you what is at stake. Globalization-Americanization is supposed to be an unstoppable force, but if Americans, who are most comfortable in this environment, and presumably most susceptible to it, are immune in this case, then perhaps other people in other countries may be immune as well. That is, perhaps the idea that globalization-Americanization is inevitable is what I call globaloney. Briefly, here are five ways to try to explain the American exception to soccer globalism.

Explanation One: there is no American exception. Soccer has been thoroughly embraced by America and Americans (even if most of them could not pick David Beckham out of a line-up). Soccer is, indeed, the most played sport in America. More school-age Americans play soccer than baseball, football, or anything else. But whereas young people who play baseball in school tend to follow the professional teams as spectator or fan (and many who do not play do as well), young people who play soccer grow up, for the most part, to be followers of other professional sports. Soccer is a game to be played by the young in the Untied States, not an adult spectator sport (apart from the ubiquitous soccer moms and dads who loyally attend their children's games). Americans seem to identify with soccer as participants, not observers. This answer has accuracy in its favor–soccer really is number one–but it really raises more questions about why this is so than it answers.

Explanation Two: soccer is not currently a major American sport, but it will be. And soon. Nike will see to it! This answer returns to the Nike theory of globalization–anything that Nike and the media moguls want they can get. The argument runs like this. Nike intended that basketball, Michael Jordan, and the new global capitalism would sweep (or maybe "swoosh" is a better verb) the world, starting from the United States and expanding steadily outward. But they did not take into account the strength of soccer, which steadfastly held on to its position as the world's number one sport. So, it is argued, Nike decided to reverse its strategy. They signed major soccer stars and teams to lucrative contracts and then set about both conquering the soccer world and extending that domain to include the U.S. Having failed to conquer the world with basketball, Nike aims now to conquer the U.S. with soccer–an inside-out conquest.

Any argument set in the future is impossible to prove or disprove, but Nike certainly seems to be taking soccer seriously. One building on the Nike corporate headquarters campus is named for Michael Jordan, but another honors Mia Hamm, the best [known] U.S. female soccer player. Nike has indeed vigorously entered the world soccer market, signing their share of the super-teams and super-players in the super-leagues. It does have competition in this, however, from companies with longer histories in soccer such as Adidas, Umbro, Puma, Lotto and Kappa. So Nike's success abroad, although likely, is not assured.

It is also clear that Nike is trying to build a U.S. market for soccer. In summer 2003, for example, it sponsored a U.S. tour by Manchester United, its most famous team, which played a series of matches around the country against other super-league teams. (The tour was repeated and even expanded in 2004.) Several stadiums set attendance records, an indication of the power of the best to attract an audience for a one-off event even in an otherwise unpromising market. More significant, to my mind, was what went on at the Nike campus in Beaverton, Oregon. Elite youth teams from around the country and around the world came to rub shoulders with the "swoosh"-emblazoned Manchester United players, to train and to play in tournament games. The top-down strategy of the touring super-teams was matched by a bottom-up strategy to develop American players who can attract American fans.

The third explanation for the American exception suggests why Nike's initiative might work where previous attempts to inject soccer into the American sports culture have failed. Answer three is taken from Markovits and Hellerman (2001). Markovits and Hellerman explain that there have been several attempts to introduce professional soccer in America and all have failed, at least so far. One reason they cite for the failure (there are many) is that soccer has generally been presented as a foreign sport and professional leagues, at least at the beginning, have relied upon foreign players. This strategy was effective in attracting an immediate audience of immigrants from soccer-playing countries and some well-educated Americans who sought status and elevated self-esteem by identifying with an international sport (that would be me, I suppose). But a focus upon foreign players to appeal to immigrant fans did little or nothing to develop a distinctly American constituency for the game. The teams and leagues just died away.

My personal experience as a fan of North American Soccer League (NASL) and Major Indoor Soccer League (MISL) soccer teams in the Pacific Northwest bears out this point. I remember the 1977 NASL championship game between the Cosmos, with Pelé and a squad of mainly aging European internationals, versus the Seattle Sounders, which featured a number of players from the 1966 England World Cup squad. Each team had several American players besides the "internationals," but the fans clearly came to see the exceptional skills of the foreign players, even if they were a little past their prime. The NASL folded relatively quickly, despite substantial financial backing, in part I think because the fans identified with the foreign players, who inevitably had to move on or out, not with their "home" teams themselves. How many fans came to see a Cosmos game? How many came just to be able to say that they had seen Pelé play?

Perhaps because the Pacific Northwest is soccer-mad, at least compared to the rest of the U.S., interest remained after the Sounders faded away with the rest of their league. Indoor soccer (soccer played, basically, on an astro-turfed hockey rink) caught on, at least for a while, and I attended the finals series between the Tacoma Stars and the Dallas Sidekicks. There were many more American players on these teams, but the stars were still foreigners. Steve Zungul, from Yugoslavia, was the most famous and productive player in the league followed by another young Yugoslav named Preki (Preki later acquired U.S. citizenship and played on U.S. World Cup teams). Only one player on the top ten all-time MISL points scorers (Dale Mitchell of Tacoma) was American, for example.

If you want an audience to embrace a sport as their own, it seems that the worst way to do this is to present it as a foreign game played by foreigners, yet this is what soccer promoters did in the United States until very recently. It is interesting how careful the NBA has been about this as more and more non-U.S. players have arrived in the league. The NBA calls them international, not foreign, players (at least in that part of their publicity focused on the U.S. audience). But there are other problems. The structural organization of soccer is, in many respects, foreign to America audiences. Most American professional sports leagues are organized in a very simple way. Teams play each other within roughly geographical divisions (designed to minimize travel costs) to determine a playoff field. Several playoff rounds determine a league titlist. The more games a team plays the more money it earns, which exacerbates the "winner-take-all" element of the business.

Soccer in other countries has a much more complex structure. Most soccer countries have a multiple hierarchy of leagues (in Italy the leagues are A, B, C1, C2, etc.). Teams compete to be at the top of their leagues, of course, but there is also interest at the bottom because the worst teams in league A, for example, are relegated to league B and replaced by the best teams from league B, with similar movements from leagues B to C1, C1 to C2, and so forth. So there is something at stake in games at both ends of the league table, which of course gives all of the games more meaning. Good teams want to advance and be promoted, bad teams try to avoid relegation. In theory it is possible for a team from a lowly C2 league town to advance via several excellent seasons to one of the super-leagues. This actually happened in Italy in the 1990s, a story that was documented by Joe McGinnis (1999).

Teams in the middle may also compete for positions in international competitions, giving their fans a reason to care. In Italy, for example, the very top teams qualify for the Champions League competitions, but others who finish in the top half of the league table may enter the UEFA Cup competition or earn the right to compete with teams from other countries for a spot in these competitions.

Each soccer nation also features a national cup competition that includes teams from several of the national leagues, providing a C1 team the opportunity, in theory at least, to play an A team and win a major trophy (and a place in the next year's international competitions). The result of this is that fans of most teams always have something to hope for or to fear with each game. In a given week a team may play one league match plus an international or national cup game, and in general competition proceeds on several different levels at once. This system is confusing to the outsider and represents another "foreign" barrier to American acceptance.

If Markovits and Hellerman are right, then the current Nike strategy is trying to have it both ways – to get attention through international super-teams and star players while also developing a distinctive American soccer identity. Perhaps it will work. But maybe it is too late.

Markovits and Hellerman are optimistic about the chances of soccer finally catching on in America, but the timing is bad, they say (this is the fourth potential explanation of American soccer exceptionalism). They note that the major spectator sports cultures around the world emerged during the period of the 1890s through the 1930s. This was the period when the urban middle class emerged in the industrial democracies and when the "space" of sports culture was created and filled. In the United States, they argue, this space was occupied by "the big three and a half" sports–baseball, basketball, American football and, to a certain extent, ice hockey. Together these sports spanned the four seasons and provided a year-round outlet for the sports consumers' interest, enthusiasm, loyalty and money. It is very difficult, they argue, for new sports to invade this space either in the U.S. or elsewhere around the world. What about basketball, you might ask (thinking about the theory that Michael Jordan and Nike have created a world hoops culture)? It was already there thanks to YMCA missionaries. What about baseball in Japan–it was introduced in the 1940s and 1950s? Yes, but it was introduced through the forces of U.S. military occupation, which perhaps indicates how unusual the circumstances must be for a new sport to enter the arena.

Why didn't soccer take a place in the U.S. sports space a hundred years ago? Markovits and Hellerman suggest that it could have done so, but didn't. The "foreign" element worked against it, of course, but there is a better reason. American football emerged during this period instead. Elite colleges in the Northeast began to play a form of soccer in the 19th

century, but it was the rough rugby-type game that was popular in England. It could have developed either way–into the Beautiful Game of association football or into the more violent game of rugby. Harvard seems to have been the key here. Just when it looked like Harvard would adopt rules like those in soccer today, the team played a series with McGill University in Canada, which played the rugby-style game. The team preferred this approach and published rules that evolved into American football. Ironically, American football, like "American" basketball, owes its emergence to Canadian influence. Professional football leagues eventually developed, building on but not replacing the college game, and the space that could have been occupied by soccer in the United States was filled instead by American football.

Is it too late for soccer in America? Maybe not. Markovits and Hellerman are optimistic that soccer can succeed as an important spectator sport this time around by developing a home grown product and finding ways to span the gaps between youth, college and professional strata. They are hopeful that current attempts to develop domestic soccer leagues that feature and develop American talent will be successful.

A new professional league structure was launched in the mid-1990s, shortly after the successful U.S. World Cup. Major League Soccer (MLS) is the top U.S. league with ten teams at this writing (New York/New Jersey, Columbus, Chicago, New England, Washington, D.C., San Jose, Dallas, Los Angeles, Colorado, and Kansas City) all owned by the League itself, which limits competition for player rights as a way of controlling costs. It began its eighth season in 2004. Just below the MLS is the A-League, with sixteen teams in Calgary, Edmonton, Vancouver, Seattle, Portland, Milwaukee, Minnesota, Atlanta, Charleston, Montreal, Puerto Rico, Richmond, Rochester, Syracuse, Toronto, Virginia Beach. Several lower layers of developmental leagues also exist. Taken together MLS and A-League include many cities with relatively strong local soccer traditions (former NASL cities such as Seattle, Portland and Dallas), strong college soccer traditions, or relatively high foreign or international fan bases (Virginia Beach has a large military-related population, for example, and San Jose's potential fans include both Hispanics and people from many nations attracted to near-by Silicon Valley). Competition with the MLS and A-League is strictly American-style: no relegation and promotion.

If it is to be successful, MLS must master several delicate balances. One goal of MLS is to develop American players and create a following for an American game, but foreign players are useful both on the field and to attract fans. Teams are therefore limited to three senior international players and must include some American developmental players on their rosters. Salaries are controlled by the league (so many of the best players leave the U.S. to play in the European super-leagues). Audiences have been slow to build, but MLS does now have an ABC/ESPN television contract, which is a positive sign.

The future of MLS is perhaps best represented by Freddy Adu, who was 14 years old when signed by D.C. United to the highest contract in MLS history. Born in Ghana, Adu emigrated to the United States with his parents, the happy winners of a green card lottery. He became a U.S. citizen in February 2003, quickly became the star of the U.S. Under-17 team and, in November, a member of D.C. United. Interestingly, Adu did not play organized soccer in Ghana, it seems. Classmates in Virginia were impressed by his schoolyard skills and talked him into joining their local team.

Adu will likely be a star on the U.S. national team in a few years and MLS has made a commitment to pay enough to keep him out of the European super-leagues, at least for a while (Inter of Milan was also interested). I think MLS would like Adu to become the Michael Jordan of American soccer (or perhaps its Tiger Woods) and to use him to raise the league from the periphery of American sports culture into its core. This will be a delicate undertaking, however. It remains to be seen if economic imbalances can be avoided and if the foreign versus American versus "international" issues can be dealt with successfully. Perhaps Markovits and Hellerman are right: the time is ripe and the MLS can avoid the problems that have doomed earlier attempts.

But I have my doubts. People thought that the 1994 World Cup, which was played in the United States, would give this process a jump start and it did not. And then there is the core-periphery factor. If the new American leagues are indeed successful in developing local talent, it seems inevitable that they will be swept away into the super leagues, depriving the U.S. teams of their feature players.

Perhaps, however, there is hope–for women's soccer. The U.S. women's soccer team competes at the highest level internationally, a statement that cannot be made about the men's side. There are professional women's leagues in other parts of the world, but they have not yet formed anything like a global winner-take-all market. Perhaps the United States could embrace women's soccer and be the center of the professional women's game? Perhaps, but that would require a greater change in U.S. sports culture than just accepting a foreign game with foreign players. It would require U.S. society to accept female athletes on the same terms as they do males. That may be a challenge even greater than globalization.

NOTES

1. Excerpted from "The Beautiful Game and the American Exception," in Michael Veseth, Globaloney: Unraveling the Myths of Globalization (Lanham, MD: Rowman and Littlefield, 2005).
2. These aspects of the history of the globalization of soccer are discussed in Veseth (2005: 91-101).
3. All data in these tables is from fifaworldcup.com (20 January 2004) Information on transfers is from *www.footballtransfers.info* (20 January 2004).
4. For a deeper study I recommend Giulianotti (2000).
5. Quoted in Rachman (2002: 6). Significantly, Valdano does not characterize the Argentine style.
6. One of the racist issues involves "monkey grunts" that the fans use to insult opposing players, particularly black players. This practice certainly seems racist to me, but my impression from reading Parks' book is that his fellow ultras simply tried to pick the most insulting possible response to each opposing player–and "monkey grunts" seemed to work against black players. When they were accused of racism, one reaction was to chant "monkey grunts" against opposing white players, too. They saw themselves as harsh and aggressive fans, extremists, but not racists.
7. Which, I think, makes this a globalization effect.
8. See the film's website at *www.finelinefeatures.com/sites/cup/* (8 June 2004).
9. Franklin Foer has recently argued that the American exception goes beyond indifference to resentment of soccer. Foer, a political journalist, claims that the American reaction to soccer mirrors the social divisions created by globalization. I don't agree with this conclusion, but I still find Foer's (2004) book very interesting in other respects.

REFERENCES

Bell, J. (2004). Soccer Report, New York Times (national edition), January 20, p. C16.

Bellos, A. (2002). Futbol: Soccer, the Brazilian Way. New York: Bloomsbury.

FIFA. (2004). *www.fifaworldcup.com.*

Giulianotti, R. (2000). Football: A Sociology of the Global Game. Cambridge, UK: Polity Press.

Hammond, D. (2004). Class War! FourFourTwo (January): 83-86.

Rachman, G. (2002). Passion, Pride and Profit, The Economist special section, June 1.

Murray, B. (1994). Football: A History of the World Game. Aldershot UK: Scolar Press.

Parks, T. (2002). A Season with Veron. New York: Arcade.

Foer, F. (2004). How Soccer Explains the World: An (Unlikely) Theory of Globalization. New York: HarperCollins.

Markovits, A.S. and S.L. Hellerman. (2001). Offside: Soccer & American Exceptionalism. Princeton: Princeton University Press.

McGinnis, J. (1999). The Miracle of Castel di Sangro: A Tale of Passion and Folly in the Heart of Italy. New York: Little Brown.

Wallerstein, I. (1979). The Capitalist World Economy. Cambridge: Cambridge University Press.

Weil, E. (2003a). Carry On Selling. World Soccer (September), 26.

Weil. E. (2003b). Buenos Aires: Busyness as Usual. World Soccer (June), 22.

White, D. (2004). Choice Between Demands of Club and Country Puts Africa's Soccer Stars in a Dilemma. Financial Times (January 24/25), 3.

www.footballtransfers.info (20 January 2004).

www.finelinefeatures.com/sites/cup/ (8 June 2004).

NETWORKS, POWER AND REVENUE IN CONTEMPORARY FOOTBALL:
An Analysis of the G14

4

Peter Millward

INTRODUCTION

In this article, I discuss the role of G14 upon the transnational football landscape and consider the criteria for gaining membership. G14 are a lobby group of European superclubs who work together to challenge the existing football power authorities, such as national associations and international bodies (i.e. FIFA and UEFA). G14 were formed in 1998 and legally constituted in 2000 (Banks 2002: 129-30) with the award of EEIG status (European Economic Interest Grouping).[1] Currently, there are eighteen members of the group. The fourteen original members are Real Madrid, AC Milan, Bayern Munich, Liverpool, Ajax Amsterdam, Juventus, Internazionale, Barcelona, Borussia Dortmund, Marseilles, PSV Eindhoven, Paris St. Germain, Porto and Manchester United, and four more were invited in 2002: Arsenal, Bayer Leverkusen, Valencia and Lyon. This article will critically question who G14 are, what they represent and how membership to the elite group may be gained.

Boyle and Haynes (2004) argue that G14 epitomise the advanced capitalist principles of contemporary European football in that their main purpose is to maximise their own revenues, principally through television income. This opinion is shared by many within sport, although the group argue that this is not the sole reason for their existence. Instead, G14 secretary-general Thomas Kurth (2002) stated that their priorities are 'to bring [G14 football clubs] closer into the decision taking process' (G14 website). Indeed, G14 list their aims as:

- promoting co-operation and unity amongst member clubs;

- promoting the interests of the member clubs and analyse all matters of common interest;
- performing economic activities to the benefit of the consortium, and,
- contributing to decisions on formal and administration of International club football or clubs related activity (and to) promote co-operation with UEFA, FIFA, other clubs Institutions, etc. (G14, September 2002)[2]

However, Boyle and Haynes (2004) argue that these aims, like many other statements from the G14, are embedded within managerial principles that promote the maximum economic gain through a tightening grip on football governance. They also claim that this rhetoric is consistent with the birth of the organisation, which was brought about by the structural changes to UEFA club competitions in the 1990s. At the centre of the transition was the rebranding of the European Cup as the Champions League in the 1992/93 season after pressure was placed on UEFA through an alliance of Glasgow Rangers and Real Madrid. These two teams joined AC Milan owner (and future prime minister of Italy) Silvio Berlusconi in creating the temporary 'Media Partners' group which sought assured entry to the European Cup and a greater share of the overall prize money.[3] The problem was that this clearly contradicted UEFA's pledge to provide equal opportunities to clubs from all member associations. Ultimately, UEFA compromised their position by offering large clubs an improved chance of Champions League qualification (particularly from the 1997/8 season) and a greater share of television monies, by allowing leagues which had large national television markets more Champions League qualifying places. G14 was created as a result of this success. A senior G14 executive, who wishes to remain anonymous, acknowledged this point:

> *When you stand up as a collective group, you have much more weight than when you stand up on your own. Whilst UEFA has influence in Europe, they are always there–if Bayern Munich goes there and says you should change 'this and that', they say 'well, this just benefits you, you are selfish, we wouldn't change just for you', but if a massive group stands up and says, 'you should do this, you should do that', they should be more sensitive to such a request.*
>
> *Anonymous G14 executive (personal interview, 29th September 2005)*

Therefore, G14 was created with the intention of challenging the way UEFA ran the Champions League. As a formally constituted EEIG, they are politically better organised than the Media Partners movement, which means that they can exert greater influence. The pressure group initially manipulated structural changes to the Champions League when for the first time, the team finishing in second place in the leading national leagues across Europe was granted access to the Champions League competition in 1997/98. Also, the group were not entirely happy with the way TEAM (UEFA's marketing partners) were attempting to maximise income from the Champions League and proposed restructuring its selling policies from individual games to complete packages. Therefore, they successfully argued that companies from the largest national television markets– England, Italy, Germany, Spain and France–should be charged significantly larger fees for exclusive national television rights. Ultimately, this meant that clubs from these countries were awarded a greater share of television incomes (King 2003; Martin 2005). Banks (2002: 128) points out that in the 1997/8 season the Champions League generated £185m, with £100m awarded to participating clubs. The remainder was split between UEFA's then-51 member football associations (£55m)–to aid smaller professional clubs and promote youth development–and TEAM (£35m). Yet the pressure group believed that the rewards should be even more heavily weighted toward the leading clubs and argued that the total generated figure could be substantially higher if the tournament further increased the number of competing clubs from the strongest football nations. As a result, the number of teams from England, Italy, Germany, Spain and France continued to expand, reaching a maximum of four teams in the following years. To compensate, the number of participating clubs grew from 24 to 32 teams. Due to these changes, key boardroom members of clubs from the 'big five' nations began to have 'informal meetings–without minutes or agendas–just sitting together sharing dinner and having fun. They found out that even though they were the 8 who had at least 5 European titles, there were some clubs missing. So they thought about who was missing and they came up with 14 teams' (anonymous G14 executive, personal interview, 29th September 2005). G14 was established from such meetings.

This article will build upon this literature by asking: What are the motivations behind the formation of the group? Can G14 be theoretically understood? What future directions could the organisation take? However, I will first critically explore the grounds upon which membership to the group is awarded.

G14 MEMBERSHIP CRITERIA

The common consensus of opinion is that G14 clubs were originally invited into the organisation on the basis of European Cup/Champions League success. Table 1 tests this theory and finds that 13 out of the original clubs 14 clubs had won Europe's premier club competition prior to the groups' formation in 1998. This means that this claim is generally, but not strictly, true.

Table 1
Winners of European Cup/Champions League

Rank	*Club*	*Country*	*Number of European Cup/ Champions League wins (post 2002 in brackets)*	*G14 Member?*
1	Real Madrid	Spain	7 (1)	Yes
2	AC Milan	Italy	5 (1)	Yes
3	Liverpool	England	4 (1)	Yes
=4.5	Ajax Amsterdam	Holland	4	Yes
=4.5	Bayern Munich	Germany	4	Yes
=8	Benfica	Portugal	2	No
=8	Internazionale	Italy	2	Yes
=8	Juventus	Italy	2	Yes
=8	Manchester United	England	2	Yes
=8	Nottingham Forest	England	2	No
=11.5	Barcelona	Spain	1 (1)	Yes
=11.5	Porto	Portugal	1 (1)	Yes
=17	Aston Villa	England	1	No
=17	Borussia Dortmund	Germany	1	Yes
=17	Feyenoord	Holland	1	No
=17	Glasgow Celtic	Scotland	1	No
=17	SV Hamburg	Germany	1	No
=17	Marseille	France	1	Yes
=17	PSV Eindhoven	Holland	1	Yes
=17	Red Star Belgrade	Former Yugoslavia	1	No
=17	Steaua Bucharest	Romania	1	No

I decided that I would take 2002 as the key point in the table because it was the year that four new members were invited into G14. The European Cup/Champions League was defined as the significant achievement because it is seen by many to be the pinnacle of European club success (even though I recognise that the anonymous G14 executive referred to all European titles).[4]

The table displays a strong relationship between original G14 membership and past European Cup/Champions League success. Only

Paris St. Germain of pre-2002 members have not won the tournament. The club is a relatively young, having been first founded in August 1970 through the union of two teams, F.C. Paris and Stade Saint-Germain. The new club played in the *Nationale* (second) division in its first season but immediately won promotion to *Le Championnat* (first division) in its first season. However, after finishing 16th in 1971/72, the club split after Paris City Council placed pressure upon the club to remove any reference to St. Germain. The professional part of the club joined C.A. Montreuil and remained in the top division under the guise of Paris F.C. while the amateur part of the club retained its name but played in the third division. In 1973/74, Paris St. Germain returned to the top division, replacing Paris F.C., which was relegated. Since then, the club has remained in *Le Championnat.* The justification for the club's membership may come from its five consecutive UEFA competition semi-final appearances (1993-1997) and securing the now-defunct Cup Winners' Cup in 1995/96. Despite experiencing a number of successful runs in the Champions League, it has never progressed beyond the semi-finals. Therefore, the motivations behind the group's inclusion of Paris St. Germain were probably not on the grounds of European success. It is also interesting that Paris St. Germain were given the invitation preference of the group before Benfica and Nottingham Forest, which had both won the European Cup twice. This has only been bettered by five G14 members. Indeed, although Benfica's fellow Portuguese club, Porto, have now won the trophy twice, at the point when G14 were founded, they had only done so once. Therefore, Benfica could lay stronger claims to membership than Porto.

It also appears that a greater selection emphasis has been placed upon more recent Champions League wins. While the likes of Benfica, Nottingham Forest and Glasgow Celtic have not achieved membership, more contemporary competition victors, such as Marseille, have been invited. This implies inconsistencies in the 'membership criteria' because not all competition triumphs are equally weighted. Most interestingly, none of the four second-wave members have won either the European Cup or Champions League. This suggests that European competition victories do not define contemporary membership, which means that there are other criteria that must be met to attain G14 status. I will now look at average match day attendances as a second selection criterion.

Table 2 illustrates that 11 out of the top 20 average attendance ranks are taken by G14 clubs; only AS Roma, Glasgow Celtic and Newcastle

United and Lazio prevent the top 12 positions being monopolised by members. This means that there is 55 percent likelihood that an elite club will achieve one of the twenty best average gates in Europe, or viewed another way, that about 61 percent of the 18 clubs in the G14 are amongst the twenty best attended in Europe. Six G14 clubs–Ajax, Juventus, Porto and PSV Eindhoven from the original group, and Arsenal, Bayer Leverkusen and Lyon as post-2002 members–did not rank amongst the top 20. Bayer Leverkusen is the most interesting case, given that they were the lowest ranked G14 club (62nd) with an average attendance of 22,471. This was a little over one third of AS Roma's mean home gate. This shows that G14 membership loosely follows attendance rank, but is not defined by it.

Table 2
European Premier Leagues Average Attendance (2000-2001)

Rank	*Club*	*Country*	*Attendance*	*G14 Member?*
1	Manchester United	England	67,490	Yes
2	Real Madrid	Spain	64,475	Yes
3	Borussia Dortmund	Germany	63,729	Yes
4	AS Roma	Italy	63,370	No
5	Barcelona	Spain	62,632	Yes
6	Glasgow Celtic	Scotland	59,353	No
7	AC Milan	Italy	52,448	Yes
8	Newcastle United	England	51,309	No
9	Internazionale	Italy	50,950	Yes
10	Marseille	France	48,508	Yes
11	SS Lazio	Italy	48,498	No
12	Bayern Munich	Germany	48,471	Yes
13	Glasgow Rangers	Scotland	47,532	No
14	Sunderland	England	46,791	No
15	Schalke 04	Germany	45,623	No
16	Liverpool	England	43,699	Yes
17	Hamburg SV	Germany	42,893	No
18	Valencia CF	Spain	42,737	Yes, invited
19	Paris Saint Germain	France	42,586	Yes
20	Herta BSC Berlin	Germany	40,337	No

Source: www.european-football-statistics.co.uk/attn/2001/aveeur.htm

As G14 are a transnational organisation, the two criteria of European Cup/Champions League titles and average match-day attendees can be considered to be reasonable ways in which prestige can be measured. However, in the era in which '[f]ootball is ... also a business' (Szymanski and Kuypers 1999: 1) it likely that Boyle and Haynes' (2004) claim that G14 exist for commercially driven purposes is at least partially valid. For these reasons in Table 3, I look at the mean revenue-generation of the top 31 football clubs across the world.

Data in this table are taken from Deloitte's *Annual Report of Football Finance* (2006). Since the 1996/97 season, this accountancy group have annually collated the revenue data of all professional football teams. From this, they release the *Rich List,* which focuses upon the 'top 20' clubs. I have aggregated the ranked positions given in the *Rich Lists* in Table 3, to show which consistently generate the highest revenues. In the annual *Rich List*, the 20 clubs with the highest yearly revenues are ranked. In Table 3, I have used these data by awarding 20 points to each first place finish (a position dominated by Manchester United), 19 points to each runner up, and so on. Twentieth place is valued at 1 point. These scores have been aggregated and displayed in Table 3. All available data have been included, even though the 2002 enlargement was taken as a key point in Table's 2 and 3. I decided to do this because the data are cumulative, which means that it is simple to view the positions of the clubs up until the enlargement.

It is clear that prior to 2002, the only non-G14 members that were consistently ranked amongst the top 10 wealthiest clubs were Chelsea and Lazio. Indeed, post 2002, only Chelsea breached this monopoly and from the other wealthiest clubs, just Arsenal was not originally in G14. In one respect it would be foolish to decide that the income of the top clubs may be a criterion for selection because elite membership would be likely to generate larger revenues for its constituents. However, the results in 1996/97 and 1997/98-the years prior to the creation of G14-are fairly consistent with those aggregated over the full period of time. That said, there are two main ways the pre-G14 results have become outdated. First, in 1997, Brazilian club Flamengo was the tenth richest club in the world, whereas from 1998 onwards, it failed to rank amongst the top 20. Second, Chelsea was not considered to be amongst the top 20 richest clubs in 1997, but over the nine years has averaged an overall position of seventh. Given that neither Chelsea nor Flamengo are members, it can be argued that the position of G14 clubs have not been greatly improved by membership, which may have been awarded because of existing wealth.

There is certainly a positive relationship between the capacity of a club to generate massive revenues and the chances of it of being a G14

Table 3

Rank of Wealthiest 31 Clubs in Europe (1996-2005): Source Deloitte

Rank	*Club*	*1996/97*	*1997/98*	*1998/99*	*1999/00*	*2000/01*	*2001/02*	*2002/03*	*2003/04*	*2004/05*	*Points*	*G14 Member*
1	Manchester United	20	20	20	20	20	20	20	20	19	179	Yes
2	Real Madrid	18	19	18	19	15	15	17	19	20	160	Yes
3	Juventus	17	17	16	16	19	19	19	16	17	156	Yes
4	Bayern Munich	16	18	19	18	18	18	16	12	14	149	Yes
5	AC Milan	15	14	14	17	17	17	18	18	18	148	Yes
6	Barcelona	19	15	15	13	9	12	8	14	15	120	Yes
7	Chelsea	0	12	17	14	11	14	11	17	16	112	No
8	Internazionale	11	13	12	12	10	9	15	13	12	107	Yes
9	Liverpool	12	11	10	2	14	16	13	11	13	102	Yes
10	Arsenal	1	8	11	10	8	13	14	15	11	91	Yes, invited
11	Newcastle United	13	16	9	1	7	8	12	10	9	85	No
12	AS Roma	6	2	5	11	12	11	10	9	10	76	No
13	SS Lazio	2	9	13	15	13	7	4	6	1	70	No
14	Borussia Dortmund	14	10	7	9	0	6	9	0	0	55	Yes
15	Tottenham Hotspur	5	3	6	4	5	5	6	7	8	49	No
16	Leeds United	0	1	4	8	16	10	5	0	0	44	No
17	Glasgow Rangers	7	5	3	6	4	0	0	2	0	27	No
18	Parma	3	7	8	3	2	3	0	0	0	26	No
19	Glasgow Celtic	0	0	1	0	0	4	3	8	5	21	No
20	Schalke 04	0	0	0	0	0	0	7	4	7	18	No
21	Paris St Germain	8	6	0	0	0	0	0	0	0	14	Yes
22	Flamengo	10	0	0	0	0	0	0	0	0	10	No
24	Athletico Madrid	9	0	0	0	0	0	0	0	0	9	No
24	Lyon	0	0	0	0	0	1	2	0	6	9	Yes, invited
24	Manchester City	0	0	0	0	0	0	0	5	4	9	No
26	Marseille	0	0	0	5	0	0	0	3	0	8	Yes
27	Fiorentina	0	0	0	7	0	0	0	0	0	7	No
28	Hamburg	0	0	0	0	6	0	0	0	0	6	No
29	Aston Villa	0	4	0	0	0	0	0	1	0	5	No
30.5	Valencia	0	0	0	0	1	0	1	0	2	4	Yes, invited
30.5	Ajax Amsterdam	4	0	0	0	0	0	0	0	0	4	Yes

member. Indeed, about 83 per cent of G14 are ranked amongst the top 31 wealthiest clubs with only Bayer Leverkusen, PSV Eindhoven and Porto missing. The case of German club Bayer Leverkusen is particularly interesting. Unlike Paris St. Germain, it is not a young club, having been initially established in 1904. However, it only won its first major trophy in 1988, as it beat Espanyol on penalty kicks in the UEFA Cup final. Rather, the club has staked its reputation from being perennial 'almost winners', achieving four 'top four' *Bundesliga* finishes (1997-2002) and making the Champions League final in the 2001/02 season. However, it has not won the European Cup/Champions League and is not amongst the best supported or wealthiest clubs, so there are no clear reasons why it has achieved membership. Although I did not question the G14 executive about Bayer Leverkusen's membership, I did ask him about Arsenal, given that like Bayer Leverkusen, they had never won the European Cup/Champions League. His response was to argue:

> *[M]embership was [originally] awarded upon the basis of international, not just European success, and then came the pressures to change... and it was decided to go 'three, three, three'..., across the major nations and Arsenal were the next ones down, in terms of international success and prestige.*
>
> *Anonymous G14 executive (personal interview, 29th September 2005)*

The case of Bayer Leverkusen can be taken as similar to Arsenal. The G14 executive pointed out that Arsenal had been invited into the group because associates had made a decision to expand by including three members from the most lucrative national television markets ('three, three, three'). As there were only two members from England, France, Germany and Spain, the decision was made to invite Arsenal, Lyon, Bayer Leverkusen and Valencia because they were considered to be the 'next ones down, in terms of international success and prestige.' The decisions to invite Arsenal (when Nottingham Forest had won the European Cup twice and Aston Villa once) and Bayer Leverkusen (which was preferred to other German clubs such as the better supported 1983 European Cup winner SV Hamburg) were not in line with the initial selection criteria of winning a number of European titles. Yet both Arsenal and Bayer Leverkusen regularly qualified for the increasingly lucrative Champions League and it seems, from the G14 executives, comment that this now defines 'international success and prestige.'

However, it can be assumed from the executives' claim ('three, three, three') that national television markets are also important when G14 decide which new clubs gain membership. This, after all, is where a significant proportion of all major clubs' revenues come from, which makes it an important consideration when trying to formulate the grounds upon which membership is decided. This also makes Porto's position particularly contentious. Given that it was preferred to Benfica (which had won the European Cup twice) it is interesting to note that the Portuguese national television market is much smaller than any of the 'big five'. Indeed, in 2002, its national television contract ranked eighth amongst European leagues (accounting for just over one third of the annual value of the ill-fated English Football League television contract with ITV Digital) with a value of £38m per year (Roche 2004). According to UEFA, the Portuguese rights to the 2004/5 Champions League season sold for €1.9m. The same rights sold for €56.8m in England and €6.3m in Scotland. Viewed in this way, we could legitimately ask why Scotland does not have a G14 representative (especially given Glasgow Celtic's European Cup win in 1967 and Glasgow Rangers' active participation in the Media Partners grouping) when Portugal does.

G14 AS A NETWORK: USING CASTELLS TO UNDERSTAND TRANSNATIONAL FOOTBALL CLUBS

The next part of the article shows that it is important to understand the power structure of G14. I argue that G14 takes on a network power structure to exercise authority and maximise economic gain. To understand the idea of G14 as a *network*, it is necessary to recognise the significance of such structures in the broader global society. In contemporary sociology, the network has become tied to the theory in Manuel Castells's *Information Age* trilogy (Castells 1996/2000; 1997/2004; 1998). It is generally agreed that a network could be defined in geographical space as discrete points bound together by links and people, where capital and ideas can flow between nodes (Jõnsson et al 2000: 23). According to Castells, networks are becoming the primary form of social organisation throughout the world and this is making established national boundaries increasingly porous (Castells 1996/2000). The defining feature of Castells' theory is that network power cannot be centralised, but instead resides 'somewhere' within its nodal points, although exactly where is unknown because power is in flux and entirely dependent upon situational context. This gives each node a point in time when it is most powerful. Melucci (1996: 207-221) concurs with this view by arguing that contemporary societies are increasingly controlled by a myriad of networks. For instance, he argues that a range of networked new social movements challenge (and shape) the central, bureaucratic decision-making hierarchies in both national, but more often transnational, settings. Castells (2000a: 14) argues that in most cases networks are threatening the central, hierarchical, power structures of 'the state' because mega-cities are classically the nodes of the global network society.

The UN define mega cities as 'very large agglomerations of human beings ... with over 10 million people in 1992 ... and four of them projected to be well over 20 million in 2010' (Castells 2000: 434). However, for Castells (2000; 2000a), their defining qualities are their crucial importance to the global economy by connecting huge segments of the human population to the global system. Also, the national media are located in mega-cities, which gives them a distinct advantage in the quest for the politics of power and the symbolic capacity to create and diffuse messages. Above all else, Castells views mega cities as functioning as magnets for the whole country or regional area in which they are located. For instance, Hong Kong and Guangzhou are not just cities with populations of six million and six and a half million people but a sole mega city of 40-50 million people connecting Hong Kong, Shenzhen, Guangzhou, Zhuhai, Macau, and other smaller towns. It is interesting to note that Paris, the city which is home to Paris St. Germain, is defined as a mega-city. Paris St. Germain may have been invited into G14 because they are based in such a vibrant urban locale that offers massive potential for future development. The mega-city network demonstrates two inter-related and key factors. [First, that in the network society, the global forces of capitalism are fully realised with anything of little or no value subsumed by other firms, territories, resources or cities] (Castells 2000a: 15) and second, that mega cities are simultaneously allied to both the global network and to local segments of their own country (Castells 2000: 436). Castells argues that in the information age, a mega city becomes more economically viable than the nation it belongs to because it connects to other mega cities in the global arena. The role of *capital* is all-defining in the network; so, whilst the nation-state is sustained, it becomes a tertiary consideration falling behind the lure of local, city based interests and the wider, more lucrative transnational space. Therefore the role of the nation states and the network society become counter-posed, because networks have 'no centre' and their flexibility sees them supersede nation states as the primary focus of loyalty (see also Jõnsson et al. 2000).

Another possible crisis for national sovereignty is created by the global flows of wealth, communication and information which lead citizens and institutions to question the legitimacy of national authority. However, Castells (2000) argues that neither the nation nor state disappears, although they are diminished by the elusive power structure of networks and have to adapt to retain any status. There are two ways in which this can be carried out. Nation-states can devolve and decentralise power to regions and local governments, or they can form partnerships with other nation-states in order to share mutual influence (Castells 2000). Indeed, both Castells (1998) and Rumford (2000) have argued that the continued development of the European Union can partly be seen as a way that European nation-states attempt to retain power in the era of transnationalism. Therefore, although the network society is not deliberately opposed to nation-states, its key agents are ultimately in search of the wealth that can be achieved by operating in larger markets than those merely in the national 'space'. This prompts the move toward the international arena of the network society.

In football, G14 constitute many of the nodes of a *super club network.* In much the same way that Castells' classic nodes of the network society are defined as the 13-UN defined mega-cities, plus a select number of non-UN defined mega-cities, G14 plus a small number of other mega football clubs make up the *network*. On this basis, it is worthwhile to give an extended consideration of what G14 represent and how their future may be shaped in the future.

THE THEORY OF THE 'NETWORK' APPLIED TO G14

In much the same way that the nodes of the wider network society question the legitimacy of hierarchies, G14 have caused problems for national associations. On this basis, club-country disputes break out. These typically come in at least three guises. The first two of these relate to player availability. As seen through the eyes of Manchester United supporters in King's (2000; 2003) research, it is difficult for those with solely club based loyalties to understand why national teams should be able to take their star player and potentially injure him in the process. The problem may not be as acute in major tournaments such as the World Cup finals–in which the rewards of victory are clearly prestigious and tangible–or local major tournament qualifying games. However,

G14 take umbrage to international 'call ups' for their players in either 'friendly' international games or mid-season tournament qualifying matches of non-European players. Yet FIFA Articles 36 to 40 stipulate that clubs must allow international players to appear for national teams. However, during the data collection period, England manager Sven Goran Eriksson was consistently sympathetic to super club distress by refusing to play star players from G14 clubs such as Manchester United, Arsenal, Liverpool, Real Madrid and Bayern Munich for the full 90 minutes in non-competitive games. At the same time, Eriksson was less sympathetic to the concerns of non-G14 clubs–aside from Chelsea-who have not lobbied the FAs. Therefore, small club players are often played for the full duration of 'friendly' internationals.

G14 also have a problem with star employees playing in a midweek fixture in another continent when they have club duties to perform the following weekend. The travelling involved means that players are often tired or fatigued by 'jet lag', which inevitably affects club performance. The anonymous G14 executive recognised these tensions by arguing:

> *There has been very little problem about the availability of English players. It would all be sorted out because the English clubs are proud of the English national team, and the English national team is proud of the English teams and the players. It would all be sorted out because they support each other. They belong to the same culture and address the same culture and group and supporters, because the Manchester United supporters are England supporters, the Aston Villa supporters are England supporters. You cannot nurture a conflict inside this, because they want to support both their club and national team... But after the Bosman ruling things have changed with the abolition of the European 'foreigners' rule... This means that nowadays the English clubs have some English players but also some Nigerian, French, Italian, Swiss, Brazilian, Colombian, whatever. Now you have the problem because the interests of the association are not the interests of the club. [For instance t]he French FA don't have to respect the interests of the English club.*
>
> *Anonymous G14 executive (personal interview, 29th September 2005)*

The executive's general argument is that home football associations have learned to co-operate with the demands of their G14 clubs, although the presence of *foreign* players has created new dilemmas as similar transnational understandings have yet to be developed. This creates clear institutional tensions between club and national football teams.

The second, related issue that causes unease from G14 towards national associations is the question of who pays player wages. Currently, even if a player is on international duty, the club who employs him continues to pay his wages. This issue becomes particularly pressing if a player is injured whilst on international duty, as FIFA Article 37 stipulates that a club has no right to any financial indemnity and is solely responsible for insurance costs. While Charleroi player Abdelmajid Oulmers was playing for Morocco in a friendly match against Burkina-Faso in November 2004, he ruptured his left ankle ligament, causing him to miss a large number of club matches through injury. Although Charleroi is not a G14 member, the group have long shared this particular grievance and sponsored the cost of the case which will be considered in the European Courts. If G14 and Charleroi win the case, FIFA's policy on player release will have to change. This will inevitably favour the position of large clubs. At face value, the demands of G14 are not too problematic, yet in the age of transnational football labour markets, highly paid players often hail from countries where national associations are not well endowed. It would be problematic if, in the future, players' international 'call-ups' were decided by whether the national team could afford to reimburse his club for his wages.

The third point of contestation concerns the lack of financial return clubs receive from major international tournaments. G14 argues that the World Cup and other football mega-events are highly lucrative–the 2006 World Cup was predicted to generate more than £1.5billion in direct revenue–but the clubs who employ the players do not receive any direct return. This point is made by the G14 executive:

> *Financial compensation should be given to the clubs–not every time when a player goes to an international game–but when significant revenue is generated [a share of the revenue should go to the clubs who make the players available...] That cost is not just simply salary cost, we calculated, roughly speaking, that the cost of each player is €5,000 per game. Chelsea is not in it–there are big clubs in there, but not Chelsea. But there are also small clubs in there, such as Ajax Amsterdam, PSV, Porto. They have turnovers which are far beneath certain English clubs' turnovers. I think that could be a target, if we take €5000 and say, okay, 'how many players days does the Euro Championship require?' You come to a figure which is a bit below 10,000 player days – if you include the 14 days preparation and then you have so many days for group matches and then so many days for each of the knockout stages and you come up for a figure which is about 10,000. Which means that you have 10,000 days at the cost of €5,000 you come up with a*

figure of €50m. For a World Cup the pattern is larger as you have more than 22,000 days, because there are 32 as opposed to 16 teams, making €110m. You can say let's remove 10 per cent of the overall revenue and give 7 per cent to those clubs who have made players available and 3 per cent to all those others who have given players during the qualifying round.

Anonymous G14 executive (personal interview, 29th September 2005)

Therefore, G14 battle against the precedence of national teams on three levels, echoing Castells' model in which nodes of the global network society challenge the authority of nation-states. The role of *capital* in the football configuration can also be considered to be an accurate application of Castells' theory as he sees it as the all defining mechanism of power. Therefore, in the age of Information and Communication Technologies (ICT), it is the neo-liberal flexibility of industry in mega-cities which make them more appealing than rigid nation-state power. In the *network of superclubs*, the same principle applies as clubs gain power over national associations because the disparities of wealth are becoming smaller, with some clubs now wealthier than national associations. Underlining this point, Giulianotti (2004) pointed out that in 2004, the Euro Championship winners Greece gained £13m prize money. This compared unfavourably to the £70m that Porto received for winning the Champions League just two months earlier.

FUTURE G14 DEVELOPMENTS

This section of the paper will synthesise the findings of the membership criteria section, Castells' theory of networks and the apparent goals of the organisation to predict future developments in the G14. There are two issues which I will look at: where the group are likely to expand in the middle-term future, and whether the group would like to develop a *European Super League*.

It is impossible to accurately predict how the future of G14 might develop, but it is extremely likely that the group will continue to expand. This view was validated by the anonymous G14 Executive, who stated:

In the future, we will expand further: Turkey, Scotland, Brazil, Argentina to clubs with international reputations...

Anonymous G14 executive (personal interview, 29th September 2005)

As earlier documented, network association was initially based upon the criteria that members had experienced pan-European competition success. Yet, it is certain that now national television markets also play an active role in determining membership. Arguably the most significant *super club network* achievement pre-dated G14 and came under auspice of the Media Partners when, as earlier mentioned, they encouraged UEFA to rename the European Cup as the Champions League. According to Banks (2002: 129), such changes took the 'financial relevance of the Champions League to a whole new level' and–in the era of G14 - with the award of a further eight extra Champions League places divided between clubs in the five major television markets in the 1998/9 season, UEFA's television income rose to a new high of £670m. Of this, £490m was distributed to participating clubs, with the largest shares awarded to clubs from the 'big five' national television markets. This means that for super clubs who hail from such nations, a place in the Europe's premier competition is worth an estimated £10m upon qualification; winning the tournament is conservatively worth £70m (Giulianotti 2004), although according to some sources, this figure is more like £100m (Andrews 2002). Therefore, it would be foolish to argue that the role of the nation has been rendered insignificant in the age of the *super club network*. While the national space has become secondary to local club interests in the transnational space, the nation continues to have the role of revenue facilitator for super clubs. This prompts critical questioning into the anonymous G14 executive's claims. Specifically, he refers to clubs from Turkey, Scotland, Brazil and Argentina joining the elite group of clubs. This is particularly interesting, given that fifteen out of the eighteen current members are located in the five largest (exclusively European) national television markets. If the proposed future expansion was legitimate, it would mirror a more diffuse and inclusive G14 institutional structure. However, it is more likely that other large clubs from lucrative national television markets, such as AS Roma (Italy) or Chelsea (England) would become third-wave members. Indeed, when asked about the likelihood of Chelsea joining G14, the anonymous executive replied:

> *Well, perhaps. Chelsea are now of that standard. I mean, Peter Kenyon was at Manchester United for many years and attended the G14 meetings. Just because he has changed clubs does not mean that he is not the same man. He still understands the same things... I mean, they have a very good team and you have to give them time. They will do well and, of course, have Roman Abramovich.*
>
> *Anonymous G14 executive (personal interview, 29th September 2005)*

The vague nature of the comment is interesting. First, he does not define what 'that standard' refers to: standard in football terms often refers to playing quality, and since the accession of Arsenal in 2002, Chelsea have greatly improved, especially given the investment of Russian billionaire Roman Abramovich in the teams playing staff. However, because the executive partially qualified his statement by referring to the role of Chelsea Chief Executive Peter Kenyon (who was hired in 2003 after resigning from his similar post at Manchester United) it seems likely that 'the standard' probably meant commercial awareness. If this was the case, it would reaffirm G14 as a business-led enterprise, which would almost certainly mean that members would continue to hail from the most lucrative national television markets and operate in the Champions League. Nevertheless, despite Chelsea and AS Roma's lack of G14 membership, they along with similarly wealthy and successful clubs would still form nodal points in a *super club network* and would be likely candidates for entry should G14 decide to expand.

A second way that G14 may develop is by attempting to seize a greater degree of control over the Champions League and other international football events. News stories reporting G14's latest attempt to gain greater power broke in spring 2006 with the leak of *G14 Vision Europe* document to the British newspaper, *The Guardian*. This manuscript was interpreted to suggest that UEFA's role in organising the Champions League should be reduced in favour of a G14-run competition:

> *The clubs would... have the right and power to shape ... the rules and development which impact upon them, and to an appropriate degree. Clubs participating in top international competitions would take control over the organisation of such competitions as well as the commercialisation of the rights involved.*
>
> *G14 Vision Europe (in Scott 2006)*

It was widely interpreted that G14 wanted UEFA to reduce 'solidarity payments' to less affluent nations by reallocating this revenue to successful clubs and award G14 members with guaranteed entry into the Champions League (Scott 2006). Predictably, G14 would exert pressure by threatening to withdraw its teams from UEFA competition and set up its own 'superleague.' However, Dan Jones (2006), a partner in Deloitte's 'Sport Business Group,' argues that this threat is unlikely to be realised for two main reasons. First, G14 clubs realise that meritocracy produces uncertain results, which makes exciting and saleable sporting events. Currently this exists in UEFA competition with those teams who fare the best in domestic competitions qualifying for European competition, irrespective of the size of the club. G14 are unlikely to want to lose this marketable excitement. Second, Jones (2006) argues that if G14 carried out their threat, it is uncertain that it would receive more lucrative television deals than UEFA currently do. He believes that this represents a risk that G14 would be unwilling to take. Given that Boyle and Haynes (2004) argue that G14 exist to generate revenues, Jones' argument may be valid, although it is likely that the organisation will manipulate the situation to enter into talks with UEFA in an attempt to make the competition even more favourable for G14.

CONCLUSION

The results that have been generated do not allow us to accurately predict the criteria which clubs must meet if they are to attain G14 membership. In fact, it seems as if only a mysterious combination of pan-European success, the enduring capacity to generate revenue, numbers of live match attendees and a lucrative national television market might herald an invitation to join the new elite of global football. Even then, there may be hidden factors which grant membership. It is unlikely that these could be highlighted in any empirical studies and may have more to do with positive business associations than any sporting achievement.

It is certain that there was previously a heavy degree of team past-performance which granted group accession, but in the post-2002 era, membership has become more heavily tied to the size of national television markets. For this reason, the commercial value of G14 becomes more obvious, even though it seems likely that the motivations behind the group were revenue-driven since inception. The group's capitalist nature and transnational tendencies draws heavy parallels to Manuel Castells' theory of the 'network society'. In particular, to the argument that G14 functions as a revenue-orientated network which pursues further profit. The Champions League is highly lucrative and so this becomes the level at which the clubs are principally defined.

The role of the nation is potentially important if it is defined by the size of its television market. However, if the nation is defined in terms of its national football team, G14 render it worthless and continuously challenge it. Using Castells' theory, it is possible to predict future likely trends in the organisation. First, if it expands, it will probably move to include a small number of clubs from strong national television markets rather than teams from countries which sell their Champions League rights for smaller sums of money. This means that clubs from the 'big five' television countries may further dominate the group. If this happens, it remains to be seen if/how the long-term constitution of the group may be altered. The second prediction is that the Champions League will prove to be too lucrative for G14 to risk setting up an alternative competition. However, the threat of a breakaway will continue because it is a powerful way for G14 to place pressure on UEFA. Despite the mystery surrounding the group membership and the underlying goals of G14, it is almost certain that the influence of the network will not go away. Indeed, if transnational club football competition continues to become an increasingly commercial enterprise, G14's significance is likely to grow.

NOTES

i. An EEIG is an association linking organisations from different countries within the European Union that need to work together, enabling them to do business across boundaries. EEIGs work within a neutral framework that is independent of individual national legal systems, meaning that G14 are on a equal footing in terms of familiarity with the law. It is noted that an EEIG should not make a profit for itself, but should be apportioned between members and taxed accordingly.

ii. Available from *www.g14.com*.

iii. Again, in 1994/95 the Media Partners placed pressure upon UEFA to dramatically change the Champions League fixture structure. Under this new system, there were four qualifying leagues, from which the top two teams qualified, leading onto a two-legged quarterfinal. This appeased members of the clambering superclubs, by decreasing the chances of critical early round 'giant killing' results and meant that the chances of smaller teams progressing to the later rounds, at the expense of 'superclubs' became smaller; this appealed to UEFA as it increased the market value of television rights.

iv. The European Cup is the Champions League before it was 'rebranded.'

REFERENCES

Andrews, N. (2002). 'Fergie faces harsh reality,' BBC Sport Online, 15th August, *http://news.bbc.co.uk/sport1/hi/football/champions_league/2195159.stm* [accessed 4/2004].

Banks, S. (2002). Going Down: Football In Crisis, How the Game Went from Boom to Bust. London: Mainstream.

Boyle, R. and Haynes, R. (2004). Football in the New Media Age. London: Routledge.

Castells, M. (1996 [2000]). The Rise of the Network Society. Oxford: Blackwell.

Castells, M. (1997 [2004]). The Power of Identity. Oxford: Blackwell.

Castells, M. (1998). End of the Millennium. Oxford: Blackwell.

Castells, M. (2000a). Materials for an Exploratory Theory of the Network Society. British Journal of Sociology, 51(1): 5-24.

Deloitte. (2006). Annual Review of Football Finance: All eyes on Europe. Manchester.

Giulianotti, R. (2004). Cash Cow Gets One Up on 3 Lions. The Times Higher, 11th June.

Jones, D. (2006). Foreword. In Annual Review of Football Finance: All Eyes on Europe. Manchester: Deloitte.

Jönsson, C., Tägil, S. and Törnquist, G. (2000). Organising European Space. London: Sage.

King, A. C. (2000). Football Fandom and Post-National Identity in New Europe. British Journal of Sociology, 51(3): 419-42.

King, A. C. (2003). The European Ritual. Aldershot: Ashgate.

Martin, P. (2005). The "Europeanisation" of Elite Football: Scope, Meaning and Significance. European Societies, 7 (2): 349-368.

Melucci, A. (1996). Challenging Codes: Collective Action in the Information Age. Cambridge: Cambridge University Press.

Roche, M. (2004). Europe, 'the Cosmopolitan Condition' and International Sport: 'Cultural Europeanisation' and EU Regulation in the Case of European Football. Paper presented at Europe and Cosmopolitanism Conference (April), Royal Holloway College: London.

Rumford, C. (2000). The European Union: A Political Sociology. Oxford: Blackwell.

Scott, M. (2006). European Body Alarmed by Big Clubs'Blueprint.' The Guardian, 18th March.

Szymanski, S. and Kuypers, T. (1999). Winners and Losers. London: Viking.

SOCCER, POST-COLONIAL AND POST-CONFLICT DISCOURSES IN ALGERIA:

Algérie-France, 6 Octobre 2001, "ce n'était pas un simple match de foot"

Mahfoud Amara

"...il me semble que le fait même d'écrire sur mes origines algériennes me montrent à quel point je ne suis plus exactement Algérien comme ceux qui sont restés là-bas, mais que je ne suis pas exactement Français comme ceux d'ici..." It seems for me that the fact, in itself, of writing about my Algerian origins shows how far I am not exactly Algerian as those who stayed there, but I am not exactly Frkench like those of here (Azouz Begag, 1998).

France greeted me with open arms ... and that's why I live here now. Here, I have the opportunity to perform 20 concerts a month with good musicians and good technicians. That doesn't mean I've forgotten my roots. I feel fine almost anywhere in the world, but the place I come from is always a part of me. In fact, it's nonsense to separate these things. Anyone with a modicum of intelligence can link the traditional with the modern world (Souad Massi, Algerian singer living in France, in Dombrowski, 2005).

The core of my discussion is directed toward deconstructing the sense of being of an Algerian community (or of Algerian origin) in France. I suggest that an analysis of (Algerian) media content around a 'friendly' international soccer game between France and Algeria can be used as lens through which to look to understand the process of making Beurs (word inverted from rebeus, which designates Arabs) and French-Algerian (called also Maghrébins, North Africans) identities. Hence, the paper seeks to shed light on the importance of studying sport, not only as a form of practice but as a symbolic space for remembrance which may involve the process of forgetting (not yet forgiveness), or at least appeasing memory, of past Franco-Algerian colonial history. Furthermore, the staging of the soccer match between the two national teams was an occasion to reposition Algeria in the international sporting map and to re-assert Algerian social ties, an important constituent in the course toward post-conflict 'reconciliation' after more than two decades (since 1988) of generalised violence. Before I begin the discussion about Algerian newspapers' coverage (of pre-and post-game events between France and Algeria in 2001) in regard to the identity of the Algerian community in France, including that of French-Algerians and French of Algerian origin, in order to comprehend the contemporary (conflicting) discourse(s) about Algerian national identity, I will first examine the impact of colonialism and decolonisation in that country.

THE IMPACT OF COLONIALISM AND DECOLONISATION IN THE RECONSTRUCTION OF ALGERIAN IDENTITY

Colonialism was one of the direct causes of (forced) immigration, the violent uprooting of thousands of Algerians who saw migrating to (then metropolitan) France as a means, sometimes the only one, of improving their economic and social conditions. According to Manceron (1996), nowhere was the colonial 'conquest' so violent, brutal and radical in its destruction of the pre-existing social structure than in Algeria. In the same vein, Khan (1991: 286) states that

> *[French colonialism] not only worked to expropriate the Algerian tribes and destroy the rural economy, but also to wipe out handicraft and guild-type organisation, pillage the cities, suffocate the few extant intellectual élites, steal or burn archival documents and entire libraries, wage ceaseless war on Arabic language and Islam, and try to drive them into permanent inferiority by setting up a native school system designed mainly to enhance a servile education necessary for the advancement of colonialism and a degree of acculturation apt to ensure the maintenance of foreign domination.*

The damage caused by the violence of colonialism and decolonisation have affected the raison d'être of the Algerian sense of being. It subjected the society to a real déculturation;[1] the colonial past, after forty years of Algerian independence, is still at the roots of an unappeased conflict, described by Manceron (2002) as the latent tension between two

(Algerian-French) memories. This has prevented, or at least contributed in slowing down, the normalisation process between the two nations, making the task of organising and staging a 'friendly' soccer game between the two national teams a complex endeavour.

After Algeria's independence in 1962, the flow of immigration continued for different political and socio-economic reasons. One can argue that the reconstruction of identity based on total rupture between the coloniser and the colonised, achieved through revolutionary action where 'the native would simply bury colonial society,' did not happen as Fanon and Sartre predicted it would.[2]

That said, as a result of the official interruption by the French government of working immigration rules in 1974, the phenomenon previously conceived by migrant workers in terms of forced uprooting (déracinement) and displacement, turned to that of a permanent project of settlement (enracinement) and definite "sédentarisation" (Césari, 1998: 49). Subsequently, a gap in the models of identification emerged, particularly for those of the second and third generations who are negotiating their identity today between the values of French universalism transmitted by the (republican) school and that of their parents' original culture. Both forms of identity-making are in crisis. The former because of the challenge of American (Anglo-Saxon) hegemony, characterised according to Naïr (2003: 84) by the spiritualisation and essentialism of the particular (ethnic, cultural, linguistic, religious) sense of belonging, and the latter as a consequence of globalisation, synonymous for some of material civilisation and hyper-consumerism, which increased, according to Habermas, (in Borradori, 2003), the sense of fear of the violent uprooting of traditional ways of life. Furthermore, the previous economic approach of the 1960s and 1970s toward immigration has given place to more political and cultural approaches, transforming the debate, previously discussed in terms of costs and advantages, to that of control of flows, citizenship-nationality, national identity, integration, Islam, communautarisme, multiculturalism (Withol, 1995).

SOCCER VECTOR FOR 'PEACE' AND 'RECONCILIATION'?

As part of the Algerian struggle for independence, soccer 'l'héritage de l'occupant' was used to counter the colonial cultural hegemony on its own terms. Sports clubs, after being a space for cultural "co-existence" between different ethno-religious groups, had become a place for the nationalist struggle for independence and, thanks to the FLN-team, an effective tool for the internationalisation of the Algerian cause. During the Algerian revolution (1954-1962), the FLN soccer team became a symbol of Algerian resistance and struggle for independence, and therefore sport was viewed as an effective tool for international recognition of this struggle. According to Fates, the FLN succeeded, through its national soccer team, in ensuring an honourable participation in international life by achieving high quality sporting performances and thus becoming a model for other revolutionary movements fighting for their independence around the world (e.g. the Palestinian national soccer team). In this way the phenomenon of sport became an effective diplomatic tool for the promotion of the Algerian cause in international society. After independence, Algerian and French national teams met only twice. The first "confrontation" was during the 1975 Mediterranean Games held in Algiers. Organising a mega event, such as the Mediterranean Games after only 13 years of independence (followed by the African Games in 1978) was an occasion for the Algerian government's so-called 'revolutionary regime' under the leadership of Boumedienne to show to 2700 athletes and 15 participant nations (and thus to the world) the first results of its socialist programme for development. This is exemplified in the following El-Moudjahid newspaper reports:

> *The revolutionary regime in Algeria has always accorded major importance to the youth of this country. The proof is in the building of sports facilities in wilayates [departments]. This approach is symbolized by the Olympic complex of 19 June [the day of the military coup, called officially the readjustment of the Algerian revolution], where the Mediterranean Games of Algiers will take place. ... Those projects were promoted for a precise objective, the building of a large-scale infrastructure aimed at facilitating the promotion of sports participation for all young Algerians ... (El-Moudjahid, 23 August 1975; original text in French).*

In Scagnetti's (2003) terms, Algiers' Mediterranean Games constituted an important sporting event in the history of the independent country. Algeria succeeded in winning 30 medals, including 5 won by citizens of immigrant origin (a gold medal in boxing, 3 silvers in track and field and boxing, and two bronzes in judo and boxing). The other important event during the Games was Algeria's victory over France (the former enemy) in the soccer final.[3] Algeria won the gold medal with a team coached by Rachid Mekhloufi.[4]

The last 'confrontation' between the two national teams, the focus of this paper, took place on 6 October 2001, thirty-nine years after independence, in a soccer game which ought to be a new page in the relations between the two nation states. But it finished in an unexpected manner, described by one Algerian newspaper as "a sad end for a historical match."

Although it should be noted that the main objective of the paper is not to discuss the different use of soccer in the colonial and post-colonial eras, for nationalist, political and ideological purposes this part of the country's sporting history has already been investigated by a number of Algerian and European scholars (Fates, 1994; Dine, 1994; Lanfranchi and Wahl, 1996; Lanfranchi and Taylor, 2001; Amara and Henry, 2003). The paper is directed toward the study of an international soccer match which happened under different circumstances and of time, together with differing sporting and political contexts. On one side, you have France, an ex-coloniser of Algeria, which at the time was the World Cup holder and one of its best players, Zinedine Zidane, a French national of Algerian origin (voted on many occasions as the personality of the year in France). On the other side, you have Algeria, an ex-colony of France, its team managed by *Rabah Madjer*, the country's first soccer superstar after independence (Dine, 2002) and supported by millions of Algerians in Algeria and elsewhere. Particularly in France, where the Algerian community (or those of Algerian origin) represents the biggest immigrant community, their hope (at least in the way portrayed by the Algerian media) was to beat the French soccer 'master' (the world champions), as they had done in 'the battlefield,' forty years earlier.

As previously discussed, the major focus of this paper is the Algerian community living in France (called also Beurs, Maghrébins and North Africans–at least for a segment of this population–since the notion of Beur/Maghrébins/North African community masks great internal diversity of gender, class, generation, religiosity etc.)–for whom the soccer game between the two national teams was highly symbolic. It was another occasion for the Algerian community in France to celebrate their own double sense of belonging to a 'hybrid' identity. That is an amalgam of some aspects of both Algerian culture and French citizenship, neither expressed in terms of fully belonging to 'French culture' or that of (Algerian) 'culture of origin.'

TOWARD AN INCREASED 'HYBRIDISATION' OF IDENTITY

The so-called Algerian immigrant population is today facing multiple dilemmas concerning the complexity of combining multiple identities: (a) ethnic nationalism characterised by social, political and cultural ties to the motherland (pays d'origine), mixed with a universal sense of belonging to Islamic Umma (community of Muslim believers); (b) civic/civil nationalism, to express[5] (at least for the second and third generations) their belonging to the French republican (laïque) values of democracy; (c) identification, specially for younger generations, with a global (transnational) youth culture, i.e. MTV, hip hop, Nike, NBA.

Césari (1998: 42) explains this complex variety of belonging(s) as the contradiction between individual, collective, and national identities. The dialectic between these three (although not exhaustive) systems of identity making in the everyday life of populations of immigrant origin, and for younger generations in particular, can be illustrated with Kepel's (1994) example of the French (republican) schooling system:

> *... In France, the Republican school is the place par excellence where the common belonging of pupils to the common laïque nation undermines individual differences. It [the school as system and space] aims at training of equal citizens whose main reference is a sum of shared values – where there is no need for religious sphere to interfere because it is considered as part of private domain[6] (Kepel, 1994: 165; translated from French).*

Moreover, the debate on post-colonial discourse is also a debate of the antagonism between two different (essentialist) world views. The first could be described as 'universalist;' propagating universal values of democracy and enlightenment, but also ethnocentric in presenting itself as the sole guardian of rational thinking. It symbolizes the culture of the dominant (ex-coloniser) as the "only legitimate culture that could ensure the universal communication of knowledge" (Finkielkraut, 1987: 77). It is explained as well as being the most able to bring light (enlightenment and reason) to those dominated classes or ex-colonised nations–who were previously deprived of 'modern science.' This universalist project, as asserted by Finkielkraut, who is usually criticised for privileging ethnico-religious arguments in his analysis of the French society, hides two missions: (a) "un déracinement" or déculturation (the gradual loss of cultural distinctiveness) which consists of snatching a social group (ethnic-religious-linguistic minorities) from their web of habits and attitudes comprising their collective (ancestral) identity; (b) dréssage, or taming, characterised by the inculcation to the dominated group of the values (the ideal culture) of the dominant.

Today the impossibility of transcending those contradictions makes integration–particularly in the sense of assimilation as conceptualised in the French political and intellectual spheres–an unthinkable project.

The second world view can be described as 'particularist.' It is a discourse which calls for the return of ex-colonised societies to the communitarian logic of identity, in contrast to that of the neo- colonial (individualist) logic. It separates the colonial and original cultures and refuses to accept any other "corrupted" form of culture, including that of a hybrid (Beurs) culture, which is considered as not identical and even an immoral deviation from the initial (motherland) local (Muslim) culture.

Building from the above discussion, we can argue that both universalism (in the name of enlightenment) and particularism (in the name of local identity) represent two faces of the same coin, i.e., nationalism.

Billig, in his discussion of the psychological, ideological and historical bases in the construction of nationalism (we and them), states that:

> *We imagine* ourselves *and* foreigners *to be equally ruled by the sociology of nationhood. This governing sociology produces countries in which* we *and* them *are reproduced as peoples bound both uniquely and universally to our places. Armed with this vision of nationhood, not only can* we *claim to speak for* ourselves *but also* we *can speak for* them, *or for* all of us *(Billig, 1995: 83; emphasis added).*

In the same vein, it could be argued that the national identity of the French of North African origin have been constructed by the French media and political spheres on the foundation of French universalism (French republican values). The universality of 'our' French nationalism and 'our' secularism (laïcité) refuses or denies 'their' particularism, even in the name of 'our' pluralism and tolerance. As Billig claims:

> ... our *tolerance is threatened by* their *presence;* they *are [les jeunes des banlieues] either intolerant or cause of intolerance; thus* we *seek to exclude* them *not because* we *are intolerant but, quite the reverse, because* we *are tolerant (Billig, 1991: 82; emphasis added).*

The discourse of exclusion that particularly Maghrébins and the African community living in the French national space are facing, is often projected in a manner that 'they' are too 'culturally different'[7] to be absorbed into the French society. The analysis of Algerian newspaper reports shows that these notions of differentiation when talking about the Algerian community living in France exist also within Algeria's national space. This time it is addressed in the name of 'our' (Algerian) 'cultural identity' and 'authenticity,' which views the success of 'others' (from Algerian origin) as a natural result of 'our' (Algerian) 'specificity' (the example of Zidane) and explains, on the other hand, 'their' social failure as a result of 'their' déculturation (Doukhan, 1998) which can be defined as the process of uprooting a social group–immigrant populations and minorities–from their web of habits and attitudes which comprise their collective (ancestral) identity. The 'collective self' of 'us' (in-group), representing Algerian national identity, and unity against any forms of violence, in comparison to 'them' (out-group-i.e. Beurs/ jeunes des banlieues) also exists (although with dissimilar meaning and intensity) in the discourse of Algerian journalists.

It could be stated that the tendency to include or exclude (consciously or unconsciously) individuals/groups into the Algerian national space, depends in today's post-conflict process of rebuilding national unity in Algeria, on the attitudes (association/dissociation) of individuals/groups with any forms of 'violence,' 'incivility' and 'disorder.' This is what makes today's process of rebuilding national unity in Algeria, emphasizing 'reconciliation,' different from that of (past) post-independence strategies for nation-state building, which for some historians, have over-glorified the recourse to (legitimate) violence and armed struggle to attain independence. Moreover, the analysis also confirm that 50 years after Algeria's independence, the historical memory (du passé franco-algérien) is still evident in Franco-Algerian (sporting and non-sporting) relations[8].

DISCOURSE AND THE REFORMATION OF IDENTITY

It is argued that the making of an identity is not something discovered but which has to be made. In the same line of reasoning, Said (2000: 315) claims that:

> *To see others not as ontologically given but as historically constituted would be to erode the exclusivist biases we so often ascribe to cultures, our own not least. Cultures may then be represented as zones of control or of abandonment, of recollection and forgetting, of force or of dependence, of exclusiveness or of sharing, all take place in the global history that is our element.*

Arguably, it could be stated that identity is a socially constructed reality, built on the logic of the differentiation process of 'we' that includes 'our' national, cultural, political, ideological and local identities, in relation to 'others' history, geography, traditions and life styles. 'Others' become the antagonist (mirror-like) reflection of 'our' self-identity. For the purpose of this paper, data drawn from newspaper articles were used to analyse the perception of Algerian journalists about French-Algerians, also called Beurs, Maghrébins, Franco-Maghrébins, North Africans, les immigrés de France, les Arabo-Berber-Musulmans français, Français-plus (Hargreaves, 2001). They are also branded in the Algerian dialect as z'mmagra, usually used in a negative sense, to designate (particularly during the 1960-70s socialist period) Algerian 'others' who come there every summer to show their material wealth and to confirm their (consumerist) cultural differences. The aim of the analysis is to grasp these plural/conflicting realities surrounding the construction of immigrants' (or from immigrant origins) identities in Algerian national newspapers. This involves the homogeneity/heterogeneity and dichotomy doubleness existing between the designation of Algerian journalists of the 'we' (in-group) and 'others' (out-group). The paper argues that the designation of 'us' and 'them' in the Algerian context has been deeply affected by both past and present conflicts.

It should be emphasised that our focus is not a linguistic one, but is problem-oriented, concerned with the language used by Algerian journalists to define or situate Algerian immigrants' identity in comparison to Algerian 'local identity.' For this rationale, articles from the Algerian francophone press, published before and after the game, were gathered. The French (rather than Arabic) language was selected for its similarity with the history of soccer in Algeria. Both cultures or modes of expression could be regarded as a product or the legacy of the French colonial society, absorbed and transformed (créolised)–at different stages of Algerian history–for diverse political and cultural ends. They were mobilised, at list during the colonial era, by the colonial administration to affirm its dominance on French Algeria[9], and by Algerian nationalist movement in its struggle for an independent Algeria. The creolisation of French language by Algerian intellectuals and leaders of Algerian revolution was described by Brian (2002), in line with Franz Fanon, as the process for a deterritorialization of French, the creation of a minor (Algerianized) French, in order to speed the breakdown of the French imperial relationship to Algeria[10]. In the same manner, Muslim soccer clubs became the place for the training of leaders of the national movement and for a wider political mobilization (Amara and Henry, 2003)[11]. Furthermore, the media landscape in Algeria is extremely diverse with about thirty daily newspapers and about 150 weekly or monthly newspapers, mostly state's owned and the rest, the leading ones, are privately owned by cooperative of journalists and businessmen (e.g. Issad Rebrab, the owner of Cevital, the leader of oil and sugar industries in Algeria, is the co-owner of Liberté newspaper). However, apart from the daily arabophone newspaper, El Khaber, which has the highest circulation rate with 400 000 copies per day, francophone newspapers, have a greater readership, reaching broad segments of the literate-urban population (most of the Algerian urban population lives in the northern 10 percent part of the country)[12].

The other point that needs to be raised concerning the selection of newspapers is the issue of accessibility. Only those newspapers electronically available or with free access online archives at the time of collecting data (in 2002) were selected. More Algerian newspapers are electronically accessible today but not all offer access to online archives. Finally, even though the question of representativeness in the quantitative sense of the term is not a concern for this paper, because of the qualitative nature of the study, it could be argued that the selected national newspapers are still the main elements of the Francophone (or Francophile) press in Algeria.

The selected newspapers are usually classified (in ideal type) for their editorial line as liberal (laïque) such as private owned newspapers El-Watan, Liberté and Le Matin; centrist, for example La Tribune; nationalist-conservative, for instance the state owned newspaper El-Moudjahid. Having said this, it should be emphasized that the distinction between democrats-liberal versus conservative-nationalists in the Algerian politico-intellectual arena is not clear cut. Algerian journalists paid a high price (113 journalists were assassinated between 1992-1998) because of their positions, or the nature of their work, in what is now portrayed as the red decade, to describe more than ten years of civil war in Algeria (a term which is still unsaid for its sensitivity in a nation which declared itself to be unified in its struggle against colonialism). Secondly, all Algerian newspapers are still dependent in their day to day management (e.g. printing and publicity) on public funds, which makes them politically and financially vulnerable[13]. Thirdly, the meanings of nationalism and conservativism, on the one hand, and liberalism and democracy on the other (at least in its actual form of a controlled, top-down multiparty system), which were presented in the past socialist Algeria as contradictory concepts, are accepted today, in post-socialist and post-conflict (yet to be achieved) Algeria, as the norm by all political and social movements.

It needs to be noted here that the present political debate in Algeria is oriented toward re-negotiating the sense of both:

(a) modernism; which accepts some notion of progress and controlled political pluralism (but not necessarily the secular values of western modernity). Incorporating also (modernist) Islamist parties which are present members of the government coalition;

(b) radicalism, associated with those armed movements which reject the notion of the Algerian state, declared to be the (poisoned) legacy of colonialism, calling instead for the return to the Umma or nation of believers. That said, in the aftermath of the massive popular vote in 2005 for the president, Abdelaziz Bouteflika, a project for national reconciliation may lead in the future to a general amnesty. The meaning of "radicalism" usually applied in the official political discourse refers to armed groups and is in itself in the process of continuous redefinition involving only those armed groups refusing to put an end to violence and to join the platform for national reconciliation.

ALGÉRIE-FRANCE, 6TH OCTOBER 2001

The organisation of the 'friendly' game was agreed upon by the two governments a year before in 2000, after the visit of Algerian president Bouteflika to France. We should highlight here the highly historical significance of the 6th October 1961 date in the Algerian collective memory. Particularly for those Algerian immigrants who lived and witnessed the struggle for independence from 'metropolitan' France (since Algeria was a province of France), it was the day when the chief of the Police, Maurice Papon, famously known for his repressive methods, decided as part of security measures against what were described as 'criminal activities of FLN terrorists' to establish a curfew for Algerians living in the suburbs of Paris from 8:30 pm to 5:30 am. Following this decision the FLN, which managed to impose itself as the sole representative of the revolution in Algeria and elsewhere, decided to organise a large and peaceful demonstration in the centre of Paris for the night of 17 October. The response of the national police was extremely violent. Hundreds were massacred, and their bodies were thrown in the river Seine, or imprisoned (including everyone who looked like a North African, i.e. southern Europeans who happened to be in the wrong place that day). A dark page in Algerian-French history which has still to be opened.

The international soccer game was also played while the world media, politicians, sociologists and historians were busy discussing the aftermath of the 11 September attack in New York and its consequences for world security as well as the manner in which the US was going to respond to stop the treat of 'world terrorism.' The latter is claimed to became after the end of the Cold War the new threat to world stability and western democracy. In this context of hypertension, a security plan named 'Vigipirate' to thwart the menace of another terrorist attack on French territory (after that of 1995 bombing) was reactivated. The objective was to face the threat of what the French media, particularly after 11 September, described as sleeping cells (les cellules terroristes dormantes). In addition, the match was played at a time when France was still under the shock of another tragedy, the explosion of a chemical factory in Toulouse. First, the French media attributed it to 'Islamist' groups, but after investigation it was established to be an accident brought about by a technical failure and human neglect. For El-Moudjahid newspaper, this was another occasion for the enemy of Algeria and "some mistaken associations which cultivate hatred of Algeria ... to tarnish the image of Algeria and displace the match from its normal context, while placing pressure on the organiser to cancel it." According to the same newspaper, the French media wanted at all costs to link the match between Algeria and France with 'terrorism.' This was described as "the fruit of fertile imaginations– des scénaristes de l'information–of news' scriptwriters" (El-Moudjahid, 09/10/01).

However, for the majority of Algerian newspapers the match was a historical moment. According to Liberté,

> *[the match] is highly symbolic for our country, which will face France for the first time after the independence. But this time in a soccer field ... it will be a battle between two countries which have lived through difficult times (Liberté, 07/10/01).*

The same newspaper chose to cover the pre-match atmosphere in the streets of Paris, particularly those known for their important concentration of the Maghrébins community:

> *Algerian immigrants succeeded to create an outstanding atmosphere ... in Barbés. They were hundreds to go out to express their joy and pride ... they even stopped traffic for one hour, to transform the street to a panorama of a mega festivity (Liberté, 07/10/01).*

The act of stopping the traffic for an hour, even if not legally authorised, is justified as an expression of joy and festivity. This could only happen in the multicultural streets of Barbés, which reinforces, at least in the reporter's account, the distinctiveness/uniqueness of Barbés as a space, inside (outside) French territory.

According to El-Moudjahid (09.10.2001), the soccer match was a meeting in the service of "an appropriate and sought after fraternity." As for El-Watan, the match was a challenge and an occasion to de-sensitise (décomplexer) "passion, nostalgia, and suspicion ... in the relations between the two nations. As a consequence, soccer, this highly mediated activity, becomes for this occasion the most appropriate tool, "to go beyond certain direct and indirect [psychological and historical] blockages" (El-Watan, 07.10.2001).

One can argue that journalists' language used to describe the pre-game atmosphere reinforced the attitude, the readiness, of Algerians toward forgetting (and even forgiveness) of the colonial past, with the hope that this feeling was shared among the French population and political leaders. To illustrate this position, we can read in Le Matin's article that those types of events could serve as a bridge between two countries, linked most of the time by a passionate and conflicting history. Above all, "because of the international events [post 9/11] ...which have transformed more instinctive the rejection of others and normal the distrust of foreigners, the source of evil" (Le Matin, 07.10.2001).

LE JOUR J

The following are the words chosen by a reporter from Liberté newspaper to describe the atmosphere before the kick off:

> *19h29 French time, Stade de France, "les verts" get into the field ... everybody stood, shouting "One, Two, Three, viva l'Algérie." We felt to be in the 5th July temple [referring to the Algerian Olympic stadium] ... the world champions [except for Zidane of course] were welcomed as if they were playing outside their base, by thousands of Algerian supporters coming from all over France.*

France has discovered other colours: green, white and red [the Algerian flag] ... It was simply magnificent, with all supporters standing for Tahia El Djazair [long life to Algeria] ... sublime images which only soccer knows how to produce. The participation of Dahleb and Zidan's kick off, the two symbolic figures of plural Algeria,[14] announces the starting of the game. (Liberté, 07/10/01)

All this happened in a stadium, according to Liberté newspaper, which had known the joy and triumph of the French "melting pot" (Black, Blanc, Beur) during the World Cup final, but which for this occasion has given an image of a "conquered territory."

The same mixed feelings of pride, joy and hyper-nationalism were expressed by other daily newspapers. One of El-Watan's reporters had even claimed that "... we had the impression to be in the 5th of July stadium" (the biggest stadium in Algeria, named after the day of independence).

> *Supporters' hearts present that night belonged only to the green of Algeria, and Kassaman [the Algerian national anthem] ... was sung in an enclosure which has borrowed its voice to be the echo for a strong presence of Algerian supporters.*

On the other hand, la Marseillaise was faced by protest[15] by the so-called les jeunes des banlieues (the youth of suburban Paris) who waited for this occasion, according to the same newspaper, to

> *take a psychological step upon the social difficulties that they are going through ... the Algerian flag raised by les jeunes des banlieues was largely dominant....*

It was an occasion for Algerian supporters to express their identities:

> *the Algerian flag had occupied the French land, at least for the time of one night (El-Watan, 07/10/01).*

It is worth highlighting here ways that the notion of space, being inside or outside Algerian/French land, and thus of "our" and 'their' supporters present that day in Stade de France, was constructed. The same supporters of the Algerian national team were one time described as Algerian (like 'us') and another time as les jeunes des banlieues. The place itself, the famous Stade de France, became the 5th of July stadium in Algiers and therefore part of Algerian territory. Thus the displacement of space caused also a displacement of supporters' identities. The voice of 'other' French (including those of North African origin) supporters, who may have represented the majority that day, became nearly silent and therefore absent.

AFTER 76 MINUTES OF OFFICIAL TIME

The atmosphere described above of partying and joy and of a soccer match supposedly between two nations sharing hard moments of history, but willing to forget and even to forgive, was bungled by what Liberté (7/10/2001) described as 'prétendent supporteurs' or pseudo-supporters of the Algerian national team.

> *the happiness was transformed to sadness, real supporters des verts, do not find the words to describe their desolation...*

After 76 minutes of official time, while the score was 4-1 for the World champions, the referee decided to stop the game[16]. The reason was 'envahissement de terrain', supporters spilling out into the pitch portrayed by the same newspaper as

> *they were rascals who emerged from nowhere and they have nothing to do with Algerians... Shameful, despicable, the words are never strong to describe what really happened.*

According to El-Watan,

> *it was a violent form of expression by a group of 'jeunes Beurs' marginalized, who waited for this occasion to protest against their social exclusion...By the fault of a well determined group ... a bench of agitated supporters who came to spoil the party (El-Watan, 07.10.2001).*

Many reactions were offered to explain what happened. For some journalists, it was the expression of internal (French) socio-economic problems and the failure of those in charge of security in Stade de France. Other newspapers chose to minimise, or at least to de-dramatise, the importance of the incident.

For La Tribune (08/10/2001) the interruption to the game was another aspect of the continuous history of conflict between Algeria and France "which does not have an end." In El-Moudjahid's view, the incident was in fact a "banal" event and an "isolated" act of "two or three agitated supporters."

> *...There was absolutely not a will of violence by those who swept onto the pitch...they entered for the sole reason to express their enthusiasm and joy without violence or aggressiveness... (El-Moudjahid, 09/10/2001).*

In a similar vein, the journalist from El-Watan (09.10.01) claimed that the event was unpredictable and irresponsible, but non-violent.

> *... There was a sympathetic sweep onto the pitch ... by number of supporters who wanted to live the party much closer.*

The same newspaper pointed out that in addition to Algerian supporters, who spilled onto the pitch, there were also others from Tunisia, Morocco, Portugal:

> *a multitude of nationalities not animated by bad intentions but not safe though from manipulations ... despite the negative effect of such irresponsible behaviour aggravated by minority of supporters, we are far from the hooliganism that European and French stadia are so familiar with.*
>
> *In other places hooliganism is a fashion, causing enormous damage. In this perspective we cannot teach neither the French or the initiators of soccer [English] who have had at numerous occasions to witness much more serious scene (El-Watan, 08/10/2001).*

For El-Watan and El-Moudjahid, those in charge of Stade de France security were held responsible for what happened 15 minutes before the end of the game. The others responsible are, of course:

> *hidden groups whose sole obsession is to derail the train of friendship between Algeria and France (El-Moudjahid, 09/10/01).*

The different positions of Algerian newspapers in discussing the significance, and the moral responsibility for what happened, divided between aggravation and de-dramatisation and using terms ranging from despicable to sympathetic to clarify what 'really' happened, can be explained as part of the ongoing reconstruction (renegotiation) process of what is acceptable, common, suspect and unjustifiable in the present Algerian post-conflict outlook.[17] Some Algerian newspapers reasserted that aspects of public disorder and incivility (provoked by a minority) are not unique to Algerian supporters. Acts of hooliganism (more serious) take place week in and week out in the European stadia (e.g. in France and England) as a reminder of the global dimension of this phenomenon, and thus an argument against the ethno-cultural explanation of violence which tends to associate violence (thus terrorism) solely to Arabo-Muslim culture.

CONCLUSION

In conclusion, it could be stated that the construction of Beurs/French-Algerian identity, etc.–at least in the account of Algerian newspapers–varied considerably. This could be assumed to be linked to the following issues: (a) the influence that colonial history had, and still has, in the definition and positioning of Algerian immigrants' identities in French society; (b) the projects for society, i.e. liberal versus conservative (although it is hard to distinguish between these two political positions in the Algerian context) which each of those Algerian newspapers adhere to; (c) the recent history of internal generalised violence and the process of post-war trauma Algerian society is going through. It imposes a certain revision, re-examination, and renegotiation of the meaning of what it is to be an Algerian,[18] and the conditions which contribute to prevent the recurrence of collective violence (as a means for political change) in the Algerian society.

The general observation we could make from our analysis is that the Algerian press employed multiple uses of rhetoric to portray the identity (psychological types) of Algerian supporters, incorporating (consciously or not) dual and antagonist types of categorisation. The same Algerians (supporteurs des verts) previously depicted as members of the Arabo-Berber and Islamic community, and Maghrébins proud of their cultural distinctiveness and 'their' Algerian flag, had become in a space of 76 minutes, "rascals who emerged from nowhere and they have nothing to do with Algerians or Algeria." They were also described as Jeunes Beurs, marginalised, who waited for this occasion to protest against 'their' (thus nothing to do with Algeria) social exclusion, in France ('their' homeland).

Other newspapers such as El-Watan and El-Moudjahid preferred to talk about a minority of 'sympathetic' and 'non-violent' jeunes Beurs, who were not safe from manipulation by 'hidden forces.' In other words, the French media were depicted by Algerian newspapers also as 'scriptwriters of fictional news' in reference to their negative portrayal of Algeria between 1992-1998, during the hardest period of internal political violence. Their main aim, from the Algerian perspective, particularly El-Moudjahid's (the official government newspaper), was to tarnish the image of Algeria and to destroy any chance of amity and partnership between France and Algeria.

A comparison of French and Algerian press discourses regarding the match event, particularly in connection with the reaction and behaviour of the so called Beurs and Maghrébins supporters, before, during and after the game, could deliver some aspects of the complex identity that this category of population is going through today.[19] A comparison between Francophone and Arabophone newspapers in Algeria, knowing the sensitivity of the debate between Francophones and Arabophones around the building of post-independent Algeria,[20] can also shed light on interesting themes.

It could be stated that the problem of identity (not to forget the socio-economic problems) among the Beurs/Franco-Maghrébins population in France (not to use the term 'minority,' being highly sensitive in the French republican context) can be located in the complex and ambivalent sense of living in 'between-ness' and even 'emptiness.' This may be more pertinent for the third generation. This is a generation, according to Breviglieri, whose immigrant consciousness is not questioned. Therefore, the issue of integration their parents had to deal with should not be part of their daily life problems for the simple reason they consider themselves as French 'like others.' Their view about their (parents' or grandparents') societés d'origine (le bled) is not always nostalgic, but it is equivalent also with étrangeté (foreignness), political totalitarianism, corruption, imposed (selective) history,[21] political violence and social inequality (Geisser & Kelfaoui: 2001).

> *Ici [in France], we are in the presence of a generation, that naturally 'forget' or they do not find indispensable to possess patrimonial culture*[22] *(Doukhan, 1998).*

We should mention here the specificity of the Harki population in France and their descendents (second and third generations), which are absent (silenced) in the Algerian newspapers' analysis of pre- and post-game issues between France and Algeria. Harkis are the Algerian Muslim[23] population who chose (or it was imposed upon them) to fight against their fellow Muslim Algerians to uphold French colonialism in Algeria. For this category of the population, the previously discussed notions of forgetting and the possibility of forgiveness in relation to the Franco-Algerian past are impossible or difficult to conceive. Because they chose to fight for the French flag against Algerian independence, and therefore against a Muslim Algeria, they thus (voluntarily) decided to be part of the French national space for ever. Consequently, to be accepted or not as Harki (for cultural or religious reasons) in the French national space and history, becomes an internal French problem. The same rhetoric of Harki or fils de Harki (the sons of Harki) "who are thirsty for vengeance against Algerian independence" was used by the media, and by the Algerian government to depict the armed groups. By doing this the Algerian authorities contributed, according to Harbi, in bringing to the surface all these unresolved historical issues concerning the Algerian war for liberation (1954-1962). As he puts it,

> *[regarding] questions such as terrorism against civilians, Harkis, Algerian cultural identity etc. We have to remind ourselves that some political groups in Algeria, particularly those who are against the Islamist project [to establish an Islamic state], sought in the last years to carry the internal Algerian conflict into France. The problem is not to be against the Islamists. They have enough convincing arguments why they are against the Islamist project. The problem is in the discourse that these groups utilise which is close to the discourse of French settlers [pied noirs] and most French political factions which are embittered by the Algerian cultural experience after independence (Harbi 2006, from Aljazeera news web page, translated from Arabic).*

The constructed stereotype, while referring to the specificity or particularism of Maghrébins, which is usually presented as one homogeneous group, is projected (consciously or not) with a logic of differentiation, if not exclusion. For instance, when talking about national belonging, cultural identity and religious faith, the image projected by the media (in Algeria and France) is that of struggle, identity crises, violence, chauvinism, fundamentalism and isolationism. It is characterised also by le repli (the-tactical-return) toward the community, family and religion (i.e. the process of ghettoïsation), an image which Geisser and Khelfaoui (2001) reject and describe as dramatic, discriminatory, and even pathologic. The origin of that negative imagery has roots, according to Césari, in past colonial history, with consequences still persistent, particularly in the social imagination of the French. As Césari points out,

> *Those young are victims of post-colonial syndrome, which makes [their] Arab and Muslim origins the object of a sum of negative imagery which is rooted in the colonial past (Césari, 1997:39).*

This is to say that what is needed today, more than a symbolic 'friendly' soccer game, is un travail de mémoire, in other words a de-colonisation (deconstruction) of the shared memory between France and Algeria. This memory has only been established in terms of invasion, conquest, battles, domination, defeats, victories; in other words, through war and violence. A product also of an ideologised history on the one hand, as well as a selective memory on the other hand. A tendency, according to Ravenel (1996), for amnesia (even negations[24]) on the French side and that of hyper-commemoration on the Algerian side.

I finish the paper in the same way I started by quoting, this time from Tahar Ben Jelloun's novel, Les raisins de la galère. This perfectly describes the pluralist (double, and even ambiguous) sense of belonging to the French among those of Algerian origin (represented in the novel by Naima):

> *We were conceived in an improvised manner, for the provisory, we are the children of the cities of transit, we arrived without warning ... we found ourselves living here with human-like faces, expressing ourselves with civilised-like language, and with French-like manners and customs, we are here, and what is left for us [to do] to deserve staying here [in France]? (Ben Jelloun, 1996:117; translated from French by the author)*

NOTES

1. Described by Bourdieu as a catastrophic experience of social surgery, "the war made a clean sweep of a civilisation which we only can speak about today as part of the past" (see Bourdieu, 1974: 123; translated from French).
2. On the intellectual debate about Algerian war of revolution see Le Sueur (2001).
3. This symbolic sporting victory intervened after the (first) official visit, from 10 to 12 April 1975, of the president of the French Republic, Valery Giscard D'Estang, to independent Algeria.
4. In April 1958, Mekhloufi (named by Boudjedra 1981, as 'le footbaleur de la révolution' in a novel dedicated to the FLN team) abandoned the French national team, which was preparing for the World Cup finals in Sweden and instantly became an Algerian national symbol. A few months earlier he had been part of a French team that won the world military soccer competition in Buenos Aires on Bastille Day, 14 July 1957. (See Lanfranchi and Wahl, 1996; Amara and Henry, 2004).
5. Through institutionalised channels, such as the act of voting as well as participation in political and other associative (and non-political) activities.
6. The school system in Britain, which is not considered "laïque" in the French term, functions according to another logic, that reflects the disassociation between citizenship and nationality (see Kepel: 1994).
7. The core justifications of cultural differentiation is based particularly on presumed attitudinal differences toward separation of religion and state (see Lamont et al., 2002).
8. At the time of writing this article, the Algerian President Bouteflika has asked the French government to officially recognise its crimes against humanity in Algeria as a precondition for the signing of traité d'amitié between the two countries. "Bouteflika persiste et signe, La colonisation

française a été brutale et génocidaire", Liberté, Edition N° 4145 du Lundi 08 Mai 2006.

9. To increase the foreignness of the Arabo-Islamic cultures of pre-colonial Algeria, Arabic was declared as a foreign language , in French-Algeria.

10. French language has become, as the Algerian writer Kateb Yacine has said, one of the spoils of war.

11. The majority of the names of 'indigenous' clubs began with the words 'club Musulman', or 'Union sportive Musulmane'. Islam was thus a fundamental element and symbol of differentiation, between Muslim and non-Muslim (European settlers) clubs.

12. The Arabic, Berber and French languages are all connected to the country's history and culture. For Berger (1998: 61) "many Algerians, perhaps the majority, live in several languages, often switching from one to the other in the same sentence. To deny Algerians the possibility of being at the same time Arabophone and Berberophone, or Berberophone and Francophone, might amount to denying them the very possibility of being Algerian".

13. For instance, Le Matin newspaper is no longer in the market and at the time of writing its director had been in jail since 14 June 2004 for "financial infraction". He was released on 14th June 2006.

14. Zidane and Dahleb because of their creativity and soccer performance have become the symbols of "plural Algeria", and not that of "plural France".

15. La Marseillaise faced the same protest by the supporters of FC Bastia (from Corsica) in the French Cup final against L'Orient held on 12 May 2002. In this form of protest, supporters showed their objection to Chirac's policy regarding Corsica's nationalist (separatist) movement.

16. The first time that an official game was interrupted before its term since the creation of the French Soccer Federation in 1904 (Gastaut, Y. Les soccereurs algériens en France a l'épreuve des identités nationales, *http://www.wearesoccer.org*).

17. For similar works on understanding peace after post-conflict see Pouliny (2004).

18. This involves also the negotiation of the meaning (codes, beliefs, values) of nationality, collective 'self', social ties, religion, solidarity, the organization of collective work .

19. "You could read in Liberation's front page "France–Algeria, after forty years of stoppage time", Marianne responded by naming those who were involved in the interruption of the game as "boys of divorce" (between France and Algeria) whereas Le Monde regarded the match of reconciliation between France and Algeria is still on" (Gastaut, Y. *http://www.wearesoccer.org*).

20. For some the arabisation policy has been imposed and over-politicised by the regime to maintain its control of political life.
21. See the work of Ricoeur (translated in 2004) on history and memory and the notion of (institutionalised) inertia, selective memory and even forgetfulness.
22. They do not express either their full belonging for social and historical considerations to "French culture" nor to their culture of origin.
23. It should be mentioned here that the war of resistance in Algeria was not exclusively a war between 'Muslims' and 'Christian' French, because there were many Christians who fought for Algerian independence and many Muslims fought against independence. Although reaffirming Islamic identity as a form of differentiation and resistance was important against the colonial order because of its ambiguous game of defining colonialism in Algeria as a secular (civilising mission) endeavour and at the same imposing on Algerians (the indigenous population) a denial of their Islamic identity as a condition to be accepted as full citizens (not indigenous) in the colonial society.
24. It was only in 1998 that the French Parliament recognised that what happened between 1954 and 1962 in the "Algerian territory" was not an internal conflict but a war. This recognition was a setback with the recent French Parliament's voting on 23 February 2005 on article 4 of law n° 2005-158 which glorified the positive enterprise of French colonialism (the article was abrogated by presidential decision on February 16, 2006).

REFERENCES

Amara, M. & Henry, I. (2004). Between globalization and local 'modernity: The diffusion and modernization of soccer in Algeria. Soccer and Society, 5, (1): 1-26.

Begag, A. (1998). Ecrire et migrer, Ecarts D'identité, Revue trimestrielle sur l'intégration, N86. Migration, Exil, Création.

Begag, A. (2002). Les relations France-Algérie vue de la diaspora algérienne. Modern and Contemporary France, 10(4): 475-482.

Ben Jelloun, T. (1996). Les raisins de la galère. Paris: Libres Fayard.

Berger, E.A. (1998). Algeria in Other(s)' Languages: Toward a rethinking ofAlgeria's linguistic predicament, Parallax, 4 (2): 43-46

Billig, M. (1995). Banal Nationalism. London: Sage Publications.

Boudjedra, R. (1981). Le vainqueur de coupe. Paris: Gallimard.

Borradori, G. (2003). Philosophy in a Time of Terror, Dialogue with Jurgen Habermas and Jaques Derrida. The University of Chicago Press: Chicago and London.

Brian, E. (2002). Fanon's al-Jaza'ir, or Algeria Translated. Parallax, 8(2): 99-115.

Breviglieri, M. (2001). L'étreinte de l'origine: Attachement, mémoire et nostalgie chez les enfants d'immigrés maghrébins. Confluences Méditerranée, 39 (Automne). Retrieved from http://confluences.ifrance.com/confluences/.

Césari, J. (1997). Faut-il Avoir Peur de l'Islam? Paris: Press de Science PO.

Césari, J. (1998). Musulmans et républicains: les jeunes, l'islam et la France, Paris: Complexe.

Dombrowski, R. Souad Massi Melancholy and Hope. Translated from the German by Patrick Lanagan, Qantara.de 2005. Available in http://www.qantara.de/webcom/show_article.php/_c-310/_nr-244/i.html.

Doukhan, R. (1988). Atouts et pièges de la particularité. Confluences méditerranée, 28, Hiver). Retrieved from http://confluences.ifrance.com/confluences/

Dine, P. (2002). France, Algeria and Sport: From colonisation to globalisation. Modern and Contemporary France, 10(4): 495-505.

Fabienne R. (2000). D'un imaginaire national à un autre: comment peut-on être français quand on est d'origine algérienne? Confluences Méditerranée, 39 (Automne). Retrieved from *http://confluences.ifrance.com/confluences/*

Fates, Y. (1994). Sport et Tiers Monde, Pratiques Corporelle. Paris: Presses University of France.

Faucault, M. (1997). Il Faut Défendre la Société, Cours au Collège de France, 1976. Paris: Gallimard, Seuil.

Finkielkraut, A. (1987). La Défaite de la Pensée. Paris: nrf, Gallimard.

Flick, U. (1998). An Introduction to Qualitative Research. London: Sage Publications.

Gastaut, Y. Les soccereurs algériens en France a l'épreuve des identités nationales. In "we are soccer, association (cultures, mémoires, histoire)" *http://www.wearesoccer.org* (accessed, 28/03/06).

Geisser,V. and Kelfaoui, S. (2001). La nation d'origine réinventée La persistance du «mythe national» chez les Français originaires du Maghreb, Confluences Méditerranée, 39, (Automne). *http://confluences.ifrance.com/confluences/*

Gessey, P. (2001). Balancing acts: Family and integration in the fiction of Franco-Magherbi. In Ireland. S., Proulx. P. S. (eds.), Immigrant Narratives in Contemporary France. Contributions to the Study of World Literature, Number 106, (pp. 57-68). London: Greenwood Press.

Harbi, M. (2006). Awsat Aljazaeeria asshamat bi aoudat khitab Tamjid al isstiamaar (Algerians have contributed in the return of the colonial discourse which glorifies colonialism). Interview with Yacine Temlali for

Aljazeera net. Retrieved 24/01/06 from (http://www.aljazeera.net/NR/exeres/5F8FE1A6-9662-4DB3-87D3633B1A21DBCC.htm).

Hargreaves, A. G. (2001). Perceptions of ethnic differences in post-war France. In Ireland. S., Proulx. P. S. (eds.), Immigrant Narratives in Contemporary France. Contributions to the Study of World Literature, Number 106, (pp. 7-22). London: Greenwood Press.

Kepel, G. (1994). A L'ouest D'Allah. Paris: Edition du Seuil.

Khan, A. (1991). Algerian intellectuals: Between Identity and Modernity. In El-Kenz, A. (Ed.) Algeria: The challenge of Modernity.. London: CODEBRIA Books series.

Lanfranchi, P and Wahl, A. (1996). The Immigrant as Hero: Kopa, Mekhloufi and French Soccer. International Journal of the History of Sport, 13 (March): 115-127.

Lanfranchi, P. and Taylor, M. (2001). Moving with the Ball: The Migration of Professional Soccerers. Oxford: Berg.

Lamchichi, A. (1999). Islam et Musulmans de France: Pluralisme, Laïcité et Citoyenneté. Paris: L'Harmattan.

Lamchichi, A. (2002). Pluralisme et citoyenneté L'islam de France à l'épreuve de la laïcité et du «vivre ensemble» Confluences Méditerranée, 41, (Printemps). *http://confluences.ifrance.com/confluences/*

Lamont M., Morning A., and Moony M. (2002). Particular universalism: North African immigrants respond to French racism. Ethnic Racial Studies, 25(3): 390-414.

LeSueur J. D. (2001). Uncivil War: Intellectuals and Identity Politics During the Decolonization of Algeria. Philadelphia: University of Pennsylvania Press.

McKinney, M. (2001). Le jeu de piste: Tracking clues to the emergence of Maghrébins-French literature in Farida Belghoul's Georgette! In Ireland, S., Proulx. P. S. (eds.), Immigrant Narratives in Contemporary France, Contributions to the Study of World Literature, Number 106, pp. 105-116. London: Greenwood Press.

Maldidier, D. (1972). Discours politique et guerre d'Algérie: approche synchronique et diachronique, La pensée, 7/8 (June): 57-86.

Manceron, G. (1996). Algérie, comprendre la crise. Brussels: Interventions.

Manceron, G. (2002). "Colonisateurs et colonisés, face au souvenir colonial." Migration et Société, 81/82, (May-August): 121-138.

Naïr, S. (2003). L'Empire Face à la Diversité, Paris: Hachette.

Pouliny B. Re-imagining peace after massacres: a trans-disciplinary and comparative effort towards the rebuilding of functioning societies. Summary proposal, CERI-Sciences Po/CNRS, Paris, September 1, 2004.

Ravenel, B. (1996). Mémoire, Histoire et Politique. *Confluences Méditerranée*, 19, (Automne). Retrieved from *http://confluences.ifrance.com/confluences/*

Ricoeur, P. (2004). Memory, History, Forgetting. Translated by Kathleen Blamey and David Pellauer, Chicago, IL: University of Chicago Press.

Said, E. W. (2000). Reflection on Exile, and other Essays. Harvard University Press: Cambridge, Massachusetts.

Silverman, D. (ed.) (1998). Qualitative Research: Theory, Method and Practice. London: Sage Publications.

Scagnetti, J.C. (2003). Sport et retour au pays: l'exemple de l'émigration algérienne en France, 1973-1978. Migration 22(2): 40-46.

Van Dijk, T. A. (1985). Handbook of Discourse Analysis (Vol. 4). Amsterdam: Academic Press.

Wetherell, M. and Potter, J. (1982). Mapping the language of racism: Discourse and the légitimation of exploitation. London: Harvester & Wheatsheaf.

Withol, D. (1995). L'immigration, objet du débat politique, confluences Méditerranée, 14, (Printemps). Retrieved from *http://confluences.ifrance.com/confluences/*.

Newspaper articles

El-Moudjahid, « 78 minutes de bonheur, rubrique Sports», 07/10/01.

El-Moudjahid, «Après France- Algérie- Le sport et...le rest», 09/10/01.

El-Moudjahid, « Un enthousiasme débordant et bon enfant », 09/10/01.

El-Watan, «Envahissement pacifique du terrain lors du match Algérie-France: une fête gâchée», 7/10/01.

El-Watan, «Ce n'était pas des hooligans», 08/10/01.

El-Watan, «C'était le 5 juillet», 07/10/01.

La Tribune, "Rien ne ce termine entre l'Algérie et la France," 07/10/01.

La Tribune, "Match historique," 07/10/01.

Le Matin, "Le Match de trop," 07/10/01.

Liberté, "Hélas la fête tourna court, de nos envoyés spéciaux a Paris," 7/10/2001.

Liberté, "Après les événements du match France-Algérie: la thèse du "coup monté," 08/10/01.

FROM THE TERRACES TO THE BOARDROOMS: *Reviewing Theories and Perspectives on Racism in Football*

6

Tim Crabbe

INTRODUCTION

During the 2006 FIFA World Cup finals in Germany, FIFA President Joseph Blatter, World Cup Organizing Committee President Franz Beckenbauer, German Federal Interior Minister Wolfgang Schäuble and South African civil rights activist Tokyo Sexwale came together in Berlin to promote a campaign against discrimination and racism. Following the launch of the initiative, and directly before each of the tournament's Quarter Final matches kicked off, the team captains of the competing countries made statements condemning all forms of discrimination before the teams joined together for a photo behind a "Say No to Racism" banner. Indeed, this slogan was displayed before every game on a banner laid out in the centre-circle. Furthermore, prior to the tournament, FIFA announced new, strict penalties that would be invoked in the event of racially-motivated incidents. The FIFA President made it clear that the revised Article 55 of the world governing body's disciplinary code, which includes the power to expel national associations from the organization, would be enforced.

This degree of institutional opposition to racism lies in stark contrast with the situation just a few years ago, when racism was easily dismissed by the football authorities as an insignificance that lay beyond the game and its realm of responsibilities. The reality is that football represents one of the tapestries onto which social achievements and problems, claims and counter claims are ritually etched. Prior to their World Cup victory in 1998 France's National Front leader Jean Marie Le Pen famously rebuked the French team–particularly those whose family origins lay outside the country–for their lack of zeal when singing the *Marseillaise*. Later, in the aftermath of their glorious victory on home soil, the team was lauded as a symbol of a new multiracial nation. Today the pendulum has swung once more as ethnic conflict on the terraces is related to wider social tensions in the *banlieue*, whilst the infamous head-butt on the Italian defender Marco Materazzi by the French captain Zinedine Zidane in the World Cup Final became emblematic of the racial undertones associated with the 'War on Terror.'

This growing awareness of how racism is connected to football operates through a discursive framework which locates it as a problem which is 'out there' in wider society and, where it does touch the game, it is manifest among players and supporters rather than the institutions of the game itself. Whilst acknowledging that 'we must ensure our sport isn't destroyed by racism from within,' even the FIFA President declared at the launch of the initiative in Berlin on the 28th June that 'racism is society's problem, and not a problem typical of football'. In this way the presentation of racism in football provides something of a paradox. At once it is a problem but it is not a problem. It can be rhetorically opposed whilst its presence cannot be contemplated. This approach reflects the pattern established in the UK, where the commitment to challenging racism has been most firmly established but where fans and players take centre stage.

In the UK the phenomenon of racism in football first became a subject of widespread concern in the late 1970s and 1980s. This was a time when there was increasing evidence of racist behaviour related to football and attempts by extreme right-wing movements to use the game as a basis for recruitment (Buford, 1991; CCS, 1981; Fradley, 1983; Robins, 1984; Leeds Trades Council, 1988; Turner, 1990). Groups such as the National Front were regularly seen distributing and selling their literature outside football grounds. But interest in the issue was also partly related to the increasing presence of black players amongst the ranks of professional footballers. With the emergence of black players at all levels of football, phenomena such as racist chanting and abuse became a common occurrence at many football grounds.

The pervasiveness of such displays during this period is by now well established, both by recent research and by anecdotal evidence in popular publications and books. It is perhaps not surprising then that most studies of racism in football have tended to concentrate either on the nature and extent of racist abuse in and around football stadiums (Holland, 1995), or are preoccupied with the recruitment activities of extreme right-wing movements (CCS, 1981). In addition, a number of writers have analysed the phenomenon of the growing presence of black players in football, notably Cashmore (1982), Woolnough (1983), Hill (1989), Orakwue (1998) and Vasili (1994, 1998, 2000). What was missing, until recently (Back, Crabbe & Solomos, 2001), was a serious analysis of the multiple formations and social sources of racist practice and the extent of its reach into wider sectors of the game.

FOOTBALL CULTURE, RACISM AND THE 'HOOLIGAN'

Part of the explanation for the absence of a serious analysis of race and racism in football cultures can be found in the discourse of fan 'hooliganism' that has tended to establish the parameters of academic debate about virtually every aspect of football culture. This emphasis is not surprising, since it is clear that the emergence of football as a field of academic study in the 1960s and early 1970s was from the outset related to an interest in manifestations of violence within the game, and more particularly (and peculiarly) in the violent tendencies of English football supporters. But the question that needs to be addressed is the adequacy of seeing the issue of racism as merely a constituent element of the broader cluster of 'anti-social' forms of behaviour which form the basis for the concern around football 'hooliganism.'

Some of the early studies of football disorder touched on the relationship between racism and football in the context of wider research into football culture and 'hooliganism.' These studies, however, tended to be largely descriptive and to document rather than *explain* the extent of racist activity in football grounds (Melnick, 1988; Waters, 1988; Holland, 1995).

Some qualitative research on football supporters, such as Robins (1984), Dunning, Murphy & Williams (1988), Williams, Dunning & Murphy (1989) and Murphy, Williams and Dunning (1990) has provided many valuable insights into the popular culture around football. The ethnographic work of Armstrong (1991 and 1993, 1998) has also led to a useful debate about the key issues facing researchers when analysing the social context and everyday practices of 'football hooligans' (Dunning et al., 1991; Hobbs and Robins, 1991). But these studies do not provide a rounded analysis of the development and role of racist cultures in football. In fairness to these authors, this issue was not central to their research focus. Comments about fan racism are appended to wider concerns and seen as an extension of the problem of football violence and disorder.

Without being drawn into the prolonged and at times personalised debate over the 'hooligan issue,' it is useful to reflect on how the question of racism in football has been mapped onto this field of enquiry. Among the first academic interventions in this field were a number of articles by the late Ian Taylor. Taylor attempted to relate the development of 'football hooliganism' to a Marxist analysis of changes in the game of football itself and, more particularly, changes which were occurring in the relationship between the (male) working class supporter and his home team (Taylor, 1971). The 'football hooligan' was thus initially defined in romanticised terms as a defender of football's traditional working class communitarianism against a growing embourgoisement of the game. This perspective gained support from others writing about football culture in the 1970s (Cohen, 1972; Hall and Jefferson, 1976; Clarke, 1978) and those concerned about the use of media led 'moral panics' in generating populist attitudes towards dealing with crime (Hall, 1978; Hall *et al.*, 1978).

Explicit references to the racist attitudes of 'hooligans' and the activities of the far right were made within this early football literature. Contemporary concerns about the political affiliations of Eastern European football hooligans were pre-figured in England by the report of the Centre for Contemporary Studies (CCS, 1981) which stated that as a result of racist activity at football matches 'the arbitrary and random violence of the skinhead becomes the political and organised violence of the Nazis.' It was also in this context that Taylor (1982) re-assessed his original perspective, with support from Robins (1984), after considering the emergence of the skinheads (see Clarke, 1973) and other 'fighting gangs' associated with 'racist-populist politics.' Taylor argued that 'the repertoire of some of these ['hooligan'] groups now extended far beyond the 'taking of ends' and the property vandalism of the 1960s to involvement in National Front-inspired attacks on blacks' (1982: 158) and other violent activities. The 'hooligan' was now depicted as a member of a lumpen 'underclass,' ripe for manipulation by fascist elements, rather than in romanticised 'class fighter' terms.

Perhaps the most influential body of research on football violence over the past few decades came from researchers at the University of Leicester (Williams *et al.*, 1989; Dunning et al., 1988; Murphy *et al.*,

1990). These studies combined statistical and ethnographic material to produce a theory of 'football hooliganism' grounded in Eliasian sociology and Suttles's (1968) concept of ordered segmentation. The approach suggested that English 'football hooligans' since the mid-1960s have come predominantly from the lower working classes. This is the group who have been less influenced by the 'civilising processes' which Eliasian theory (Elias, 1978) suggests have historically moderated aggressive violent behaviour.

The centrality of this theoretical approach to the Leicester teams' work led their analysis of racism in football to become something of an extension of their broader analysis of 'hooliganism' and the social processes underpinning it. The life experience and values of the lower working classes are seen then to generate racist behaviour in the football context:

> *Probably only a handful of football fans support or even understand the political aims of movements like the National Front and the British Movement in their entirety. Many more, however, perhaps especially those from the lower working class, the ones we have identified as most centrally involved in football hooliganism, appear to be attracted by the pro-white, anti-immigrant stance and proclivity for violent demonstrations of these organisations (Williams et al., 1989: 150).*

While a number of these studies of football hooliganism have much of value to say about the culture of football supporters, they have also tended to reinforce understandings of the nature of football racism within fairly narrow terms of reference which have since been extended to other national contexts in continental Europe. The portrait of racism offered in most of these studies is limited to a focus on the behaviour of young working-class men, often connected closely with aggressive support for the national team or more local variants of nationalism. This way of framing the issue has since transcended the academic arena and has had a far-reaching and lasting influence on the way football authorities both in the UK and in the international context have tackled the issue.

SOCIAL POLICY, RACISM AND THE RACIST/HOOLIGAN COUPLET

The conflation of the issues of hooliganism and racism has had wider significance than merely identifying specific acts of fan racism. What has emerged is the formation of a sporting person, namely the 'racist hooligan,' as the effect of a certain kind of knowledge (Wickham, 1992). Here, following Foucault (1979), we might usefully connect this process of person formation with a project of governmentality in which fan populations are subjected to strategies of maintaining order and establishing new codes of behaviour. The *racist/hooligan couplet* makes it possible to both establish a moral pariah, and then in contrast to this image of deviance promote new codes of propriety and 'acceptable behaviour' inside football stadia. The point here is that 'anti-racist' responses of this kind are the result of a very particular set of discourses which in order to perform their work conceal the complexity and variety of expressive racism at all levels of football.

This is best illustrated by the experience of anti-racist campaigns in football. The primary model for these campaigns, which has since been taken up by FIFA and UEFA in their partnership work with the Football Against Racism in Europe (FARE) network, was established by the Commission for Racial Equality (CRE) and the English Professional Footballers Association with the launch of the *Let's Kick Racism Out of Football* campaign in England in the early 1990s. The CRE had recognised the fact that football provided a useful platform for wider anti-racist strategies but it is also clear that their understanding of the issue of racism in football was still dominated by the concept of the 'racist hooligan.' This was made explicit in the CRE's press release, which accompanied the campaign launch on 12 August 1991 and spoke of the emergence of a '...new generation of football hooligans using the game as a front for a mixture of serious crime and far right politics [involving] the leafleting of racist material at matches' (CRE, 1991).

There are clear benefits in this approach as a political strategy since it has the effect of galvanising a range of football authorities, government, fan organisations and other professional bodies who otherwise share little by way of a common political or organisational agenda. However, the participants in such alliances may well be around the same table for starkly different reasons. For some, it seems clear that the campaign against racism is merely a convenient way to promote greater constraints on fan behaviour. A related consequence of this is that racism in football is defined in a very narrow and unrepresentative way. Thus, the political advantage of representing racism in this way ultimately becomes a constraint. The dependence on the 'racist/hooligan couplet' means that fans do not recognise the image of racism which is presented. Rather what is more familiar, and in some ways more challenging, are the intermittent and often banal forms of racism practiced by strikingly ordinary fans.

Ambiguous and contradictory expressions of racist practice get ignored because their perpetrators don't accept them as racism. A man in his seventies who shouts abusive racial epithets at a black player; coaches who make stereotyped appraisals of Asian players' sporting abilities; and all white boards of directors do not comply with the image of what 'racists' are supposed to look like. For racism to 'count' within this logic the exponent has to fit the category of person we have identified as the 'racist hooligan.' In order to widen our understanding of the issue of racism in football it is imperative to (i) recognise how these regimes of knowledge work; and (ii) to transcend their terms of reference. With this in mind it is worth considering some more recent shifts within football research and writing.

RE-THINKING RACISM IN FOOTBALL

The failure to ground policy interventions in an understanding of manifestations of football racism and its forms of legitimation has been recognised by some writers who have chosen to focus on specific aspects of the problem such as the 'political racism' of extremist groups. Holland et al., in their consideration of the influence of racism and the far right, recognise 'that it is impossible to identify uniform patterns of racism or prejudice or race relations' (Holland *et al.*, 1996: 169), and rationalise their own choice of focus on the basis that 'terms such as race, ethnicity and sport have to be specifically "unpacked" in terms of content, time and place' (Holland *et al.*, 1996: 183). This emphasis on carefully situating the expression of racism was a particularly useful development, for it challenges us to identify the specific ritual and cultural mechanisms through which football culture is racialised. The language of race works differently within different local and national contexts and what holds in the context of one national team and its fan base may not be the case in particular local settings.

Williams's work was one of the first to develop a more nuanced notion of the politics of racism within English football. Interestingly he used Phil Cohen's (1988) use of Hannah Arendt's notion of 'nationalism of the neighbourhood' to discuss the ways in which minorities can win contingent inclusion within local working-class collectivities. Equally, intense working-class localism, often organised around allegiance to particular football clubs, can also provide a strong obstacle to entryism from right-wing political groupings:

This is a key reason why racist organisations have had relatively little success in achieving support for their ambitions which cut across local club allegiances (Williams, 1991: 170).

Equally, Williams (1992) pointed towards the way issues of racism were being played out inside the institutions of the game itself. Here he described the 'naturalness' of racist assumptions and how football 'simply, "has a way of saying things", an accommodative code or a form of (racist) "banter" which incorporates rather than alienates the growing number of black players in League football' (1992: 2). It is within this context that he recognised that 'racism on the football terraces and in the stands is rather more overt and, for most people, easier to identify than the semi-institutional forms that tend to characterise professional football culture'. The paper does not explore these issues inside the professional structures of football, returning instead to the influence of the far right and the relationships between hooliganism and terrace racism. However, Williams pointed the way to another research agenda which transcends the traditional preoccupation with annexing the issue of racism within broader discussions of crowd violence.

Williams also reflects more deeply on the institutionalised basis of racism in football in an account of the history and experiences of the playing members of a local amateur black football club in Leicester (1994) which raises a number of important questions with regard to the attitudes of football institutions as a whole to the position of black clubs and players. Over the past decade European professional football has witnessed an unprecedented growth in the number of black players, largely from African-Caribbean and African backgrounds. This has been accompanied by a small but important increase in black representation in management and coaching. But while black players and managers have made important advances at the occupational level, this has not generally been the case for south Asians and other ethnic minority communities. This leads to a related question about the variety of forms of racism that affect particular minority groups. Jas Bains and Raj Patel in their path breaking work *Asians Can't Play Football* (1995) pose this issue strikingly and provide one of the few discussions of the multi-accented forms of racism that are generated inside football. This diversity of Asian football experiences was given full treatment in Jas Bains and Sanjiev Johal's excellent *Corner Flags and Corner Shops* (Bains and Johal, 1998). The book explodes the myth that there is no interest in football in south Asian communities in Britain and provides a unique insight into these passions through the personal testimonies of south Asian fans themselves.

Some recent texts have attempted to provide a more rigorous analysis of contemporary forms of racism across football culture. Fleming and Tomlinson (1995), for example, sought quite consciously to provide a fuller analysis of the processes of normalisation of racism in football culture and to provide an insight into the wide variety of forms of instrumental racism in the game. They recognised that:

> *Football can embody a popular aesthetic of collective endeavour, but it can also encourage prejudice, discrimination, stereotyping and ethnocentrism. It can bring different cultures together in common celebration, but it can also provide the basis for extreme, and very public, forms of xenophobia and racism (Fleming and Tomlinson, 1995: 2).*

Refreshingly, their understanding is built around a much broader conceptualisation of the processes at work in the generation and normalisation of racist behaviour. While the activities of the far right and hooligans are highlighted; they are recognised alongside the equally important vernacular cultures of football (as expressed by supporters, players, managers, administrators, directors and elsewhere), as well as in the relationship between popular racism and the social institutions of the football industry. This point is also made by Chas Critcher (1991) and leads to a broader sense of the context in which racism features within football.

NEW RESEARCH AGENDAS

As we have seen, until the mid-1990s a focus on fan behaviour was the key way in which the football authorities both addressed the issue and diverted attention away from the forms of racist practice and racial inequality manifest inside the professional game itself. Indeed it is striking that, in the UK at least, the growth in public attention to this issue and the increase in anti-racist campaigning has taken place at a time when there has been a decline in the type of overt mass racial abuse that preoccupied earlier writers. As such the *Kick It Out* Campaign, which was established as an extension of the *Let's Kick Racism Out of Football* initiative, has attempted to develop a new agenda for tackling racism in football which is now beginning to influence approaches in other parts of western Europe. The current campaign has embraced the critique of the conflation of racism and hooliganism, focusing on localised strategies which bring the aspirations of the campaign closer to local activists and practitioners within particular regions.

While a reframing of the campaigning priorities has occurred in this field, the academic analysis of racism and sport remains within a limited analytic framework and isolated from wider debates about race and racism. There is a real gap between contemporary social theory relating to questions of race, social theory and the politics of difference and the literature on the sociology of sport. This has been identified elsewhere (Jarvie and Reid, 1997). A case in point is the controversy about John Hoberman's *Darwin's Athletes* (1997). Hoberman's book caused a considerable uproar in the United States and elsewhere. Writing as a cultural historian Hoberman sees racism as a historical legacy whose echoes are replayed constantly within American life. An example of this is his observation about the lineage between military segregation and the profound lack of black athletes in the cerebral spheres of sports coaching and management. His central contention is that sport is implicated in the perpetuation of the myth of race which binds black and white Americans in a racialised straightjacket of stereotypes. More than this, multi-racial sport becomes:

> *[...] a Darwinian theatre, which has preserved like no other public forum the evolutionary drama that transformed the human image during the nineteenth century (Hoberman, 1997: 13).*

While there is much of interest in these observations, and the points made by Harry Edwards (1969) much earlier, the problem with this account of racism is that it doesn't adequately deal with the possible ruptures and transformations within the culture of racism(s). The recognition of the plural and multifarious nature of racial power is one of the key contributions of recent theorising in this field (Goldberg, 1993; Solomos and Back, 1995). Such nuances are missed when racism is reduced theoretically to a Darwinian inspired discourse of racial biology. Equally, there is a growing consensus that suggests it is necessary to carefully situate the processes of racialisation with specific national, class and gendered contexts.

It is in this sense that the 'racist/hooligan couplet' is not an adequate way of framing the complex forms of racist expression that are part of football culture. In order to understand more fully the culture of racism in football it is necessary to identify the range of *sporting contexts in which processes of racialisation occurs*. In this sense racism can be seen as a mutable and changing phenomenon in which notions of biological or pseudo-biological cultural difference are utilised to explain and legitimate hierarchies of racial dominance and exclusion (Solomos and Back, 1996). The processes of racialisation are both fluid and changing, yet it is also clear that they can play an important part in maintaining patterns of privilege, domination and white supremacy. This perspective sees patterns of racist discourse as changing in line with the dynamics of a particular social formation. For example, the intense fan racism sometimes directed at black players provides a key episode in the racialisation of football. Yet, racism and racist discourses are by their very nature volatile and adapt to new circumstances. So, the disappearance of this particular form or style of racism in contemporary English football need not necessarily be a measure of greater tolerance or unambiguous 'progress.' Whilst new forms of racism have emerged in the English context it is clear that these 'older' formations of racist practice are alive and well in other parts of continental Europe.

It is possible to appreciate then that real changes have occurred in football in relation to questions about race. But equally, continuities remain with past styles of racism which may well combine with neoteric forms of racial discourse. Some of the stereotypes relating to the attributes and playing skills of black players have been exploded by the variety of black players in the professional game. These were classically articulated through suggestions that 'black players couldn't play in the cold,' 'while skilful they lacked the grit and determination of their white counterparts,' and lastly that 'black players had attitude problems, were lazy and with insufficient application to the game.' The sheer presence of black players has shifted some of the ideological terms of these stereotypes and muted their expression. In the wake of this displacement, however, other forms of racial discourse are being generated.

This is not merely the return of pseudo-biological racism which codes athletic prowess 'black' and mental acuity 'white' (Hoberman, 1997). Rather, older strands of racial ideology are invoked and applied alongside new variants contrived to suit present circumstances. In particular, prospective black managers have to face preconceptions about their assumed incapacity to manage multi-racial teams even-handedly, or cope with the organisational load of football management and its associated responsibilities.

In order to establish an overall sense of how the processes of racialisation work within the broader structure of football culture, we need to distinguish between specific arenas in which racism may feature. In Figure 1 four fields are identified within football culture. These are distinct but inter-related sectors providing specific contexts in which particular forms of racialisation can be analysed. For example, the cultural industries provide a distinct set of issues, in the main concentrating on how difference is represented in a range of media from advertising to news and electronic media. Here the key issue is the ways in which different sporting bodies are represented and racialised. Sportive racism provides the device through which black and white bodies are given specific meanings. Hoberman comments that the fetish for racially integrated sport in the United States promotes both a mollifying spectacle and a means by which invidious pseudo-biological stereotypes flourish (Hoberman, 1997: 28-51). Another related question here is the degree to which the racial difference of these sporting figures is marketed as a resource to be exploited economically (Jarvie and Maguire, 1994: 101) by the saccharin forms of corporate multiculturalism that often result (Solomos and Back, 1996). Multi-national corporations use black sporting heroes as exemplary 'super organisms,' reinforcing the aesthetics of racialised sporting prowess, while allowing black athletes to coalesce synonymously with the company's brand identity (Katz, 1994; Barber, 1996).

In addition, media discourses are an important context in which ideas about the relationship between race, nation and entitlement are articulated. This point is developed by Hugh O'Donnell in his discussion of national stereotypes within sports journalism (O'Donnell, 1994). O'Donnell argues that a macro-discourse exists which codes European, South American and African nations within paired sets of attributes. Brazilians can thus be acclaimed for their flair, skill and physical grace. Lurking beneath this discourse is scepticism about flaws in the mercurial Latin American temperament, sexual impropriety and absence of discipline. These kinds of prosaic stereotypes flourish within football, in part because they can be articulated less self-consciously than ideas about colour-coded racial attributes. However, they share the elemental absolutism of racist ideas and equally fix and ossify the diversity of humankind within a gallery of national archetypes.

The second arena is the institutional domain of football's governing bodies. The administration and management of football in western Europe has remained overwhelmingly 'white' in its composition. This stands in stark contrast to the changes in the racial and ethnic make-up of the players. Networks of patronage operate within the sport that need investigation and, like other contexts in which the representation of black and minority ethnic groups has grown in recent years, sophisticated forms of racial discourse are tailored to resisting institutional change (Solomos and Back, 1995). This is associated closely with the third arena, the occupational cultures of the sport, including all aspects of the professional structure including scouting, player cultures, the dynamics of the transfer market, management and coaching and the under-representation of black people in marketing and administration of the clubs. Processes of racialisation here include the forms of stereotyping which fix the attributes and skills of black and white

Figure 1
Racialisation in Football: A Framework for Analysis

Arena	*Context*	*Forms of racialisation*
Culture Industry:	Advertising and marketing Sponsorship	Imaging racial difference Racialised patterns of commercial endorsement
	Print media & Journalism Electronic media	Elite racist discourses concerning race and nation
Institutional:	Administration and ruling bodies and decision making Players' organizations Club Ownership and boardroom control	Racial inequality in terms of access to decision making forums Racial discourses of exclusion
Occupational:	Scouting and patterns of recruitment	Connection between racialised attributes and sporting capacity and professional competence
	Players' occupational culture	Racialised rumours and decision making Racist abuse within the playing/ coaching arena
	Transfer market Management and coaching Administration and Marketing	Conceptions of the market and internal culture of football clubs.
Vernacular culture:	Race and nation within the context of the national side	The racialisation of entitlement and belonging' and racialisation of the National body politic
	Club, region and identity Geography of support and patronage	Racialised hierarchies and 'neighbourhood nationalism'
	Player symbols History and club rivalries Expressive rituals of support	Positioning of Black players and the club's collective identity Racialised forms of abuse The relationship between right-wing politics and fan cultures.

players respectively and the prevalence of racialised forms of rumouring regarding the characteristics of black players. These discourses may act informally as networks of 'white knowledge' that are rarely explicit. Equally, racist behaviour in this context would also include explicit forms of abuse from white coaches and players against their black counterparts.

Lastly, the vernacular culture of fans, as we have already seen, constitutes an arena in which these issues are managed. This works differently within supporter cultures at a local and national level. Indeed, there are overlaps here with the elite discourses of race/nation discussed in relation to sports journalism. Here the relationship between fan culture and racism can be conceptualised at a number of levels, namely the ways in which ideas of race are worked through the language of nation, locality, club identity and the geography of local fan networks. One of the features of many clubs located in inner city areas is that every Saturday afternoon ethnically diverse neighbourhoods are 'invaded' by white fans from outer city and suburban areas who reverse the patterns of residential 'white flight' to support their team. Complex negotiations may also take place between fans around the construction of club identities and their forms of collective belonging. This includes what has been referred to as 'neighbourhood nationalism,' which can establish patterns of inclusion and exclusion, whereby some black fans are admitted as contingent insiders while other minority groups and opposing black fans and players are vilified and cast as outsiders. The success or otherwise of right-wing political organisations might also be discussed in relation to the local patterns of territory and identity organised around specific football clubs. Overt racist abuse and their ritual structure would also be included within this arena. In order to understand the range of racist activity, one needs to examine the relationship between processes of racialisation and the collective ritual and symbolic practices that give any particular fan culture meaning. In this sense differences with regard to the level and intensity of racism need to be understood in terms of the way racist practices are nested within the ritual and collective symbolism of each fan culture.

The framework outlined above offers one means of broadening the analysis of racism in football which helped to inform the most detailed investigation of cultures of racism in football in the UK (Back, Crabbe and Solomos, 2001) but which might not be extended to wider international contexts. Patterns of racialisation within this sporting context demonstrate a complex combination of continuity and change which challenges the adequacy of the conventional means of understanding them. While the public debate and academic writing has constructed a vivid portrait of what a 'racist football fan' looks like, little attempt has been made to define precisely what racism constitutes in specific sporting arenas. As a result this discussion of racism in football takes on a kind of everything and nothing quality, a catchall notion that is rarely explained and defined theoretically. What is presented here then is an attempt to designate the specific processes of sportive racialisation and how they are situated in institutional and demotic arenas.

Viewing racism as merely a constituent element of the wider problem of 'anti-social' behaviour has resulted in some issues being organised onto the political and intellectual agenda while others have been ruled out. It is possible to talk about racism inside football grounds but it is more or less taboo to ask about this issue on the training ground, the field of play and in the board room. The crude labelling of racists as 'moral degenerates' within what we have described as the racist/hooligan couplet, will do little to identify and tackle these broader problems. Indeed, the continued preoccupation with crowd behaviour has become part of the problem itself. The pervasive image of the right-wing 'hooligan' both feeds and gives legitimacy to a broader project of regulating fan behaviour regardless of whether or not these rituals are connected with racist practice. As such there is an urgent need to widen the terms of the sociological imagination with regard to understanding racism in football.

REFERENCES

Armstrong, G. (1998). Football Hooligans: Knowing the Score. Oxford: Berg.

Armstrong, G. (1993). Like that Desmond Morris? in D. Hobbs and T. May. (eds.), Interpreting the Field: Accounts of Ethnography. Oxford: Clarendon Press.

Armstrong, G. and Harris, R. (1991). Football Hooligans: Theory and Evidence. Sociological Review, 39, 3: 427-458.

Back, L. (1991). Social Context and Racist Name-Calling: An Ethnographic Perspective on Racist Talk Within a South London Adolescent Community. European Journal of Intercultural Studies 1, 3: 19-38.

Back, L. (1996). Urban Culture and New Ethnicities. London: UCL Press.

Back, L., Crabbe, T. and Solomos, J. (2001). The Changing Face of Football: Racism, Multiculture and Identity in the English Game. Oxford: Berg.

Bains, J. and Johal, S. (1998). Corner Flags and Corner Shops: The Asian Football Experience. London: Phoenix.

Bains, J. and Patel, R. (1996). Asians Can't Play Football. Birmingham: D-zine.

Barber, B. (1996). Jihad v McWorld: How Globalism and Tribalism are Reshaping the World. New York: Ballantine Books.

Buford, W. (1991). Amongst the Thugs. London: Secker and Warburg.

Centre for Contemporary Studies. (1981). Football and the Fascists. London: CCS.

Cohen, P. (1972). Subcultural Conflict and Working Class Community. Working Papers in Cultural Studies 2. Birmingham: CCCS.

Cohen, P. (1988). The Perversion of Inheritance, in Cohen, P. and H. Bains (eds.), Multi-Racist Britain. Basingstoke: Macmillan.

Commission for Racial Equality. (1991). Press Release, 12 August 1991. London: CRE.

Cashmore, E. (1982). Black Sportsmen. London: Routledge and Kegan Paul.

Clarke, J. (1973). Football and the Skinheads. Occasional Paper. Centre for Contemporary Cultural Studies, University of Birmingham.

Clarke, J. (1978). Football and Working Class Fans: Tradition and Change, in Ingham, R. (ed.), Football Hooliganism: The Wider Context. London: Inter-Action.

Critcher, C. (1991). Putting on the Style: Aspects of Recent English Football, in Williams, J. and S. Wagg (eds.), British Football and Social Change: Getting into Europe. Leicester: Leicester University Press.

Dunning, E., Murphy, P. and Waddington, I. (1991). Anthropological versus Sociological Approaches to the Study of Soccer Hooliganism: Some Critical Notes. Sociological Review, 39, 3: 459-78.

Dunning, E., Murphy, P., and Williams, J. (1988). The Roots of Football Hooliganism: An Historical and Sociological Study. London: Routledge.

Edwards, H. (1969). The Revolt of the Black Athlete. New York: Free Press.

Elias, N. (1978). The Civilising Process: The History of Manners. Oxford: Basil Blackwell.

Fleming, S. and Tomlinson, A. (1995). Football, Xenophobia and Racism-Europe and the old Britain. Draft Submission to European Union Human Mobility Network. Chelsea School Research Centre, University of Brighton.

Foucault, M. (1979). On Governmentality. Ideology and Consciousness, 6: 5-23.

Fradley, K. (1983). Football Hooliganism Demystified: An Examination of Football Crowd Disorder in the West Midlands. MPhil Dissertation, University of Birmingham.

Goldberg, D. (1993). Racist Culture. Oxford: Blackwell.

Hall, S. (1978). The Treatment of Football Hooliganism in the Press, in Ingham, R. (ed.), Football Hooliganism: The Wider Context. London: Inter-Action.

Hall, S., Clarke, J., Critcher, C., Jefferson, T., and Roberts, B. (1978). Policing the Crisis. London: Macmillan.

Hall, S. and Jefferson, T. (eds.). (1976). Resistance Through Rituals. London: Hutchinson.

Hill, D. (1989). Out of His Skin: The John Barnes Phenomenon. London: Faber and Faber.

Hobbs, D. and Robbins, D. (1991). The Boy Done Good: Football Violence, Changes and Continuities. Sociological Review, 39, 3: 551-579.

Hoberman, J. (1997). Darwin's Athletes: How Sport Damaged Black America and Preserved the Myth of Race. Boston: Houghton Mifflin Company.

Holland, B. (1995). "Kicking Racism Out of Football:" An Assessment of Racial Harassment In and Around Football Grounds. New Community, 21, 4: 567-86.

Holland, B., Jackson, L., Jarvie, G. & Smith, M. (1995). Sport and Racism in Yorkshire: A Case Study. Heriot Watt University.

Jarvie, G. and Maguire, J. (1994). Sport and Leisure in Social Thought. London: Routledge.

Jarvie, G. and Reid, I. (1997). Race Relations, Sociology of Sport and the New Politics of Race and Racism. Leisure Studies, 16, 4: 211-19.

Katz, D. (1994). Just Do It: The Nike Spirit in the Corporate World. Holbrook: Adams Publishing.

Leeds Trades Council. (1988). Terror on our Terraces: NF, Football Violence and Leeds United. Leeds: LTC.

Melnick, M. (1988). Racial Segregation by Playing Position in the English Footbal League: Some Preliminary Observations. Journal of Sport and Social Issues, 12, 2:122-30.

Murphy, P., Williams, J. and Dunning, E. (1990). Football on Trial: Spectator Violence and Development in the Football World. London: Routledge.

O'Donnell, H. (1994). Mapping the Mythical: A Geopolitics of National Sporting Stereotypes. Discourse and Society, 5, 3: 345-80.

Orakwue, S. (1998). Pitch Invaders: The Modern Black Football Revolution. London: Victor Gollancz.

Robins, D. (1984). We Hate Humans. Harmondsworth: Penguin.

Solomos, J. and Back, L. (1995). Race, Politics and Social Change. London: Routledge.

Solomos, J. and Back, L. (1996). Racism and Society. Basingstoke: Macmillan.

Suttles, G. (1968). The Social Order of the Slum: Ethnicity and Territory in the Inner City. Chicago: University of Chicago Press.

Taylor, I. (1971). Soccer Consciousness and Soccer Hooliganism, in Cohen, S. (ed.), Images of Deviance. Harmondsworth: Penguin.

Taylor, I. (1982). On the Sports Violence Question: Soccer Hooliganism Revisited, in Hargreaves, J. (ed.), Sport, Culture and Ideology. London: Routledge.

Turner, R. (1990). In Your Blood: Football Culture in the Late 1980s and Early 1990s. London: Working Press.

Vasili, P. (1994). The Right Kind of Fellows: Nigerian Football Tourists as Agents of Europeanization. The International Journal of the History of Sport, 11, 2: 191-211.

Vasili, P. (1998). The First Black Footballer; Arthur Wharton 1865-1930: An Absence of Memory. London: Frank Cass.

Vasili, P. (2000). Colouring Over the White Line: The History of Black Footballers in Britain. Edinburgh: Mainstream.

Williams, J. (1992). Lick My Boots-Racism in English Football. Department of Sociology, University of Leicester.

——. (1994). Rangers is a Black Club: Race, Identity and Local Football in England, in Giulianotti, R. and Williams, J. (eds.), Game Without Frontiers. Aldershot: Avebury.

Wickham, G. (1992). Sport, Manners, Persons, Government: Sport, Elias, Mauss, Foucault. Cultural Studies, 6(2): 219-31.

Williams, J., Dunning, E., and Murphy, P. (1989). Hooligans Abroad: The Behaviour and Control of England Fans in Continental Europe Second Edition. London: Routledge.

Woollnough, B. (1983). Black Magic: England's Black Footballers. London: Pelican.

FOOTBALL HOOLIGANISM AND THE MODERN WORLD

7

H. F. Moorhouse

INTRODUCTION

England is the brand leader for football hooliganism. This leadership status is acknowledged by the banners, signs, songs and chants in the English language which appear at many games in Italy and Spain, for example. But continental copy-cats have not yet outstripped the old masters. In the build-up to the World Cup in 2006 media reports indicated that one of the German police's main worries was that actions by English football hooligans might disrupt the whole tournament. In addition, English academic analysis of hooliganism has dominated the field or, at the least, entrenched basic lines of thought and discussion and, here too, most European and South American analysis has never quite broken free of this hegemony.

Agenda setting as it has definitely been, the debate about football hooliganism in England suffers from a number of debilitating failings. Among the most enfeebling of these are tendencies to:

- over-emphasize the social significance of the subject;
- avoid or misrepresent what other people have written about the phenomenon;
- avoid cross-cultural comparisons except in the most generalised of forms;
- ignore relevant debates in other areas of social analysis, especially those concerning the complexities of contemporary class stratification.

In this paper, I intend to examine this dominant approach to the academic analysis of football hooliganism and amplify my criticisms of this branch of sociological scholarship.

EARLY ENGLISH THEORISING

The analysis of hooliganism hegemonised the study of football from the late 1960s until very recently. The theories assumed that hooliganism increased in the early 1960s and that it was the result of stresses occurring in the cultural and social position of certain sections of young working-class males. This view was contrasted with a rather romanticised portrait of the traditional soccer crowd. Early English theories tend to focus on what was believed to be new departures from old norms occurring among one segment of the post-war working class. Such theories seek to describe and explain a movement from a traditional relationship built between working class culture and the local club towards a distanced and dislocated relationship between a crumbling working class culture and a rapidly embourgeoisifying football. In all such theories, with varying nuances and emphases, hooliganism is located as a response to material and cultural stress among one group of the lower working class.

Taylor (1971a; 1971b; 1982), for instance, believes that significant changes have taken place in the ties between the working class supporter and his club. He argues that, traditionally, there was a close relation between football and the local culture (or, to be exact, a football sub-culture). This was not simply because there was an alignment between the values which arose out of working class experience and those expressed in football–values of masculinity, collective participation and victory–but also because the sub-culture was involved in, or could believe they were involved in, a participatory democracy. The players, in particular, but managers and directors too, moved in the community and their success rested directly on it. They were amenable, or were thought to be amenable, to the demands and views of their supporters, and were responsive to communal controls. The community and club were seen as a collective enterprise.

Taylor believes there always were dangers to this relationship incipient in, say, transfer policies and petit-bourgeois financial control, but it was developments after 1945 which really changed this relationship. In the post-war period, with 'affluence' for some of the working class and new opportunities in leisure, attendances began to decline and those in charge of the clubs, accepting the dominant ideologies of the time, believed that the solution was to restructure both the game and the grounds so as to appeal to a new kind of customer. Soccer's powers that be and the mass media transformed their image of the ideal turnstile-turner from working class fan to a 'classless' (i.e.

middle class) consumer. The objective was to insert football into the wider 'entertainment industry,' offering a more spectacular and expensive 'experience' to consumers who would purchase a ticket but exhibit in no excess passion. So, the essential set of relations around clubs changed from, or became more obviously not, 'democratic' and moved towards contractual ties. The value alignment of culture and game changed too as, say, masculinity, as understood by the working class, was by no means so clearly displayed on the pitch. Gradually grounds changed with more seats and amenities while the players won a freedom that served to detach them from reliance on the locality for fame and fortune.

Taylor argues that some of the working class responded to these alterations in the game and took their seats, along with the incoming middle class, in the stands, though he believes that even this group could reveal a rather refined resistance, not defined as violence or hooliganism by the media or the club. More critically, some of the working class who had missed out on the affluent 1960s remained much more traditional carriers of the values of the old football sub-culture. It was this group who educated their young, and others, into the older values of participation and passion, of a fully engaged supporter. It is these youngsters who try to assert old values and relationships through violence or, at least, new forms of violence. Football violence, or a new meaning given to such violence, is a product of the early 1960s and onwards and is both a sign of the young fans' commitment to their side's cause and also a doomed attempt to obstruct the steady bourgeosification of football and assert new kinds of control over the club rulers. Moreover, such actions are, Taylor insists, indicative of a wider alienation in their lives. For the changing relation of the club to working class culture, and so the violence, is merely an aspect of, and is caused by, a wider decomposition of the traditional working class community and traditional social relations. The new, alienated, attempts to reassert control merely lead to a spiral of official reaction and amplification as soccer's powerful, the media and state agencies seek to cleanse soccer and make it safe for the 'classless' consumer of the 'modern era.'

Clarke (1978) modifies Taylor somewhat. For example, other affinities are adduced between working class life and football along parallels of 'skill' and local identity as well as toughness and collectivity. Nonetheless, the overall argument is very similar:

> *Hooliganism comes out of the way in which the traditional forms of football watching encounter the professionalisation and spectacularisation of the game. It is one of the consequences of the changing relationship of the audience to the game (Clarke, 1978: 50).*

Again, working class youth are the inheritors of an old tradition but Clarke places much more emphasis than Taylor on inter-generational changes in the crowd itself. Class remains but working class youth are in a changing position both in the ground and in the community–they have become physically and socially separated. So while they inherit a tradition of committed support they have done so without some of the old controls on behaviour and so have altered the tradition passed onto them. Violence becomes an extension of the traditional form of support. They try to intervene in the game and, with the taking of opponents' ends, become part of a total confrontation between two sides. This also represents their appropriation of the new emphasis on spectacle. They make support the more spectacular by creating events and excitement through which they forge their own identities. This produces 'official concern' and the creation of a 'social problem,' so that not only new forms of activity but also old forms–swearing and pushing–come to be defined as deviant and as keeping away the more desired new audience.

Critcher's argument (1979) is broadly similar to Clarke's. He too sees football as an indicator of changes in working class culture, reflecting and affecting broader changes. The meshing of values between culture and the game is there in his account. Again he locates hooliganism as a problem of the early 1960s, arising for rather similar reasons: *"Into the hiatus between traditional supporter and modern consumer stepped the football hooligan"* (Critcher, 1979: 171). He summarises Taylor approvingly but thinks that his argument is somewhat overstated, particularly in what he believes is Taylor's attempt to locate the issue wholly within the game. Rather, such changes and such behaviour have to be seen as a specific, though important, example of much more general dislocations and aberrations. For the rough working class life is generally one of an uncertain cultural world in which youth try to generate a relevant code about behaviour and identity. The football ground is one established venue for the exploration and expression of their identity and so they re-orchestrate traditional values.

The Leicester School of Dunning *et al.* (1981; 1988) provide, as they note, a somewhat different theory about the relationship between working class culture and football and about the rise of hooliganism in the 1960s, based on Elias's notion of 'the civilising process' (Elias and Dunning, 1986). They locate soccer violence within lower working class communities which tend to generate norms that tolerate, indeed, reward, a high level of violence in social relationships. They pay little attention to notions of traditional democracy or to illusions about community control, and say less about changes in the game or grounds in the post-war period.

Their argument is that the football ground is one outlet for norms about masculinity current among all the working class, but that the respectable working class are able to react to 'territorial invasions' by other teams and supporters in a civilised, cosmopolitan, manner but, from the 1950s, a number of developments made the game more attractive than it had previously been to members of the rough working class who, in addition, came to define football grounds as places for expressing their own masculinity norms. So they point to a curvilinear pattern of hooligan behaviour, relatively high before the First World War, low in the inter-war years, but rising again in the early 1960s. In the early period, they say, more of the total working class lived under social conditions, and adhered to norms, approximate to those of the post-war rough working class. There was a slow incorporation to dominant standards in the early decades of the century, which increased markedly in the 1950s period of 'affluence.' So there came to be an increasing divergence and distaste between respectable supporters and a relatively few rough ones. Then the media, attracted to football by the World Cup held in England in 1966, began to report on incidents that had always occurred and presented these, as the media will, dramatically. This promoted football stadiums to the rough working class as a place where their favoured masculinity norms could be displayed and they began to attend in much greater numbers.

In contradistinction to the other theorists, Dunning et. al., locate hooliganism as a phenomenon having a long, subterranean, history but whose contemporary prominence arises because a working class group with historically rather weak ties to a soccer sub-culture have been attracted to the football grounds to flaunt their cultural values thereby serving as a significant reference group for the disaffected youth of the respectable working class.

As an interim statement on this classic theorising it should be noted that they do not fit Scottish soccer (Moorhouse, 1984). The United

Kingdom contains four football countries. Scotland, at least, has claims to be of a similar status to England with its separate league and well supported clubs. But English theories have ignored the potential for pertinent comparisons here. Taylor, who once worked in Glasgow, has some asides and footnotes in his general argument which show that he does appreciate the differences. Thus his repeated claim that the particular kind of violence, especially pitch invasions, he is concerned with, probably begins with a televised game in the 1960-61 season, is qualified in one article by a footnote which reads in part:

> *For reasons which are not obvious (and which would require explication in a comparative analysis of football in two or more cultures) invasions have apparently been 'common practice' in Scotland for many years and certainly occurred frequently long before 1960 (Taylor, 1971: 373).*

While another footnote (Taylor, 1982: 189) refers to the 'brake clubs' of young supporters of some Scottish clubs which existed before and well after the First World-War and which seem to have been heavily involved in 'football hooliganism' many decades before 1960. In fact, Taylor's intermittent references to Scotland pose problems for his theory that he does not seem to notice, let alone answer. Scottish football is arguably more 'traditional' than the English game but has always generated the apparently 'new' forms of violence that, according to all these English theorists, supposedly arose out of profound disjunctures in traditional ties. If we accept this point, then problems arise for all the theories so far summarised.

THE IMPLICATIONS OF SCOTTISH EVIDENCE

Any reading of the history of the early years of Scottish football must lead to an agreement with the general conclusion of Hutchinson (1975: 11) that:

> *Riots, unruly behaviour, violence, assault and vandalism, appear to have been a well-established, but not necessarily dominant, pattern of crowd behaviour at football matches at least from the 1870s.*

The two great Scottish clubs, Celtic and Rangers, both based in Glasgow, were, and still are, linked to ethnic communities–Catholics who often emigrated or are the descendants of emigrants from Ireland on the one hand, and Scottish Protestants on the other. Ethnic antagonism was prevalent in Glasgow from Victorian times onwards and the ethnic divide lapped into divisions in the labour market between skilled and unskilled, divisions in the community between respectables and roughs, and in some residential segregation also. However its coupling with professional football, such that it became linked to soccer violence, is a feature of the years after 1910, and, especially, after the First World War. Attention to this feature of Scottish football history would seem to disturb the cyclical trend noted by Dunning et. al.–for no curvilinear pattern of hooliganism is to be found in Scotland–while the association of skilled workers with anti-Catholicism and so support for Rangers and so violence, throws some historical doubt, at least, on the general tendency to locate 'hooliganism' with the rough working class.

In the inter-war years matches between Rangers and Celtic became potential flashpoints. We therefore get such 'modern' features of the games, in what are very traditional clubs, as the separation of fans into distinct ends of the Glasgow grounds from the 1920s and a routine long case list of offenders at magistrates' courts on the days following matches. The Glasgow teams developed a certain style of support from the 1890s, as mentioned by Taylor, whereby associations of young men in the brake clubs made a noisy and colourful way to matches in horse-drawn brakes and later in charabancs. The hooliganism of the brake clubs was by no means confined to Celtic and Rangers games. Here is how the fiscal at Ayr police court was reported following an Ayr United versus Rangers game in 1920:

> *at the corresponding match last year similar scenes of a disgraceful character took place on the part of the Rangers club. It was a singular fact that supporters of other clubs, with only occasional exceptions, behaved like ordinary citizens. The Rangers followers come to the town in brakes, charabancs and motor lorries. They were composed of a large number of young hooligans whose object seemed to be not to enjoy the football match but to create pandemonium wherever they went (Moorhouse, 1984: 298).*

So one aspect of the pattern of violence in Scotland appears to have been the development, many years before its apparent sociological time, of a youth sub-culture which revolved around soccer rivalry.

There were *notable* outbreaks of violence in Scottish football, almost all at games between Celtic and Rangers, in 1941, 1946, 1949, 1952, 1953, 1955, 1957, 1958 and on into the 1960s. The violence comprised of fighting, bottle throwing, and pitch invasions, in addition to, of course, abusive chanting, obscenities and jeering. The Scottish press denounced such incidents in a rhetoric that was to become familiar in England (and in sociological analysis) only a decade or two later. The couplet 'football hooligan,' all but unknown in England until the 1960s, was in regular use well before, in Scotland. Thus The Glasgow Herald declared on the 9th of January 1952, '*Something must be done. This hooliganism on the sports field cannot be allowed to go on. The sport of football must be cleaned up.*' The football authorities, counter-argued that trouble was caused by a few hooligans in crowds of tens of thousands of respectable fans and that violence was a much wider problem in Glasgow. As the SFA President put it in 1958:

> *We in football do not try to minimise the danger of misbehaviour in football grounds, but there is hooliganism and crime every day in the week in Glasgow's dance halls, public houses and in the streets, and we have not heard of any special powers being sought to eliminate this dreadful state of affairs (The Glasgow Herald, 3rd. November 1958).*

However sociologically prescient this observation, from the mid-1960s various Glasgow elites began to find the hooliganism increasingly irksome. Indeed, hooliganism in Scotland, and in Glasgow in particular, gets linked, much more than in England, with having an economic effect, of being in part responsible for Glasgow's poor 'image' and so of delaying inward investment and the inward migration of white collar workers. While Scottish hooliganism did not just occur at games between the Glasgow clubs, though most did, even where it occurred elsewhere it could usually be linked back to the Old Firm rivalries, and by extension to the city of Glasgow. The press (and television too) became increasingly concerned about soccer violence, in part accepting that it was economically damaging to Glasgow, but also because they echoed the new concern beginning to run through the English media about the English game. There is therefore some ambiguity in Scottish media accounts about whether the issue in Scotland in the 1970s was a matter of the traditional sectarianism and bigotry or was a simple youth phenomenon, fuelled, in Scotland, by excess alcohol.

It has to be said that, despite all the concern, violence at or around football was not a marked problem in Scotland, especially outside Rangers and Celtic matches. This was illustrated by the Report of the Working Group on Football Crowd Behaviour of 1977 (The McElhone Report), itself a product of the Scottish elites concern about the damage to the national image arising out of a hooliganism which is presumed to be on the increase and presumed to account for falling attendances. The report is largely about drink and missiles, and partly about ways of controlling the crowd. It had a profound effect on subsequent legislation. In fact, what the report actually shows is the relative insignificance of this problem in Scotland. In 1976 league games produced on average 0.28 arrests per 1,000 spectators, or just over 1,000 arrests. This comprised just over 1 per cent of all breach of the peace and assaults in Scotland and compared to 13,224 arrests for drunken driving. Not unusually, in either policy making or academic study, football hooliganism was accorded a social importance that could not really be justified by the actual harm it produced.

That said, I hope it is plain that the pattern of crowd disorder does not follow the trajectories suggested by English theory. Scottish fans have been involved in spectacular and regular violence for almost a century and thus undercut both Dunning et al. and the other English theories about hooliganism. It could be that the carriers of that tradition of violence have changed through time, but this is practically impossible to know given the extreme paucity of information about the soccer crowd in either Scotland or England. But even if Scottish youth are more involved in violent behaviour than they used to be, and this is at least doubtful, it seems clear that they are continuing a belief about appropriate behaviour passed on from generation to generation. There does not appear to be any age split in ideology or activities, in some contrast to the notions of Clarke and Critcher. Around football, as in much of the rest of life, violence can be a family affair.

Also, with regard to Dunning et. al., it is virtually impossible to say whether violence now derives more from a 'rough' section of the working class than it used to. Appropriate information about the past does not really exist, especially if we remember that 'rough' and 'respectable' are cultural definitions which do not attach to material circumstance as neatly as Dunning et. al. suggest. What can be said for Scotland is that, in the past at least, Rangers support is believed to have been drawn heavily from the skilled working class, and Catholics were labelled as, and kept in material situations supposedly conducive to, the 'roughs.' On the other hand, general Glaswegian male working class culture does seem to emphasise masculinity norms more than, say, London. One aspect of this is heavy weekend drinking, often linked to football. So, it has to be said that given valued masculinity norms, given the drinking and given the ethnic antagonism, one major theoretical puzzle concerning soccer violence in Scotland is why there is not a lot more of it, and it is not too difficult to argue exactly the same about the English situation.

In addition, attention to Scottish football points to a fallacy in the arguments of Taylor and those who follow him. 'Participatory democracy' does not necessitate an absence of violence nor do developments in the game in the last decades–the reconstruction of stadia, more advertising etc., end the possibility of, or the illusion of, communal control. If we consider Rangers policy of not signing any players who were Catholics, which held until the mid-1980s, it appears that the directors of the club believed themselves to be in thrall to their support on the issue. They may well have been sectarian themselves but it seems unlikely that they would maintain such a policy, which earned them constant ridicule in the media dock, cut them off from many of the best young players in Scotland and had implications for their continued participation in lucrative pan-European competition, sponsorship money, and so on, if it was just a matter of their own predilections. My point is that the Rangers board was sensitive to the wishes of their traditional community, though this may not equate to the romanticised working class community of the north of England in the 1930s which is the base-line of some theories.

Thus, this brief review of Scottish evidence should reveal some weaknesses in any general applicability of those English theories about the game and soccer violence with which I started. Scottish evidence seems to suggest that these theories operate with a dubious history, are severely culture-bound, and are, generally, inadequate. Other aspects of the Scottish game's relation to 'hooliganism' which I do not have space to go into here are also damaging for these English theories (Moorhouse, 1989). Such difficulties arising out of consideration of the Scottish example are extremely significant because, in most respects, it is culturally extremely similar to England. As a 'naturally occurring experiment,' a lot of variables are being held constant, but the trajectory and basis of hooliganism is at odds with those held to be important in England, and for the whole world. If the theories and causal trajectories theorists seek to create about the relation of football violence and working-class life do not hold good even for a society as culturally close to England as Scotland, then it seems quite reasonable to claim that they are fundamentally flawed. This suggestion of the difficulties posed for dominant theories of hooliganism would be all the more marked if contemporary scholarship had produced more thorough and critically judged cross cultural studies of sports violence around the world, which it has not.

LATER ENGLISH THEORISING

As we shall see, assertion of the importance of the ideas put forward in the early English analyses continues on, often in virtually unaltered forms, but, rather confusingly, often contained in what purport to be attempts to criticise these classical accounts and, seemingly, offer new insights into hooliganism. The fact is that these newer texts often commit the same fundamental errors of the works they are trying to criticise and are even less theoretically coherent.

Recent years have seen three main developments in the study of hooliganism:

- an increasing theoretical incoherence and confusion;
- a growth in cross cultural approaches of a surface kind, both theoretically and empirically;
- a shift of focus away from hooliganism associated with clubs to the national team as the game within England appears to have been pacified, while violent behaviour has marked a number of matches of the English team abroad.

One aspect of the theoretical confusion is the rise of what is self-advertised as an 'anthropological' critique of the earlier sociological theories. What this actually consists of are not extensive anthropological studies, but quite small scale participant observation accounts, expressed in an arcane academic argot derived from modern anthropology. So Robson (2000) seeks to outline the culture of the supporters of the minor London team of Millwall, and discusses how salient aspects of a localised working class cultural personality becomes embodied in boys and young men. Millwall supporters, were once believed to be at the forefront of hooliganism and have a reputation for 'hardness,' but Robson distances himself from the study of hooliganism. This is partly because he believes that, empirically, Millwall supporters have moved on:

> *Millwall fans in general appear to have significantly 'grown out' of routine hooliganism... This appears to be not merely the result of external policing and preventative measures. There is a widespread feeling that Millwall have nothing further–having written the book in the years when it really counted– left to prove on the terrain of hooligan culture (Robson 2000: 136).*

But it's also because he believes that the kind of approach exemplified in earlier English theorising is now quite 'played out:'

> *I have positioned football in a consciously delimited way as the practical medium par excellence of the continuing expression and celebration of the core practices and concerns of embodied masculinity in a specific working class variant. It is almost impossible to overstate the significance of the game in its more extended sense in the maintenance and reproduction of those practices and in the informal cultural practices of working class life generally. My interest in the game has therefore been primarily in the area of continuity of practice among these groups in their implicit resistance to and negotiation of modernity and its consequences, but without any particular focus on the hooligan phenomenon; the existing literature can be regarded as having by now exhausted the sociological potential of this particular sphere of activity (Robson, 2000: x).*

And adds:

> *I proceed from the view that 'football hooliganism' and match day disorder in general have at their core no inner truths or obscure causes awaiting revelation. The nature of the game, and the social sources from which it draws, adds itself quite naturally to 'periodic excess and the carnivalesque' and has done for centuries (Robson, 2000: 3).*

So, Robson rejects the trajectories of hooliganism outlined in early English theorising and, apparently, much of the social causation they advance. Given this kind of dismissal, it might be thought odd to find Dunning (2002: 14-15) and Williams (2001: 47) both of the Leicester School, claiming his work as, essentially, very closely allied to their own, but they are quite right. Because what Robson does is to repeat, in highly academicised language, many of the earlier assertions about the crucial net of connections between football and masculinity, parallels between values inherent in the game and those in working class life, and so on. When Robson (2000: 3) argues that:

> *Few activities offered such men the opportunity to express a deeply embodied need for physicality, competition, visceral collectivity and ludic expression.*

and goes onto to stress the value working class men put on the game's expression of hardness, stamina, courage and loyalty, rather than fairness or good manners, my feeling is that modern English theorising, rather than being any real rejection or development of earlier English theorising, is actually just a repetition of much of the earlier work. There are no real new insights but rather replays of what are now old verities in the hooligan literature.

Armstrong and Harris (1991) for example, seek through an ethnographic study of a group of Sheffield United supporters, to distinguish and criticize two main academic approaches to the study of football hooliganism:

- what they call 'a structural Marxist' approach (i.e., Taylor, Critcher, Clarke);
- another which concentrates on the actual behaviour of hooligans which divides into analyses which discuss whether this is 'real' violence and those which try to divine the backgrounds of the fighting fans the better to explain their activities (which includes Dunning et. al.)

The trouble is that their evidence is simply not adequate to cause anyone to reject either of these 'theories' nor could it be (Moorhouse, 1991). Conceptual, definitional and methodological problems intrude from the start for we are not told anything about behaviour at football matches, about why Sheffield should be regarded as a particularly salient example of the phenomenon under discussion, and we are provided with no historical information, or past or present context, within which to set and assess the (rather peaceful) events chronicled. The overall thrust of the paper is to argue for the importance of participant observation. The trouble is that any such evidence, even in more telling locales than Sheffield, may not tell scholars much about what is supposedly being discussed and certainly not in the absence of historical data.

One of the main difficulties in accepting this argument as of much significance for the study of football hooliganism is that Sheffield does not appear to provide a key case of the phenomenon. The authors are keen to lecture others about the importance of 'empirical data,' so the critic is entitled to ask why choose this example? Saying that Sheffield has many problems of poverty and unemployment is scarcely too demarcating a line for England in the last decades of the twentieth century and, anyway, since the tenor of the argument is that such material factors have little to do with violence around football, these are odd claims to make for salience. Sheffield fans have never been widely regarded as 'notorious.' So one reason to deny the theoretical claims the authors make is a doubt about whether we are discussing anything like a critical case.

What we do get, extended in Armstrong (1998), is a vignette involving around forty young men in a city not specially noted for its 'violence,' football-related or otherwise. In the end we find that males from different sections of the city and environs occasionally fight (though not too much), and that the line of demarcation of these groups is supposed to attach to professional football clubs. But we are not told whether Sheffield has always contained groups prone to fisticuffs regardless of football affiliations, though we are told that now, outside the football context, brawls around pubs are common. In short, another doubt is in what sense is what is being described 'football hooliganism' or rather a much more prevalent, new or old, low level 'rowdyism.' Part of this problem involves what activities should be legitimately denoted as 'football hooliganism.' Williams (2001: 45, and see 52) can sum up:

> *In fact, there is no useful precise definition of 'football hooliganism' available or much agreement among UK academics about its seriousness or even its causes.*

While Dunning *et al.* (2002: 1) state:

> *Probably the most important thing to stress is that the label 'football hooliganism' is not so much a scientific sociological or social psychological concept as a construct of politicians and the media. As such, it lacks precision and is used to cover a variety of forms of behaviour which takes place in contexts that are related to football to a greater or lesser degree.*

Which, in my judgment, are meagre returns for nearly forty years of study, analysis and apparent sociological discussion!

Most of those now involved in what passes for the 'debate on hooliganism' insist that what they are focusing on is gangs of young men who go to football games with the intention of fighting. But other authors, like Armstrong and Harris, seem to be 'explaining' a rather different 'violence' than some of the authors they seek to criticize. Sticking the label of 'football hooliganism' on rather disparate activities can be mystifying, especially if some of them may have much in common with other prevalent forms of rowdyism, which have no particular attachment to soccer.

More problems arise because Armstrong and Harris's account of these young men is riddled with inconsistent statements, which means their 'analysis' has a chameleon-like ability to alter page by page to match a number of tones of voice. While part of their project is to assert the symbolic nature of much violence, they are, nonetheless, keen to assert that there is something 'really' violent going on. Terms are used like: 'a threat,' 'severe beatings,' 'running battles,' 'dominate the neighbourhood,' 'upsurge of hostility,' 'gashed,' 'a menace,' 'petrol bombs were carried,' 'badly kicked,' 'damaging attacks,' and so on. Yet we are also told:

> *The worst that can be said was that most of these fans were willing on occasions to get into relatively minor physical conflict with rivals. That was all. (Armstrong and Harris, 1991: 455).*

In truth, such are the variations in the language employed and the inconsistencies in the report that it becomes quite difficult for the reader to assess just what level of 'violence' is being outlined. For example, and characteristic of the tendency in the hooliganism literature to indulge in overblown language, we are told that the Blades and the Owls are 'violent rivals' and 'the most bitter of rivals.' They are 'ardent' in their support. Allegiance commits the lad, at least in formal situations, to unswerving loyalty to his chosen club and unswerving enmity towards other fans. However, we soon find that all these attributions are fluid and lack the value-added adjectival intensity, because, when fans do confront each other, a good deal of negotiation takes place to avoid actual physical conflict because:

- some of the Blades have to move around the city and want to do so in peace;
- in 'non-football contexts' fans may have good mates, even relatives, on the other side (and, remember, we are supposedly discussing the very core of Sheffield United hooligans here);
- some have aspirations in other segments of their lives which a tangle with the law might thwart.

What then is actually meant by terms like 'violent' or 'enmity' or 'unswerving' or 'bitter'? The authors' attempt to explain away what looks like a clear inconsistency between evocative language and actual behaviour, other than by allowing the fairly prosaic point that, in most cities anyway, there are usually cross-cutting ties which will severely limit the amount and level of violence, is unsatisfactory. As always, the reader of analyses of 'football violence' should remain a sceptic and ask: if there really is so much 'real' violence around football? if it is endemic? if it stems from deep social forces, then where are the dead, the scarred and the lame? Few graves get dug under all the fearsome terminology. The sober truth, very important for locating the true social significance of this phenomenon, is that football violence is not a particularly large segment of all recorded violence. Certainly we need to wonder why policy makers, funding bodies and, yes, academics and students, are so interested in it, because on figures alone it is difficult to claim that it really is exceptional or even an important indicator of the 'well-being' of modern society or developments in it.

Armstrong's analytical aims in his later book are quite limited. He wants to *seek an 'understanding' of the fans and their various behaviours* (Armstrong, 1998: xiii). He asserts that *football hooliganism cannot really be 'explained'. It can only be described and evaluated* (Armstrong, 1998: 21). His attempts to achieve these aims sprawls over more than 370 pages, mainly being a detailed account of the activities of the Blades from the 1980s to the mid-1990s. Each minor variation in behaviour, dress, argot, comportment, positioning, and so on, over the years is lovingly catalogued. There is a careful correction of the slightest inaccuracy in the media reports of any minor fracas over fifteen and more years (and we are supposed to take the accuracy of his or the Blades total recall of all these events on trust). But all the seemingly endless detail is deployed to very little analytic effect. After 300, repetitious, pages we are told that *What the Blades do, then, is a product of choice in the pursuit of the indefinable 'crack', 'laugh', 'buzz': basically, enjoyment based in uncertainty, as the individual confronts the drama* (Armstrong, 1998: 298). This startling discovery, that this small group of young men fight because they enjoy fighting, is by no means as novel a 'finding' as Armstrong seeks to claim. In fact much of the genre consists of a Chinese boxed set of tautologies. How do we know they are 'rough'? Because they fight. Why do they fight? Because they are 'rough.' How do we know 'aggressive masculinity' is crucial to hooliganism? Because they fight. Why do they fight? Because of 'aggressive masculinity'. And so on and so on.

What the book does provide is a slice of life, but a very thin slice. The Blades are a small grouping. They are not particularly violent, sometimes disconcerted when the police do not turn up as quickly as they 'should' to terminate an encounter. Their talk about violence is *habitually exaggerated*, their violence is *negligible* (Armstrong, 1998: 247, 300). Armstrong begins his text by declaring, *The big question is: why does so much conflict take place around the game of football?* But by the end his stress is on the ritual acting out of 'violent' scripts, *The hooligan issue, is as we have seen, not so much a problem of physical violence as one of male aggressive performances in a highly controlled decontrolling of emotions and expressions* (Armstrong, 1998: 7 and 295) and this, and the stress on the importance of (certain) norms of masculinity put him a lot closer to some other writers he thinks he is criticising than he seems to appreciate. Armstrong is determined that there are no structural causes which can explain involvement in 'hooligan' behaviour, but his late assertion that it is something to do with *the state of modern living* (Armstrong, 1998: 296) reveals a lameness that all the related fashionable talk of 'carnivalesque,' 'parody,' 'plaisir,' 'revelry,' 'post-modern tribes,' and the like cannot disguise.

One last matter concerns attempts to establish the class backgrounds of hooligans. As ever in the hooligan literature there is a wild tossing about of the appellation of 'the rough working class.' Armstrong and Harris treat 'roughness' as something to do with 'poverty and unemployment,' to do with 'rough housing estates' and to do with mining backgrounds. However, what is in fact a cultural label and one by no means easily tied to any of the above social locations, then becomes half attached to a rather strange occupational gradation. Oddly these authors praise Dunning et. al.'s approach to 'roughness' for being well-researched and documented which it is certainly not, but what is more crucial here is that any such attempts to locate hooligans in wider social structures have to move well beyond the outdated Registrar General's classification, especially when even more muddled with moralizing, and attend to the more meaningful social categories carefully constructed by systematic theorists of contemporary social stratification (Marshall *et al.*, 1988).

It is noticeable that when Dunning restates the Leicester position, arguing that football hooliganism has become a global phenomenon, his 'evidence' for the presumed class location of hooligans, consists only of three extremely small scale studies dating from 1968, 1985 and 1987 (Dunning, 2002: 18-19). Counter evidence is just ignored, as when English fans trashed a few cafes and rioted around the streets in Charleroi at the European Championships in 2000 the then Home Secretary was horrified to find out that, of those arrested, few if any were 'known hooligans,' i.e. had some record with the police as being involved in football violence, and was further discomforted when he found out that many of them had rather good jobs–there were engineers, lawyers and other professionals amongst them. Once again, the study of football hooliganism seems to have made very little advance, even in its own terms, over all the years.

DISCUSSION

In recent years the English authorities have been able to claim that hooliganism within England has been controlled. A recent Home Office assessment argues that hooliganism still poses a "*lingering menace*" in the domestic game, but is now at a low level with an average of under 2 arrests per game inside and outside stadia. The highest league attendance for 35 years (over 29 million) produced the lowest number of arrests at League matches since records began (Home Office, 2005: para. 3-7, page 37). The evaluation further argues that a shift of focus has occurred:

> *Since 1977, attention has largely focused on the behaviour of English football fans overseas and the growing catalogue of incidents involving English supporters... Most of these incidents took place in connection with matches played by the English national team. The disorder typically occurred outside of grounds and during the period leading up to match days. It resulted in many thousands of English arrests and deportations with each outburst bringing shame on our national reputation." (Home Office, 2005: paras. 1-2, 1-3).*

Events during the European Championships in Belgium and Holland in 2000, where 945 English detentions and expulsions occurred, seemed to demonstrate that existing powers were not sufficient to prevent English fans from being involved in serious incidents overseas. And the need for additional measures was further emphasised to the English authorities:

> *by the reluctance of some host authorities to prosecute offenders, notably those involved in the anti-social, threatening and low level violent behaviour that is characteristic of most football disorder – a phenomenon where the overall impact greatly exceeds the individual offences committed. (Home Office 2005: paras. 2-2, 2-3)*

Which, again, points to the rather differing focus on what football hooliganism actually is.

There were three strands in the extra powers the English applied to this new problem of hooliganism:

- use of banning orders and other restrictions to prevent known hooligan fans from travelling abroad;
- maximum liaison with host authorities designed to influence their expectations of and approach to, visiting English fans and encourage the adoption of interactive, low level policing strategies;
- maximum support for independent supporters groups, fan-led initiatives and encouragement of concept of self policing.

After two, now after the 2006 World Cup, three, relatively trouble free international tournaments in a row, the Home Office claims:

> *Football disorder remains a threat and major challenges lie ahead but the measures introduced in the wake of Euro 2000 are providing an effective means for preventing football disorder (Home Office, 2005: para 20.6)*

Now, here is a problem for the academic study of football hooliganism. If the control measures deployed by the authorities really have pacified the English game domestically and in its foreign travels, then the issue simply cannot have been as socially significant as English Sociology has built it up to be. The problem laid out in the abundant literature, with all the references to underlying structural forces, contemporary problems in the display of masculinity, psychological predispositions to this, that and the other, surely could not be bounded by the issuing of just over 3,000 banning orders, more sophisticated police liaison, and much more overt control in and around stadia? The success of these simple policy initiatives suggests that both the social and sociological significance of football hooliganism has been much overstated. One could easily deduce from the above statistics that, for all the social forces supposed to impel it, the desire to fight for excitement around football exists in very few young men in England, that the capacity for low level annoyance exists amongst a much larger number, but has no particular relation other than an opportunistic one with football, and melts into an anti-social behaviour to be found in the centre of almost every British city on a weekend night, and that the vast bulk of even young male fans are involved in no sort of violence whatsoever.

Faced with this success, policy makers are unlikely to take up, for example, Williams (2001: 50) suggestion that they should be *exploring some of the causal roots of the sort of masculinist identity construction which seems to be at the heart of the hooliganism project.*

Many academics in Britain and Europe are still obsessed with the so-called 'debate' around soccer and violence, but going round and round in ever diminishing explanatory circles does not constitute a 'debate.' Interestingly, those who have studied areas round football stadia, and who have bothered to ask people who live near grounds what they think, tend to find that people cite car parking, traffic, and, sometimes, even noise and the flow of pedestrians, as much greater social nuisances to them than any 'hooliganism.' It is important to remember that football 'hooliganism' is an unimportant part of all violent crime, let alone of total anti-social behaviour. By any estimation of its social significance, violence around football has been over-studied, as well as being poorly studied. The 'debate on hooliganism' has lost all power to generate any new social insights, and will have no hope of doing so until a new methodological rigour is injected, and until there are sustained attempts to conceptualise the highly popular terms that structure contemporary discourse– 'identity,' 'carnivalesque,' 'ironic subversion' and the like. The real function of the study of football hooliganism is that it has become one of the sources of the moral panic about violence and sport that surfaces now and then. It's a career-making option for some authors, but until proponents attend to major flaws in the whole line of scholarship, some of which I have outlined in this paper, it really will not be able to tell its audience much of any significance about sport and the modern world.

REFERENCES

Armstrong Gary and Harris R. (1991). Football Hooligans: Theory and Evidence. Sociological Review, 39, 3: 427-458.

Armstrong G. (1998). Football Hooligans: Knowing the Score. Oxford: Berg.

Clarke J. (1978). Football and Working Class Fans. In Ingham R. et al (eds.) Football Hooliganism: The Wider Context. London: Inter-Action.

Critcher Charles. (1979). Football Since the War. In J Clark, Charles Critcher and Richard Johnson (eds.), Working Class Culture: Studies in History and Culture. London: Hutchinson.

Dunning E. *et al.* (1981). The Social Roots of Football Hooligan Violence, Leisure Studies, vol.1, no. 2.

Dunning E. *et al.* (1988). The Roots of Football Hooliganism. London: Routledge.

Dunning E. *et al.* (eds.) (2002). Fighting Fans: Football Hooliganism as a World Phenomenon. Dublin: University College Dublin Press.

Dunning E. *et al.* (2002). Towards a Sociological Understanding of Football Hooliganism as a World Phenomenon. In Dunning E. *et al.* (eds.), Fighting Fans: Football Hooliganism as a World Phenomenon. Dublin: University College Dublin Press.

Elias, Norbert and Dunning Eric (1986). Quest for Excitement: Sport and Leisure in the Civilizing Process. Oxford: Basil Blackwell.

Home Office (2005). Football (Disorder) Act 2000: Report to Parliament. London: Home Office.

Hutchinson J. (1975). Some Aspects of Football Crowds before 1914. In The Working Class and Leisure. Proceedings of the Conference of the Society for the Study of Labour History, University of Sussex.

Moorhouse H.F. (1984). Professional Football and Working Class Culture: English Theories and Scottish Evidence. Sociological Review, 32, 2: 285-315.

Moorhouse H.F. (1989). 'We're Off to Wembley!' The History of a Scottish Event and the Sociology of Football Hooliganism. In D. McCrone D. et al (eds.), The Making of Scotland. Edinburgh: Edinburgh University Press.

Moorhouse H.F. (1991). Football Hooligans: Old Bottle, New Whines? Sociological Review, 39, 3: 489-502.

Perryman M. (2001). Hooligan Wars: Causes and Effects of Football Violence. Edinburgh: Mainstream.

Report of the Working Group on Football Crowd Behaviour (the McElhone Report) (1977). HMSO.

Robson G. (2000). 'No One Likes Us We Don't Care': The Myth and Reality of Millwall Fandom. Oxford: Berg.

Taylor I. (1971a). Football Mad: A Speculative Sociology of Football Hooliganism. In Dunning E. (ed.), The Sociology of Sport. Cass.

Taylor I. (1971b). Soccer Consciousness and Soccer Hooliganism. In Stanley Cohen (ed.), Images of Deviance. London: Penguin.

Taylor I. (1982). On the Sports Violence Question: Soccer Hooliganism Revisited. In J. Hargreaves (ed.). Sport, Culture and Ideology. London: Routledge and Kegan Paul.

Report of the Working Group on Football Crowd Behaviour (the McElhone Report) (1977) HMSO.

Williams J. (2001). Who are You Calling a Hooligan? In Perryman M. (ed.), Hooligan Wars: Causes and Effects of Football Violence. Edinburgh: Mainstream.

8

THE GLOBALISATION OF 'BAD' MANAGEMENT PRACTICE:

The three Points for a Win Reform in soccer

Daniel Bloyce & Patrick Murphy

The English Football League introduced the three points for a win reform in 1981. It replaced the two points for a win format that had prevailed for the previous eighty-three years. In 1993, FIFA announced that the winning 'bonus' point would be adopted for the first (the mini-league) phase of the World Cup finals that were to be held in the United States in 1994. Thereafter, it quickly spread to other international and domestic competitions. The English Football League's innovation was the response to a financial crisis. The member clubs were caught in a vicious circle of salary-inflation and declining gates. The League's executive was of the view that a possible solution to these problems lay in improving the entertainment on offer. The winning bonus point was conceived as a means of encouraging more attacking football, which would produce more goals per game. As its President, Jack Dunnett, made clear at the time of its introduction, if three points for a win proved to be unsuccessful they could revert to the old system the following season (*The Times*, 26 August 1981).

However, in the event, what was presented as an experiment was one in name only because the football authorities never monitored its impact or established any criteria by which its relative success or failure might be assessed. Seemingly, they had no notion of how many extra goals would have been required to indicate that the innovation had been a success. Had the authorities bothered to monitor their 'experiment' it is difficult to see how they could have been anything other than disappointed.[1] The failure of the English football authorities to monitor the reform does not seem to have troubled FIFA's General Secretary, Sepp Blatter, or, indeed, the other football authorities that subsequently embraced it.[2] Therefore, in this paper we set out to rectify this monitoring omission, not only in an attempt to assess the impact of this 'experiment,' but also with a view to offering a sociological interpretation of the processes involved. We will focus on the impact the reform made on World Cup tournaments and then offer a figurational interpretation of these processes (See Goudsblom, 1977).

The choice of the United States as the host nation for the 1994 World Cup finals was driven by the desire of FIFA's executive to overcome the last formidable bastion of resistance to making the game more or less global. It was an aspiration that was encouraged by the promise of the United States Soccer Federation to establish a professional league on the back of the World Cup.[3] The decision was not without its risks. As one writer put it 'FIFA has never before charged its most prestigious tournament to the care of a country where the game is regarded as a minority sport, fit only for schoolchildren and a rather chic game for college students' (Morrison, 1990: 430). Not surprisingly, given the sporting traditions of America, it was a World Cup that was surrounded by much talk about the possibility of radically transforming the laws of the game. Some of the more extreme advocates of change wanted to divide the playing time into four quarters. They also bemoaned the fact that the game was not sufficiently high scoring and, in this regard, they made invidious comparisons with the established American sports. Simon Barnes reported that in 'the United States inter-Regional League... they are running a series of FIFA-backed experiments' (*The Times*, 8 June 1994). Apparently these included bigger goals, players being withdrawn after committing five fouls and the option of taking a kick-in rather than a throw-in. David Miller, also writing in *The Times*, could scarcely conceal his relief when there was an agreement 'by American television not to interrupt the 45 minute continuity of normal soccer, (an agreement) which killed the widely-rumoured intention by FIFA to introduce the "four-quarter" match' (27 November 1993).

Nevertheless, while the more radical proposals failed to find acceptance, FIFA did bring in a batch of reforms on the eve of the 1994 Finals. In addition to three points for a win in the first round they 'outlawed the tackle from behind; insisted on a liberal interpretation of the off-side rule; forced "injured" players off the field to avoid time-wasting and instructed referees to follow these new guidelines or be banished from the tournament' (Nawrat and Hutchins, 1996: 276). Two significant changes not mentioned by these authors were the modification in the 'back-pass' rule and the introduction of a new type of ball. John Goodbody reported on this latter development in the following terms: 'With FIFA anxious that the game should reach a potentially huge new audience in the United States, it wanted to arrest the steady decline in the number of goals.' To this end, they commissioned Adidas to produce the Questra ball: 'it bounces higher, flies faster and swerves more than its predecessors' (*The Times*, 25 June 1994).

The thinking behind the three points reform was revealed at a press conference in December 1993. When Blatter was asked to justify it he said:

> *The essence of football should be going for goal. In the last World Cup, this was not the case; some teams were determined to get to the quarter-finals by drawing all three matches. I expressed long ago my view that three points for a win would reward attacking football and punish those who play negatively. I think now you will see one of the best first rounds for many years (*The Times*, 18 December 1993).*[4]

Thus, it seems that the introduction of three points for a win was one element in a package of reforms whose roots may be traced back to a negative response to the football that characterised the World Cup finals of 1990 and a wish to ensure that the game was made more appealing to a potentially sceptical American public. However, the grounds for Blatter's belief in its goal generating potential remain obscure. It was, in effect, just another shot in the dark, but this time it was a shot that had global ramifications. UEFA followed FIFA down the same un-lit road and adopted the reform for the 1996 European Nations Championships. Thereafter, other nations fell into line. For example, Italy and Scotland introduced it into their domestic competitions for the 1994-95 season, Argentina, Germany and Spain for the 1995-96 season and Brazil in 1996.

The football cultures of different countries and continents are characterised by considerable variations, although an appreciation of this diversity does not preclude the recognition of global similarities. Relative success and failure in professional football tends to be measured overwhelmingly in terms of results. Few managers/coaches at the higher levels of the game will retain their jobs for very long if they consistently fail to deliver on this front. This guiding principle by which managers/coaches are judged brings with it constraints that influence the playing strategies pursued in all countries. For a manager/coach a central, if not the central, question is: what are the best results that can be achieved with the resources at my disposal? Given the ubiquitous nature of these constraints, one might anticipate that the switch to the three points for a win format in international tournaments and other national domestic leagues would have been likely to have encountered similar obstacles to those experienced in England (Murphy, 2004). The success of the reform was dependent on persuading the majority of managers/coaches that it was in their interests to adopt more adventurous styles of play.

The six World Cup tournaments between 1930 and 1958 were relatively free-scoring affairs, averaging 4.24 goals per game. In terms of goals scored, the eleven world cups held from 1962 to 2002 have been more barren affairs, averaging 2.65. Over this latter period, the variation of goals per game ranges from a high of 2.97 in 1970 to a low of 2.21 in 1990; a range of .76 and a variation that falls some way short of one goal per game. Guillerno Canedo, the chairman of the organising committee for the 1994 finals, described the 1990 finals as a 'dire, dirty, destructive combat' (*The Times*, 27 April 1994). They returned the lowest number of goals per game in the history of the World Cup–2.21. To assess the impact of the three points reform we focus on the group but not the knockout stages of the finals. Table 1[5] presents the goal scoring patterns at the group stages in the seventeen world cup finals held between 1930 and 2002.

Table 1 shows that the three points reform did coincide with a slight upturn in the number of goals scored per game at the group stage/s. When compared with the goals record for the first phases of the 1990 finals there was an increase of 0.3 goals per game at the equivalent stage in 1994; an additional goal every three games. However, the rate for the 1994 finals is still lower than that which prevailed in the group stage/s in the 1962, 1978 and 1982 finals. In fact the goal-scoring rate at the group stage/s has been remarkably stable since the 1962 finals. From 1962 to 2002 the average number of goals per game has been uniformly lower than three per game and over this period it has only varied between 2.28 and 2.71. In other words, the variation over a period of forty years has been less than one goal every second game.

Taken over the full tournament, the average number of goals per game in 1994 was 0.5 of a goal higher than that of 1990. Yet if one of the chief aims of the package of reforms had been to appeal to an American sporting public ostensibly weaned on high scoring sports, like basketball, it is difficult to see how an increase of this magnitude could

Table 1*
The World Cup Finals 1930–2002: Group Matches

Year	*Games Played*	*Goals Scored*	*Average/game*
1930	15	50	3.33
1934	-	-	-
1938	-	-	-
1950	21	80	3.81
1954	16	78	4.88
1958	24	79	3.29
1962	24	65	2.71
1966	24	57	2.35
1970	24	61	2.54
1974	36	93	2.58
1978	36	95	2.64
1982	48	129	2.69
1986	36	84	2.33
1990	36	82	2.28
1994	36	93	2.58
1998	48	126	2.63
2002	48	130	2.71

* A small number of group matches were actually played according to knockout principles and, therefore, they have not been included in this table. Only goals scored in open play have been counted, including penalties scored in the match proper. Goals scored in penalty shoot-outs have been omitted.

have been expected to register with them. While they may have made comparisons with basketball, the majority of them had no historical reference point for soccer. Nevertheless, many outside commentators greeted FIFA's strategy for the 1994 finals as triumph. For example, Nawrat and Hutchings (1996: 276) wrote:

> *The beautiful game was born again. The midwives were FIFA, who used their legislative powers to privilege adventurous play...FIFA must get much of the credit for this resurrection... Self-professed experts had dismissed FIFA initiative as something concocted by meddling bureaucrats. How wrong they were...This was not FIFA taking a sledgehammer to crack a nut – this was taking a scalpel to excise a cancer.*

The appropriateness of depicting FIFA as a surgeon deftly wielding a scalpel is open to question. As far as the three points reform was concerned, they conducted no research into the English experience and had they done so, it is difficult to see how it could have supported the introduction of a winning bonus point. Moreover, notwithstanding the fact that FIFA had four years between World Cups to pilot and assess various options aimed at facilitating more attacking football, they chose to wait until the eve of the 1994 finals to introduce a package of reforms. Introducing them en masse was bound to make it more difficult to assess their specific contributions. Blatter's instrument of choice was not so much the scalpel as the blunderbuss. The political skills recognised, even by his critics, do not seem to have extended to his understanding of the intricacies of policy (Tomlinson, 2000).

It does seem clear that unlike the winning bonus point, the new back-pass rule, the clampdown on the tackle from behind and the new ball, were all likely to have a direct and significant impact upon the game. Fortunately for our purposes, the structure of the World Cup tournament, with its two distinct forms of competition – group competition within leagues and knockout matches – enables us to probe the respective impact of the three points reform and these other changes on goal scoring rates. Table 2 presents these data.

Table 2
A Comparison of Average Goals Per Game at the Group and Knockout Stages of the World Cup Finals–1930-2002

Year	*Games Played Group stage*	*Average goals/ game Groups stage*	*Games played at knockout stage*	*Average goals/ game knockout stage*
1930	15	3.33	3	6.67
1934	-	-	17	4.12
1938	-	-	18	4.67
1950	21	3.81	1	8.0
1954	16	4.88	10	6.2
1958	24	3.29	11	3.64
1962	24	2.71	8	3.0
1966	24	2.35	8	3.88
1970	24	2.54	8	4.25
1974	36	2.58	2	2.0
1978	36	2.64	2	3.5
1982	48	2.69	4	4.25
1986	36	2.33	16	3.0
1990	36	2.28	16	2.06
1994	36	2.58	16	3.0
1998	48	2.63	16	2.81
2002	48	2.71	16	1.94

As already noted, judging by the number of goals scored per game, the finals after 1958 have become distinctively cagier affairs. Table 2 demonstrates that this trend finds expression at both the group and knockout stages. The group stages of the finals from 1962 to 2002 registered an average of 2.55 goals per game with a range of between 2.71 and 2.2. The respective figures for the knockout stages are an average of 3.06 and a range between 4.25 and 2.0. In terms of trends, while the average goals per game for the group stages have been fairly stable over this period, the average for knockout games exhibits a more marked variation. Taking 1990 – the tournament that triggered the reforms – as our base year, the average number of goals per game for the group stage of the finals 1990-2002 is 2.55. This is exactly matched by the average for the group games for the period 1962-2002. In contrast, the equivalent figure for knockout games for the finals 1990 to 2002 is 2.39. The average for knockout games for the period 1962 to 2002 is 3.06. A comparison of the group and knockout stages of the 1994 finals offers a clearer picture of the specific, immediate impact of the winning bonus point. The average number of goals scored per game at the group stage of the 1994 finals was actually 0.42 less than at the knockout stages in which the three points system did not apply.

Before drawing hasty conclusions from the above data, it is as well to appreciate the complexity of the broader human figuration. The early stages of any competition are bound to include teams with a wider range of ability and one might anticipate that the stronger teams are likely to find it easier to score goals at this phase of the competition. On this basis, FIFA's political decision to expand the number of teams entering the finals from 24 to 32 in 1998 is likely to have increased the number of weaker teams in the competition. Consistent with the above argument, it might also be reasonable to assume that goal-scoring becomes more difficult at the knockout stages of the finals because they are contested by the stronger, more evenly matched teams. Yet while the above reasoning may seem plausible it is not consistently supported by the scoring patterns of these two distinct phases of the tournament. While the scoring rate for the group stage of the 1998 and 2002 finals was higher than that of the 1994 tournament, the increase was only marginal and perhaps not as high as might have been anticipated on the basis of the above reasoning. However, while over the history of the tournament goals per game have generally been higher at the knockout stages, they are now becoming more difficult to come by. At the 2002 finals they reached a new low point with a rate of only 1.94 goals per game, the lowest scoring phase in the entire history of the World Cup. Indeed, an analysis of the goal-scoring patterns at the finals from 1930 onwards indicates that those who are concerned with the decline in goal-scoring rates should perhaps be less worried about trends at the group stage and more worried about what could prove to be an emerging downward trend at the knockout stages. As indicated above, while the average number of goals scored at the group stages has exhibited a certain stability since 1962, and in three of these eleven finals this figure has been lower than the level registered at the knockout stages, the dip in goals per game at the knockout stage in 2002 is unprecedented. In this regard, it will be interesting to monitor developments in Germany 2006.

One possible explanation for the relative stability of the average number of goals per game scored at the group stage is that at this phase of the competition, defensive strategies are already well established. Echoing Blatter's earlier cited comment, many managers have long been prepared to play for strategic draws if this served their purpose. This has become more possible because over the last decade or so the general standard of world football has risen appreciably. The market for coaches has become global and knowledge of sophisticated coaching techniques has accompanied them. The weaker teams have become better organised. There is a pervasive attachment to the importance of 'keeping clean sheets', a euphemism for a commitment to defensive football. The modern football cliché that there are no easy matches contains a growing element of truth. These developments may go some way towards explaining why the entry of more teams into the finals since 1998 has not been accompanied by any marked increase in the number of goals scored in the opening phase. At the knockout stages, where, at least until the introduction of the penalty shoot-out, there was nothing to be gained by playing for a draw, one might anticipate more uninhibited attacking football and higher scoring games. However, this possibility seems to have been countered by the growing conservatism of managers and coaches, a conservatism which seems to be rooted in the game's perceived increasing cultural, political and economic significance (Bragg 2006: 113-16). The winning bonus of $500,000 offered to each player if Italy won the 1994 World Cup is but one indication of the growing seriousness with which national governing bodies view World Cup tournaments (*The Times*, 16 June 1994). Yet the promise of such rewards can be a double-edged sword. While they may be envisaged as an incentive, in practice they can induce a fear of failure. Since only one team can win the tournament, perhaps the paramount and growing pressure on managers/coaches is to ensure that their teams do not suffer 'humiliating' defeats. The simple palliative of an extra bonus point was, and is, unlikely to dampen such concerns. It is difficult to avoid the conclusion that while FIFA have introduced a number of reforms aimed at encouraging attacking football, they still find themselves swimming against a conservative tide. It is a tide that seems to draw its strength from the growing world prominence of football and the greater risks to national prestige following defeat. The paradox is that the FIFA Executive have been at the forefront of driving this process.

CONCLUSION

In our view this process can best be understood in terms of the complex and dynamic figurations formed by human beings (Mennell and Goudsblom, 1998: 38-9; van Krieken, 1998: 55-59; Quilley and Loyal, 2004: 1-22; Bloyce, 2004). The individuals and groups involved were subject to different sets of constraints. Managers and coaches–themselves not an undifferentiated group–sought to achieve relative success for their teams and, thereby, satisfy their employers and club supporters and retain their jobs. Given the limited resources available to most of them, relative success was more or less synonymous with developing fit, well-organised teams with a high level of commitment. The numerical dominance of such clubs/teams goes a long way towards explaining the prevalence of defensive strategies. Football administrators in England in the early 1980s had different priorities. In this period the owners of the member clubs of the Football League felt themselves to be in the grip of spiralling wage costs and declining gate revenues (*The Times*, 25 August 1981). The League's administrators did not really know what to do to alleviate these problems, but felt under pressure to do something. It may be left to its then President, Jack Dunnett, to capture the collective state of mind of the Football League's executive when the reform was introduced. He conceded: 'we are in the position of a beleaguered garrison; the situation is very serious; gates have fallen 11% over the past season. All the management know something is wrong–we are not idiots. But don't ask me the solution. I don't know it.' (*The Times*, 6 June 1981). In this malaise they made the simplistic assumption that more goals would mean more entertaining football and the hope was that this would reverse the decline in attendances. The three points reform was seen as the means by which this process could be triggered, but, as we have seen, its implementation went unmonitored. As the seasons passed it simply became part of the unquestioned working environment of the football fraternity. This so-called experiment was given renewed prominence when Blatter announced that it would be one element in a package of measures introduced on the eve of the 1994 World Cup finals that were aimed at raising the game's entertainment level. The concerns that Blatter and the FIFA executive were addressing diverged from those that led the English football authorities to introduce the three points reform. They were striving to make the game more entertaining, but they also wanted to establish football as a 'truly global sport' by selling it to a sceptical 'American public.' FIFA's endorsement of the reform was sufficient to legitimise its global diffusion.

Some of the groups and individuals involved in these human figurations[6] were and are relatively powerful (Mennell, 1989). Some of them have the capacity to define what is and is not a problem and to initiate actions or strategies aimed at correcting or ameliorating the situation. However, their capacity to achieve their ends is limited by an array of inter-related and interdependent internal and external constraints (Soeters and van Iterson, 2002: 37). The internal constraints relate to their inadequate appreciation of their own limitations. This can stem from a lack of knowledge of social processes, and not uncommonly these limitations combine with considerable over-estimations of their own ability to exercise control over future developments. In addition, their capacities to develop effective policies tend to be hampered by flights of fancy. That is to say, their commitment to particular visions of the future lead them to engage in highly partial analyses of the conditions causing them consternation and hence to policies imbued with strong elements of wishful thinking. As such, the visions of the future they pursue are often unrealistic. In other words, they adhere to an unrealistic appreciation of 'what is possible.' The external constraints relate to the sheer complexity of the relational networks of which they are a part. To adequately comprehend even the immediate figurations in which they were embroiled, they needed to recognise that it was not sufficient to focus solely upon the values, priorities and intentions of the parties involved. There was a need to conceptualise the 'composite unit,' that is to say, the relevant human figuration as a whole (Elias, 1978: 71). Only in this way would it have been possible to anticipate some of the unforeseen outcomes that were bound to emerge from the combined actions of the individuals and groups involved. Appreciating outcomes as a combination of planned and unplanned human actions fosters a more realistic understanding of the limits of the possible, and what can and cannot be achieved by concerted human action. Even if policy-makers do, on occasions, realise their ends, their achievement is almost invariably accompanied by a series of unforeseen outcomes. Policy-makers may perceive some of these as fortuitous, but they are likely to view others as less welcome. The consequences of yet others may remain hidden for varying lengths of time. We should not be misled by the tendency of policy-makers to claim retrospectively that the 'positive effects' were part of their original plans or, indeed, by the countervailing tendency for them to deny the connection between their actions and what are perceived to be the unanticipated 'negative side effects.' One source of unplanned outcomes is when an executive committee pursue distinct policies that are themselves at variance with one another. For example, while, as we have seen, FIFA have initiated policies aimed at making the game more attractive by placing the emphasis on attacking play, many of their other policies have been geared to the desire to increase the global prominence of soccer. These two dimensions of policy are captured in a key phrase of FIFA's President, Sepp Blatters' mission statement: 'Make the Game better, and take it to the World' (cited in FIFA, 2005). Clearly from his perspective, part of 'making the game better' is making it more entertaining. However, 'taking it to the world' requires resources, and the generation of these have involved expanding its links with a variety of commercial organisations and political bodies. Developing such ties inevitably increases the political and cultural prominence of the game and helps to raise the amount of national prestige at stake in international competition. The increasing fear of failure seems to be a key element discouraging managers/coaches from adopting more adventurous styles of play. Thus, one policy initiative has helped to undermine another. As such, the three points saga can be seen as an example of just one of the ways in which human figurations can produce unanticipated, unplanned outcomes (Elias, 1978; Mennell, 1989; Murphy and Sheard, 2006).

In our view, the thrust of the above analysis is at variance with much of management theory because of the latter's tendency to exaggerate the power of management to influence outcomes, a tendency that reaches its apotheosis in the 'power of positive thought' literature (see for example, Srivastva and Cooperrider, 1999). In our view this tendency to exaggerate the control that managers can exercise has more to do with ideological imperatives than it does with expanding managers' level of understanding.

Throughout, we have been cognisant of the need to distance ourselves from what Elias termed heteronomous evaluations[7] (Elias, 1987; Mennell,1989). In respect of this, we are bound to point out that the term 'bad management practice' in the title of this paper is not an externally imposed judgement. Rather it springs from the experimental criterion espoused by the President of the English Football League. He viewed it as 'an experiment' which, if it failed to live up to expectations, would be repealed. Since this so-called experiment was not monitored it is clearly a case of management not abiding by its own declared standards. FIFA then propagated this 'bad practice' on a global scale. Our aim has not been to assign responsibility. Rather, we have tried to understand these processes more adequately. Given the locations of the participating parties, given their intense level of involvement in their own narrow agendas and, given the internalised and external constraints they were under and the consequent pressure to do something, the chances of FIFA raising their heads and making a more detached assessment of the relational networks of which they were a part, and which they hoped to change, were most unlikely (Williams et. al., 1984). The problem facing anyone trying to determine the impact of this reform is that it was but one element in a complex human figuration. The dynamic figuration that gave rise to the decline in the number of goals per game is itself bound to have been multifaceted. The chances of a single specific reform reversing a deeply entrenched process are fairly problematic.[8] The chances become more tenuous if the reform in question is aimed at affecting the situation indirectly. In the case of the three points reform, the chances of it being successful were dependent on it influencing the mind-set of a crucially placed occupational group– the managers/coaches. Moreover, determining its impact is complicated still further if its introduction coincides with other developments, including other reforms.

Even though this package of reforms does not seem to have generated the desired significant increase in goals per game, it should not necessarily be interpreted as an abject policy failure. It is difficult to see how the reform of the back-pass rule, a clampdown on the tackle from behind and the introduction of balls which travel faster and swerve unpredictably could do anything other than benefit sides that are more committed to attacking football. That these innovations have not found expression in a significant up-turn in goals scored might suggest that were it not for these reforms defences would have become even more dominant and scoring rates would have declined still further. It seems that the dominant trajectory of world football is in a cautious, conservative direction.

NOTES

1. The eyes of the League executive were on more entertaining football measured in terms of the number of goals scored. Managers/coaches were bound to focus on the number of points gained relative to their competitors. To adopt a more attacking approach, in the first instance with a view to turning more draws into victories, would have involved scoring more goals, but inevitably this would have made teams vulnerable to conceding more goals. Therefore, the calculation that managers/coaches would have had to make is: 'Are we likely to score more goals than we concede by adopting a more attacking style? ' For every additional goal they conceded as a result of modifying their approach they would have needed to score two. While we are not suggesting that this pattern would have had to be replicated in every game, the scale of these targets suggest that the odds were very much stacked against the League achieving their desired outcome by means of their three points reform. In practice there seem to have been three broad possible reactions on the part of managers/coaches to the introduction of a winning bonus point: (i) none of the managers were prepared to risk adopting a more attacking style, (ii) all managers/coaches responded positively to the incentive and opted for a more attacking approach and, (iii) only the more adventurous managers/coaches moved down this path. The remainder preferred a wait and see strategy. In the case of option one, little would change. Without the emergence of other changes, the goal-scoring rates would have continued to vary more or less within the prevailing parameters. In the case of option two, inevitably, given the competitive nature of a league, there would be some winners and some losers. Those who had faired better under the previous system would be likely to revert back to their earlier more defensive formations. This, in turn, would have implications for those who initially benefited from the adoption of more attacking strategies and these then might lead them to reconsider their position and so on. Option three would simply involve a variation of option two leading to a movement in one direction or the other, and possibly back again. In the event, in the crucial first season of the reform the number of goals per game fell from the 2.66 of the previous season to 2.54 in the English First Division. The respective figures for the ten years before and after the reform are 2.55 and 2.66, a marginal increase of 0.11 goals per game. This amounted to an extra goal every nine games. This suggests that the majority of elite managers in England made individual decisions to forego the in centive of a winning bonus point and stick to their previous, more defensive-minded game

plans. Had individual managers chosen to make their own assessment of the consequences of the reform, they would have been confirmed in their initial judgement, although, of course, this would have involved an element of self-fulfilling prophesy.

2. An analysis of the reform's influence on elite level football in England has been presented elsewhere (Murphy 2004).

3. In the event, Major League Soccer was established in 1996, one year later than originally planned.

4. There were eight draws in the first round of the 1990 tournament. Three were 0-0 games and in five the result was 1-1. Five of these draws were concentrated in one group (F) and only two teams–Holland and the Republic of Ireland– drew all three of their first round matches. Only Ireland progressed to Round Two. Incidentally, while no teams at the 1986 finals drew all three of their first round matches, there were eleven draws at this stage. These included three 0-0s, seven 1-1s and one 2-2 result.

5. We could have calculated and included the level of statistical significance of these data. However, this would have been a genuflection for pedantic statistical reasons only. As Atkins and Jarrett have pointed out while 'the choice of a significance level is supposed to be rational and objective, in much social research there are no purely technical criteria on which this choice could be based. This problem forces the choice straight back on to "subjective" criteria' (1981:98). In the context of this paper the FIFA executive did not make public their thoughts on what sort of variation in the number of goals per game would constitute relative success and relative failure. Indeed, the likelihood is that they did not reflect in any depth on the matter. In any case, they would not have been able to isolate the respective influence of their various reforms. As far as the reactions of the competing managers are concerned, it is not possible to know what they would have regarded as a 'significant incentive' in terms of goals scored or points acquired to modify their playing strategies.

6. By introducing the concept human figurations Elias wanted to make the study of the dynamic interdependencies formed by human beings central to sociology. In doing so he was trying to overcome what he saw as a number of prevailing and still prevailing tendencies. Firstly, he was critical of the tendency to reify social structure. To see social structure as something over and above the human beings who comprise it. Secondly, he was equally concerned to challenge the often connected tendency to conceive of in dividuals as if they live apart from society (homo clausus) rather than seeing people in the plural (homines aperti) and, thirdly, he was striving to ensure that the focus is unerringly upon process (for a more extended discussion of these issues see Mennell 1989: 188-93).

7. Elias was committed to contributing to the development of the sociology of knowledge. As such he was critical of what he saw as the unproductive objective/subjective dichotomy that pervaded and still pervades discussion of the part played by values in the understanding of the non-human and human sciences. He saw human behaviour as involving a complex blend of greater and lesser involvement, greater and lesser detachment. Moreover, he argued that in the course of human history the balance between these aspects has tended to shift more in favour of the latter. This movement has found its strongest expression in the non-human sciences. In other words, the professional orientation of scientists working in these fields are characterised by relatively high levels of autonomy. This compares with the more heteronomous, more involved, evaluations that are prevalent in the work of social scientists and, of course, people in general as they go about their daily lives (for elaboration see Elias 1987).
8. There are, nevertheless, important differences between a game and social life in general. For example, see Elias on games models (Elias 1978:71-103). It is possible to envisage silver bullet solutions to perceived problems in games. For example, the decline in the number of goals scored per game could and can be rectified by simply increasing the size of the goal. This would, however, prove to be a highly contentious move and might also have the consequence of widening the performance differentials at the highest levels in football and placing an even greater premium on prolific strikers.

REFERENCES

Atkins, L. and Jarrett, D. (1981). The Significance of "Significance Tests". In J. Irvine, I., Miles, and J. Evans (eds.), Demystifying Social Statistics (pp. 87-109). London: Pluto Press.

Bloyce, D. (2004). The Globalization of Baseball? A Figurational Analysis. Unpublished PhD thesis, University of Leicester.

Bragg, M. (2006). Twelve Books That Changed the World. London: Hodder & Stoughton.

Elias, N. (1978). What is Sociology? New York: Columbia University Press.

Elias, N. (1987). Involvement and Detachment. Oxford: Basil Blackwell.

FIFA. (2005). **need title.** Retrieved 20 April 2006, from http://www.fifa.com/en/fairplay/index/0,1255,106408,00.html?articleid=106408.

Goudsblom, J. (1977). Sociology in the Balance. Oxford: Basil Blackwell.

Mennell, S. (1989). Norbert Elias: Civilization and the Human Self-Image. Oxford: Basil Blackwell.

Mennell, S. and Goudsblom, J. (1998). Norbert Elias On Civilization, Power, and Knowledge. London: The University of Chicago Press.

Morrison, I. (1990). The World Cup: A Complete Record 1930-1990. Northampton: Brendon Books Sport.

Murphy, P. (2004). Incentive to attack? Revisiting the three points for a win reform. In P. Murphy and I. Waddington, (eds.), Soccer Review 2004 (pp. 46-53). Leicester.

Murphy, P. and Sheard, K. (Forthcoming 2006). Boxing Blind: Unplanned Processes in the Development of Boxing. *Sport* in Society.

Nawrat, C. and Hutchings, S. (1996). The Sunday Times Illustrated History of Football: The Post-War Years. London: Chancellor Press.

Quilley, S. and Loyal, S. (2004). Towards a "Central Theory:" the scope and relevance of the sociology of Norbert Elias. In S. Loyal and S. Quilley (eds.), The Sociology of Norbert Elias (pp. 1-22). Cambridge: Cambridge University Press.

Soeters and van Iterson. (2002). Blame and praise gossip in organisations: Established, outsiders and the civilising process. In A. Van Iterson, et. al. (eds), The Civilized Organisation: Norbert Elias and the Future of Organisational Studies (pp. 25-40). John Benjamins Publishing Company: Amsterdam.

Srivastva, S. and D. L. Cooperrider. (1999). Appreciative Management and Leadership: The Power of Positive Thought and Action in Organizations. Euclid, Ohio: Williams Custom Publishing.

van Krieken, R. (1998). Norbert Elias. London: Routledge.

Tomlinson, A. (2000). FIFA and the men who made it'. In J. Garland, D. Malcolm, and M. Rowe (eds.), The Future of Football: Challenges for the Twenty-First Century (pp. 55-71). London: Frank Cass.

Williams, J., Dunning, E. and Murphy, P. (1984). Hooligans Abroad. London: Routledge and Kegan Paul.

9

'IN BALANCE WITH THIS LIFE, THIS DEATH': *Mourning George Best*

Alan Bairner

INTRODUCTION

In the opening line of an article published in 2006, sports historian Tony Mason (2006: 3) writes, 'it is well nigh impossible to say anything new about George Best.' It is a curious sort of admission for any academic to make, not least one who is about to discuss the very subject about which little more can be said. This article seeks to argue that there are various aspects of George Best's life that continue to demand closer analysis, which were specifically highlighted in public reactions to his death and which have wider sociological significance.

George Best was born in Belfast on 22 May 1946 and was buried in the same city on 3 December 2005. Between these two dates, in a life punctuated by numerous highs and lows, Best became for a time arguably the greatest soccer player in the world and also an alcoholic whose long struggle with his illness came to an end with his death on 25 November 2005. This essay argues that both the varied responses to Best's death and also the choreography of his funeral accurately reflected the contradictions in his life–a stereotypically introspective Ulster Protestant obliged to live in the glare of publicity on account of his talents as a footballer. The discussion is conducted within the context of the growing literature on how post industrial societies mourn their celebrity dead and specifically of studies concerned with soccer, tragedy and commemoration. The analysis also draws upon previous work that deals with the ways in which the influence of Best's upbringing as an Ulster Protestant may have impacted on later aspects of his life (and death) (Bairner, 2004). Finally, it is intended that the article should highlight the importance of discussing celebrities as individuals rather than solely as representatives of a generic category.

CELEBRITIES, SOCCER AND COLLECTIVE MOURNING

In approaching this subject, I had initially expected to be devoting a fair amount of space to comparing and contrasting reactions to Best's death with responses to the relatively recent deaths of other celebrities, most notably that of Diana, Princess of Wales in 1997. Diana's death attracted considerable academic attention, leading to a marked expansion of the analysis of death and public mourning (Kear and Steinberg, 1999; Turnock, 2000; Haynes and Shearer, 1998; Campbell, 1988; Thomas, 2002). It quickly became apparent, however, that few if any of the main discourses linked by social scientists to the death of Diana–Britishness, gender, New Labour, the role of the monarchy and so on–were relevant to readings of George Best's life and death. Indeed, I soon came to the realisation that not only might comparison be invidious, it might also be unhelpful. This is not to ignore the extent to which public mourning was a characteristic of the deaths of both Princess Diana and Best. In the case of the latter, however, arguably more meaningful comparisons were to be found in the very sport which he had graced as a player.

According to Russell (2006: 3), 'football's culture of commemoration has altered both quantitatively and qualitatively from about 1985.' By this he does not wish to suggest that the game previously ignored the deaths of its heroes. He argues, however, that 'while football paid due respect to its dead, there was generally nothing distinctive about its public mourning in terms of frequency and style' (Russell, 2006: 3). An interesting comparison in this respect can be drawn between reactions to the Ibrox Stadium disaster' of 1971 and the Hillsborough disaster of 1989.[2] As Walker (2004: 180) notes, 'the Ibrox disaster has been much more the subject of popular inquiry and personal remembrance since the late 1980s than before' and 'whilst partly this reflects the popularity of new technology and the extent to which the internet has allowed more supporters to participate in discussion and reminiscence, yet the main factor seems to have been the general trend towards more explicit displays of commemoration in Scotland and in Britain as a whole, which was clearly visible in the fans' reaction to the Hillsborough disaster.' As Russell (2006: 6-7) reminds us, 'central here was the building by fans of shrines composed of flowers, club scarves and shirts, personal mementos, including teddy bears and photos, all often adorned with messages that connected the dead to elements of their club's history'.

Many would be tempted to refer to Princess Diana moments (Preston, 2005) when analysing changes in collective public mourning in Britain, but the Hillsborough disaster occurred eight years before the Princess's death. More generally, however, as Russell (2006: 10) observes, 'a panoply of social and cultural changes including the growth of the hospice movement, the increased role for bereavement counselling, the emergence of many public discourses over AIDS, the vogue for roadside shrines, the increased appetite from the 1990s for the minute's silence and much else are testament to both the withering of lingering taboos about open discussion of death and a new appetite for displays of public grieving.' Within this context, 'football's increasingly varied response to the passing of its heroes is part of a much wider shift in the nation's emotional ecology' (Russell, 2006: 10).

The extensive media coverage of George Best's last days was certainly part of this new approach to death and dying. What distinguished his death from those of Princess Diana and those who had died as a result of football stadium disasters was the fact that it had been anticipated for so long–arguably since his late twenties and certainly since 2000 when liver failure first put him in hospital. Even had his death been sudden, however, the choreography of public mourning was already so well established that the people would largely have known what was expected of them. Before examining the actual public response to his death, however, it is worth reminding ourselves of the more relevant facets of George Best's life.

WHO WAS GEORGE BEST?

It was only relatively recently, in the years leading up to his death, that George Best the man beneath the celebrity became a matter for serious academic attention (Cashmore, 2002; Whannel, 2002; Rojek, 2001; Bairner, 2004). One important concept to emerge in this respect was that of dislocation. Describing the travails of certain sports stars, Whannel (2002) makes reference to Chas Critcher's (1979) use of the concept of 'dislocation' to describe soccer stars for whom remaining working-class was not an option but who nevertheless sought to resist incorporation into a middle-class way of life. According to Whannel (2002: 51), 'George Best is the archetypal dislocated football hero whose talent, personality and background were insufficient to withstand the pressure, both on and off the field.' Rojek (2001: 81) adds that 'the media and fan expectations of producing a world-class performance every week resulted in gambling and drink problems'. Best's dislocation, however, was not rooted solely in an inability to negotiate rapid social mobility whilst simultaneously trying to satisfy an adoring public; he was also dislocated both spatially, and it will be argued, culturally–from his place of birth and early upbringing and from his Ulster Presbyterian parental culture.

Like many other players in the years after the abolition of the minimum wage, Best was faced with unaccustomed wealth. But he was also a young labour migrant who left behind family and friends in the quest for sporting success. In the opinion of his first wife, 'George was too young at the age of fifteen to go off to Manchester United; I think he should have been made to finish school' (Best, 2001: 57). Indeed, his first visit to Manchester lasted only one night before homesickness set in (Best, 2002). Had he decided not to go back, both English football and Manchester United would undoubtedly have suffered. One can only speculate on the consequences for Best himself.

The Calvinism of Ulster-Scottish Presbyterianism is a difficult influence to shake off. At its most sinister it is the world of R. L. Stevenson's 'Strange Case of Dr Jekyll and Mr Hyde', that Manichean creation of which George Best was a worthy representation. As his first wife recalls, 'when he was drunk, George could go either way–nastiness and meanness, or flirtation–but when he was sober he was quiet and withdrawn' (Best, 2001: 58). He was capable of jealous rage; his second wife admits that their relationship was punctuated by instances of domestic violence (Best, 2005). Whannel (2002: 113) refers to Best's 'objectification of women' and there can be no doubt that his approach to gender relations was often reprehensible. Indeed, according to Whannel (2002: 127), Best's faults and failings were such that his life 'has been transformed into a moral homily – a warning, like a nineteenth-century moral tract, concerning the dangers of giving way to emotion, desire, hedonism and alcohol.' This is an element in the mediation of Best that will emerge prominently when varying assessments of his life and career are later discussed. It should also be noted at this point, however, that Best's chosen way of life did not lead to universal condemnation even though it was clearly at odds with some of basic precepts of his parental culture.

Growing up in an ascetic and God-fearing Protestant family has tempted many a young man (and woman) to use alcohol to overcome personal diffidence with highly unpredictable consequences. In this respect, Best had much more in common with rock star Van Morrison, also from east Belfast, who includes Best in a list of exiled Irish geniuses in his song, *Too Long in Exile*, and with former world snooker champion Higgins, described by his biographer as 'a product of his time and upbringing in Protestant Belfast' (Borrows, 2002: 17), than with some of the English-born football players he has been categorized with (Whannel, 2002).[3]

Ulster Protestants are, as Steve Bruce (1992: 7) notes, 'predominantly descendants of the Scots (and some English) who settled in the north-east of Ireland in the sixteenth and seventeenth centuries.' According to Bruce, 'that the settlers were of a different 'race', were of a different religion and were in economic competition with the native Irish meant that relations between the two groups were generally distant and periodically degenerated into open warfare.' This situation would be exacerbated in the twentieth century with Ulster's Protestant population clinging tenaciously to the Northern Ireland state that was set up after partition in 1921 and to a position of economic superiority, both of which were increasingly to come under threat from Irish nationalism and de-industrialisation respectively. As poet and critic Tom Paulin, himself an Ulster Protestant, comments, 'it was bizarre to grow up in a statelet that had no future. The root of it all is Calvinism. The sense of being persecuted and a member of an elect minority, feeding its persecution complex' (McKay, 2000: 296). One of the more damaging results of this condition has been a lack of ease with ideas and an increasing inability to present an articulate defence of core beliefs, thereby explaining Tom Nairn's somewhat hysterical description of the Ulster Protestants as 'this particular band of tonguetied sons of bastards' ghosts' (Nairn, 1981: 233). With specific reference to George Best, Eamonn McCann (2005) adds, 'there's a sometime awkwardness about Prods, particularly Prods from a proletarian background, as they make their way, if they can, in the upper reaches of the wider world, sometimes expressed in drunkenness, grumpiness or uncool outbursts of atavism, perhaps resenting the way their identity isn't esteemed, perhaps resenting their identity'.

Perhaps it was this that led Geoffrey Bell (1976: 11) to comment, 'by all normal standards the behaviour of the Protestants of Northern Ireland is peculiar.' In modern times this may well have been exacerbated as a consequence of political and economic change (Bairner,

2005). Thus, according to Steve Bruce (1994: 39), 'the first and most obvious feature of the recent history of Ulster unionists is displacement.' This in turn has led to 'a decline from security to precariousness' (p. 40) and to 'a sense of inadequacy' (p. 62). A relatively privileged group has increasingly found the basis of its privileges threatened by forces beyond its control and is obliged to cope with an increasingly alien social universe. Van Morrison's biographer writes, 'Here was a man whose social skills short-circuited some time back, forced to function in a world that operated along entirely unfamiliar lines' (Heylin, 2002: 496). It is not overly fanciful to suggest that this description of Morrison could be equally well applied to the Ulster unionist family as a whole, and particularly to its male members, not least because a 'crisis of masculinity' can be often be attributed to loss of control and status (Bairner, 1999; Bairner, 2001; Segal, 1990).

According to Angie Best (2001: 7), 'George has an amazing brain, but he was never given the opportunity to use it.' This comment is uncannily similar to one made to Susan McKay by Shankill Road born artist Dermot Seymour.

> *Being a Protestant, for me, is like having no head, in the sense that you are not allowed to think. It is hard to hold an individual thought about anything... Out of that inability to think comes a lot of bizarre extreme behaviour, like the Shankill Butchers. (McKay, 2000: 302).*

It would be invidious to compare George Best with the psychopathic killers who terrorised Belfast in the 1970s. But his behaviour was, at times, undeniably bizarre and extreme. However, Best was by no means alone in this respect amongst the Ulster Protestant community's celebrities. For example, Keith Altham, an NME reporter who first met Van Morrison in 1965, comments, 'the most disturbing thing about Van is that he's disturbed and it's something to deal with someone like that' (quoted in Heylin, 2002: p. x-xi). Morrison found himself in the unfamiliar world of rock music to which few Ulster Protestants belonged.

George Best must have experienced a similar feeling of exposure to the unfamiliar when he left Northern Ireland as a boy to join Manchester United. Not only was he leaving home and the working-class Protestant culture that had shaped him, he was about to pursue a highly successful career which would bring him considerable fortune with a club that has consistently been identified with Irish Catholic culture (Bairner, 2004). Without wishing to engage in pop psychology, perhaps in the end the strains of the triple dislocation of class, geography and culture simply became unbearable.

None of this is meant to deny Best's considerable achievements on the field of play. Nor should one ignore his undoubted popularity. Nonetheless, what began as a life of glitz and glitter was transformed over time into the dark world of the alcoholic–missed engagements, domestic violence, embarrassing television appearances and so on. In July 2002, Best underwent a liver transplant operation. By mid July 2003, it was widely reported that he was drinking alcohol again. In December of that year, he was arrested in connection with an alleged assault and the following February, he was fined £1500, banned from driving for 20 months and ordered to pay £55 costs having pleaded guilty to a drink-driving charge. In April 2004, Best and his estranged second wife were granted a divorce on the grounds of his adultery with an unnamed woman. On 1 October 2005, Best was admitted to hospital with flu-like symptoms, later suffering a kidney infection. His condition worsened dramatically on 18 November and he died the following Friday. Daily reports on his condition had appeared in the British press and on television.

Before discussing responses to George Best's death, it is worth spending a little more time on the concept of dislocation. The inference to be drawn from most of the literature is that this phenomenon is necessarily harmful. It creates insurmountable problems for the individuals affected by it. At the personal level in Best's case, this is irrefutable. At the very least, the triple dislocation which he experienced may have facilitated his emotional and physical decline. Nevertheless, it may also be useful to think of dislocation as a form of challenge, the handling of which can help to produce diverse experiences denied to others from a similar background. This in turn may lead to a wide range of assessments of the person involved. This is certainly true of Best, as press and public reactions to his death, as well as the organisation of his funeral, serve to demonstrate.

JUDGING GEORGE BEST

For all intents and purposes, George Best's obituaries appeared in the newspapers before he actually died–not the formal obituaries, of course, which were not published until 26 November, but certainly the type of reviews of his life and times which would normally appear only after a celebrity's death. It was as if the country's editors were terrified that he would die shortly after they had gone to press, leaving Internet sources to broadcast the news, or that he would die on Saturday, 27 November, thereby allowing the Sunday papers to steal their glory. As I travelled by train to Manchester that Friday morning I was reading the death notices for a man who was still alive and would not die until around 1 pm that day.

Perhaps not surprisingly, the analysis prior to and immediately following his death largely consisted of regrets over the depths to which he had fallen combined with celebrations of his playing career. According to novelist Gordon Burn (2005: 8), writing in *The Guardian*, 'Best was as careless with the things his talent brought him as he was with his body.' Eamon Dunphy (2005: viii), Irish journalist and former Manchester United Player wrote in *The Independent* of 'a generosity, courtesy and sensitivity completely at odds with his public image.' As for his ability as a player, The Guardian's football writer David Lacey (2005: 1) commented that 'George Best was the outstanding British footballer of his generation and that, many would argue, is a gross understatement for he had plausible claims to be considered the greatest of any generation.' 'It is safe to say', he went on, 'that no footballer, before or since, has achieved the initial or lasting impact that Best had on the English game.' There were frequent reminders that Pele had once described Best as the greatest footballer in the world.

On Saturday, 26 November the formal obituaries appeared. In *The Guardian*, Ivan Ponting (2005: 44) began with a reflection on the word 'genius.'

> *'Genius' is a term so chronically overused in conjunction with sport that it is in danger of being comprehensively devalued. It should be rationed scrupulously, reserved for the truly sublime, rather than being squandered on the merely remarkable.*

According to Ponting, however, 'there should be no hesitation in dusting down the "g" word for a fitting recipient, and such a man was George Best.' In similar vein, veteran football writer, Brian Glanville (2005: 37), claimed that Best was 'arguably the finest player produced in Britain since the war.' Perhaps of even greater relevance to this particular study is Hunter Davies's (2005: 5) claim that 'George Best was probably the first player to become and remain a legend throughout his lifetime.'

It did not take too long, however, for more critical assessments to appear. This came as no real surprise given that throughout much of his life, as Rojek (2001: 81) notes, he had long been 'condemned by the media for squandering his gifts.' With his death, came the charge that certain sections of the media were now hell bent on the canonization of Best.

According to Berlins (2005: 7), 'Best's latest manifestation as a violent, woman-beating drunk had been paraded before us for years, forcing us to make the comparison between the god that he once was and the pathetic figure that he had turned into.' In fact, most media coverage of the Best story tended towards the former. Was it perhaps that the media—dominated still by middle-aged men—had led the way? As Preston (2005; 28) remarked, there was 'nothing strictly logical about the magic that transformed a washed-up footballer into a surrogate Princess of Wales. But there was something calculated, almost cynical, to the process.' The media had been caught out by the public's response to Diana's death; it would not be caught out again. As Walkerdine (1999: 101) argues, in relation to the public reaction to Princess Diana's death, 'the idea that ordinary people could understand something that others had missed through all the hyperbole thrown at them by the media, and could recognise what they wanted to do about it in a practice of profound social and political comment and, indeed, protest, is beyond the comprehension of many of the broadsheet and intellectual commentators.' By pre-empting Best's death in the first instance, the newspaper editors had already given a clear indication that on this occasion they would endeavour to lead the people.

Above all, it was a time for nostalgia.

> *Middle-aged football commentators relive their youth when they talk of him [Best]. The nostalgia of the beautiful game comes drenched in tinted memories. His death is cause for pause and reflection (Preston 2005: 28).*

Thus, Peter Blake, designer of the Beatles' famous Sgt. Pepper album cover, claimed that Best 'lived the Sixties as people think they were lived' (Braid, 2005). With even greater pathos, former Manchester City player and friend Mike Summerbee (2005: 76) wrote, 'I just remember what he meant to me when the world was so young and everything was before us.'

But the critics did not remain silent. On the day of Best's funeral, Deborah Orr (2005: 14) argued that 'it wasn't his glorious genius that tortured George. It was his mulish refusal to care like an adult for himself and others.' Writing in the *Sunday Mirror* the following day, Carole Malone (2005: 31) reminded readers, 'three weeks ago I said we shouldn't waste our sympathy on a man who'd quite literally drank himself to death, a man who'd been given a second chance with a new liver but who'd thrown that chance down the toilet by drinking up to 10 bottles of wine a day.' Now she opined that 'this national outpouring of grief for a wife-beating alcoholic who was 100 percent responsible for his own death is frankly ridiculous.' 'Like most alcoholics', she went on, 'he was selfish, self-absorbed and didn't care enough about the people he loved to give up alcohol for them.'

The evidence suggests that whilst male writers were inclined to wallow in nostalgia, women were quicker to identify his character flaws. Yet, recalling encounters with Best in 1968, even the renowned feminist Germaine Greer (2005: 36) was willing to make allowances.

> *One of the reasons for not entering into a flirtation with George was that, like other men I have known, George thought women were to be lied to, but if you were male, he was four-square.*

In response to claims that as a media sport star, Best had been a poor role model, Nicky Campbell commented, 'when I was a kid I wanted to play football like Best. I was never minded to treat my women, my liver or my career like he did.' Best did not lead a blameless life, but a life that combined the good with the bad, a fact that was clearly highlighted by the diverse range of responses to his passing.

BURYING GEORGE BEST

Public mourning for George Best began the moment his death was announced. Fans quickly began to lay floral tributes and football memorabilia on the pavement across the street from the main entrance to Manchester United's Old Trafford ground. By Sunday, 27 November when I visited the scene, the resultant collection stretched out for around 300 yards and included mementoes from supporters of Manchester United and Northern Ireland, Manchester City, Celtic and clubs for which he had played towards the end of his career, notably Fulham and Hibernian. Foreign visitors wandered around reading tributes to Best and taking souvenir photographs.

The most striking events, though, took place on Saturday, 26 November when football matches throughout the United Kingdom went ahead as planned. All of them were to be prefaced by a minute's silence in memory of Best. At many venues, however, including Turf Moor (where I was about to watch Burnley play a home game against Crewe Alexandra) the referee's whistle prompted not silence but enthusiastic, albeit respectful, applause. This represented a remarkable shift in the public's response to death. It is true that people had applauded as the hearse carrying Princess Diana's body travelled to its final resting place. But here was a staged minute's silence at football grounds being interrupted, not by boorish chants which is often the case, but by the sound of people clapping their hands. It became immediately clear that none of us would really miss George Best. Indeed his death had been predicted so often that in many ways he was already a figure from our past. He had not died young enough to be forever young–in the manner of James Dean, Marilyn Monroe or even Princess Diana. Towards the end he had looked older than his years, a shadow of the young man who had once been revered as much for his looks as for his sporting ability. We were not surprised by George Best's death and thus could not be stunned into silence. What we wanted to do was celebrate the man, or to be more precise, the footballer he had been. This was yet one more demonstration of the extent to which 'people are increasingly taking matters into their own hands to create their own rituals of mourning and participating in informal or idiosyncratic funerary services (Turnock, 2000: 69). Commenting on comparisons made between the response to Best's death and a longstanding Italian tradition, Tim Parks (2005: 2) noted that 'as football grounds become almost the only places where large crowds gather, it becomes more and more tempting for powers-that-be to use them for some pious propaganda or other.' Rightly fans resist by applauding instead of remaining silent although, as Parks (2005: 2) adds, 'let's remember to keep a deep silence when there is real tragedy.' In fact, few of us who were at Turf Moor that day would have had any direct experience of the Italian approach to these matters. Although someone must have taken the lead, ours was a largely spontaneous gesture, evidence perhaps of the crowd's time-honoured refusal to be governed by rationality (Le Bon, 1896; Walkerdine, 1999). But now it was time for the serious business of laying George Best to rest.

Even more than in either the media reaction and initial public response to his death, his funeral ensured a balance between his complex life and his death. Almost immediately after his death, moves were afoot to allow Best's funeral service on 3 December to take place at the Great Hall inside the Northern Ireland Parliament Buildings at Stormont, built initially to house the Northern Ireland parliament in the wake of partition. Only 32,000 people were to be allowed into the grounds of the

Stormont estate because of health and safety concerns, with 300 invited guests attending the actual service. Best's body was flown to RAF Aldergrove on 2 December. Two pipers played a lament as they escorted the coffin, draped in a Manchester United flag. The coffin was then taken to the Best family home in the Cregagh estate in keeping with Irish tradition. The following day, with neighbours congregating outside the Best home, again in keeping with tradition, the coffin was lifted into a waiting hearse and then transported to Stormont (by way of the Cregagh Road, the Knock dual carriageway and the Upper Newtownards Road. After the service, the funeral procession made its way via the Upper Newtownards Road, the Knock dual carriageway and the Ballygowan Road to Roselawn Cemetery for a private burial). Despite heavy rain, thousands lined the roads. Many clapped; some threw bouquets of flowers, football shirts and scarves on to the passing hearse. It had been predicted that this would be the biggest funeral in Northern Ireland's history although in the event the numbers lining the route fell far below those that had gathered for the funeral of IRA hunger striker Bobby Sands in 1981 (Appleyard, 2005).[4] Whilst the latter event was notable for the social and ideological homogeneity of the mourners, the service held for Best was characterised by incongruity.[5]

The service was introduced (compered, one might say) by Belfast-born television personality and Manchester United fan Eamonn Holmes. He referred in his opening remarks to Ulster and to 'our country' of 1.5 million people–this despite the fact that for most people who share Holmes's Catholic background the equation of Ulster and Northern Ireland is normally associated with unionism and the status of Northern Ireland as a country is widely contested. The first hymn was 'The Lord's My Shepherd,' a common feature of Protestant funerals both in Northern Ireland and in Scotland. The Best family, including George's 87 year old father Dickie, sang lustily. Some of the celebrity guests, such as former world champion boxer Barry McGuigan seemed more uncertain.

The coffin itself was draped in an Irish Football Association Northern Ireland flag and had been carried into the Great Hall by former Northern Ireland players Billy Bingham, Gerry Armstrong, Peter McParland, Derek Dougan and Harry Gregg and by Best's former team mate and long time friend, Denis Law. Both Armstrong and McParland are Catholics, Gregg the product of a mixed marriage.

Songs were sung by London West End musical star Peter Corry, a Protestant from Bangor, Co Down, and by Brian Kennedy, a Catholic from west Belfast who would go on to represent the Republic of Ireland in the 2006 Eurovision Song Contest. Kennedy's contributions included a reworked version in Best's honour of Don McLean's 'Vincent,' evoking memories of Elton John's 'Candle in the Wind' tribute to Princess Diana.

There had already been misplaced attempts at humour from Holmes and Law. They were followed in this by Best's old friend Bobby McAlinden with whom he had played football in the United States. At this point, the mood became less funereal and more akin to a sportsmen's dinner with speeches. McAlinden even affectionately referred to Best at one stage as 'a wee shite.' Throughout all of this the assembled members of Best's immediate family looked on impassively, in some cases betraying signs of disapproval.

Proceedings then took another twist as Pastor Roy Gordon, the family's Free Presbyterian minister, called on the guests to turn to the word of God in the form of Psalm 103. He noted that Best had been described by others as a good friend but pointed out that Jesus is the best friend of all. George Best, he observed, had been blessed with a great gift which had brought pleasure to people throughout the world. But God's greatest gift, he informed the gathering, is eternal life through his son, the Lord Jesus Christ. The pastor also referred to people 'here in Ireland,' ironically offering a mirror to Holmes the Catholic's reference to Ulster as 'our country.'

Best's son, Calum, read two poems, wiping away tears and reminding us that this was indeed a funeral for a young man's father. One of Best's sisters, Barbara McNarry, spoke. She also cried and talked of her brother's ability to bring people together even in Northern Ireland. Best's surgeon, Professor Roger Williams, reminisced fondly about his former patient. As the service came to an end, the coffin was carried to the waiting hearse as Brian Kennedy sung 'You Raise Me Up.' Best was later buried alongside his mother, Ann.

CONCLUSION

Comparing Best's funeral with that of other famous people, Brian Appleyard (2005) perfectly captured the apparent contradictions that characterised the former.

Diana's was the most emotional funeral I have ever attended, the Pope's the most awe-inspiring. But Best's was the most strange, suffused as it was with the modern cult of stardom and the ancient tribal cults of Ulster.

In the words of Michael Walker (2005: 5), 'Belfast is not a city noted for forgiveness but where George Best was concerned, among the public, it was a bottomless well.' This is, of course, a gross generalisation. One did not have to go far in the city in the hours immediately after Best's death to hear epithets like 'liver thief' be invoked. Meanwhile the 'Anyone But United' lobby, consisting of football fans who reserve their deepest dislike for Manchester United, was less forgiving than the countless Manchester United fans who live in Northern Ireland (Scally, 1998). Many nationalists with little sympathy for the Northern Ireland national team, and indeed for the idea of Northern Ireland as a political entity, also expressed their reservations. In republican west Belfast where Best's picture hangs prominently above the gantry of the Red Devil Bar (Bairner, 2004), some Manchester United fans expressed a preference for Roy Keane, born in the Irish Republic, over the east Belfast Protestant Best, and anger that the entire funeral was being confined to the east of the city (Appleyard, 2005). Undeniably, the east Belfast location of the funeral procession and the subsequent renaming of the City Airport, itself located in east Belfast in a parliamentary constituency held by Peter Robinson MP of Ian Paisley's Democratic Unionist Party, appeared to underline Best's Protestant and Unionist roots.

The actual venue for the funeral service is of course no longer home to what Northern Ireland's first Prime Minister, Lord Craigavon (James Craig), had described as 'a Protestant parliament and a Protestant state' (Quoted in Farrell, 1976: 92). With the formation of a Northern Ireland Assembly and Executive in the wake of the signing of the Good Friday Agreement, the elected representatives of the nationalist community established themselves at Stormont. Similarly, the mourners and indeed some of the key participants at Best's funeral represented more than one tradition and came from very different walks of life.

According to Sean O'Hagan (2005: 2), 'it mattered not that he was Protestant, or from a loyalist neighbourhood, only that he was Northern Irish.' This, he goes on, is 'a freedom accorded only the very few, though, in truth, he bestowed it on himself by virtue of his singularity.' In fact, it did matter to many that he was a Protestant and that his funeral procession and service took place in the most predominantly Protestant quadrant of Belfast. It also mattered to many that he had played for Manchester United and not for Liverpool, Arsenal, Manchester City or Leeds United.

But for large numbers of people, neither his religion nor his playing connections mattered. Arguably as a direct result of his dislocation, Best had acquired the gift to be different things to very different people, spawning admiration and affection despite the demons which had damaged him and which were almost certainly also a by product of his dislocated existence. The varied assessments of George Best the man and the seemingly incongruous features of his funeral service actually ensured that his death was perfectly in balance with his life–however unbalanced both of these had been.

Best's funeral and the reactions to his death were markedly different from those of other celebrities. Though celebrity is something that people can have in common, the precise relationship each person has with his or her celebrity status is ultimately determined by unique socio-economic and cultural forces. In death, as in life, George Best was different. That said, there is no doubt that the ways in which we create and subsequently treat our heroes offers great insights into society as a whole. Nowhere is this more apparent than at the time of celebrity deaths. Our willingness to mourn the loss of complete strangers suggests not only a growing incapacity to distinguish the important from the trivial but also the apparent need for a kind of secular spirituality. For many of the reasons outlined above, the canonization of George Best is nevertheless unlikely.

NOTES

1. The first part of this title consists of a line from the poem 'An Irish Airman Foresees his Death' written by William Butler Yeats. Yeats wrote,

   I balanced all, brought all to mind,
   The years to come seemed waste of breath,
   A waste of breath the years behind
   In balance with this life, this death.
   (Collected Poems of William Butler Yeats, Richard J. Finneran, Ed. New York: Simon and Schuster, 1996).

2. On 2 January 1971, 66 football fans were crushed to death and 145 injured as they tried to leave Ibrox Stadium in Glasgow after a game between traditional rivals, Rangers and Celtic. On 15 April 1989, 96 Liverpool fans died attending the FA Cup semi-final between Liverpool and Nottingham Forest at the Hillsborough Stadium in Sheffield.

3. For a more detailed comparison of the three men, see Bairner, A (2006). Simply the (George) Best: Ulster Protestantism, masculinity and the Belfast boy(s), Canadian Journal of Irish Studies. (Forthcoming).

4. At most around 60,000 people either lined the route of the funeral procession or entered the Stormont grounds. An estimated 100,000 attended Sands' funeral.
5. What follows is a distillation of the author's observations on the funeral service which was broadcast live on BBC television.

REFERENCES

Appleyard, B. (2005). Belfast gives George its best. The Sunday Times, 4 December. (*http://www.timesonline.co.uk/article/0,,2087-1903611,00.html*). Accessed 8 December 2005.

Bairner, A. (1999). Soccer, masculinity, and violence in Northern Ireland. Between Hooliganism and Terrorism. Men and Masculinities, 1 (January): 284-301.

Bairner, A. (2001). Masculinidad, musculatura y cristianismo en las representaciones corporales del unionismo en el Ulster. In C. Sánchez-Palencia and J. C. Hidalgo (Eds.), Masculino plural: construcciones de la masculinidad, (pp. 99-115). Lleida: Universitat de Lleida.

Bairner, A. (2004). Where did it all go right? George Best, Manchester United and Northern Ireland. In D. L. Andrews (Ed.) Manchester United, A Thematic Study, (pp. 133-146). London: Routledge.

Bairner, A. (2005). The age of unreason. Daily Ireland, 16 September: 17.

Bairner, A. (2006). Simply the (George) Best: Ulster Protestantism, masculinity and the Belfast boy(s). Canadian Journal of Irish Studies, forthcoming.

Bell, G. (1976). The Protestants of Ulster. London: Pluto Press.

Berlins, M. (2005). Few people in their twenties felt George Best was important to them. So why did the media give his death such attention? Guardian G2, 30 November: 7.

Best, A. (2001). George Best and Me. My Autobiography. London: Virgin Books.

Best, G. (2002). Blessed. The Autobiography. London: Ebury Press.

Best, A. (2005). Always Alex. My Story. London: John Blake.

Borrows, B. (2002). The Hurricane. The Turbulent Life and Times of Alex Higgins. London: Atlantic Books.

Braid, M. (2005). George Best by Peter Blake. The Independent on Sunday, 27 November: 48-49.

Bruce, S. (1994). The Edge of the Union. Oxford: Oxford University Press.

Burn, G. (2005). The long goodbye. The Guardian G2, 25 November: 8-13.

Campbell, B. (1998). Diana Princess of Wales. How sexual politics shook the monarchy. London: The Women's Press.

Cashmore, E. (2002). Beckham. Cambridge: Polity Press.

Critcher, C. (1979). Football since the war. In J. Clarke, C. Critcher and R. Johnson (Eds.), Working Class Culture, (pp. 161-184). London: Heinemann.

Davies. H. (2005). Rise and fall of George, simply too good to be forgotten. The Guardian Sport, 26 November: 5.

Dunphy, E. (2005). A generosity, courtesy and sensitivity completely at odds with his public image. The Independent Extra: viii.

Farrell, M. (1976). Northern Ireland: the Orange State. London: Pluto Press.

Glanville, B. (2005). George Best. The Guardian, 26 November: 37.

Haynes, J. and Shearer, A. (1998). When a Princess Dies. Reflections from Jungian Analysts. London: Harvest Books.

Heylin, C. (2002). Can you feel the silence? Van Morrison. A New Biography. London: Viking.

Le Bon, G. (1896). The Crowd: A Study of the Popular Mind. London: Fisher and Unwin.

Lacey, D. (2005). El Beatle, the artist who was greater than the team. The Guardian Sport, 25 November: 1.

Malone, C. (2005) Bestie is no hero of mine. Sunday Mirror, 4 December: 31.

Mason, T. (2006). George Best: The first of the modern celebrity footballers? Soccer History, 14 (Spring): 3-5.

McCann, Eamonn. (2005) An uncertain genius who became a pop star footballer. The Irish Times, 26 November. (*http://www.ireland.com/sports/soccer/ 2005/1125/mccann.htm*). Accessed 29 June 2006.

McKay, S. (2000) Northern Protestants. An Unsettled People. Belfast: Blackstaff Press.

Nairn, T. The Break-up of Britain. Crisis and Neo-nationalism, Second, expanded edition. London: Verso, 1981.

O'Hagan, S. (2005). Pitch perfect. Observer Review, 27 November: 1-2.

Orr, D. (2005). The enduring myth of the fatally flawed genius should be laid to rest. The Independent, 3 December: 14.

Parks, T. (2005). How to say goodbye in Italian. Guardian G2, 29 November: 2.

Ponting, I. (2005). George Best. Mercurial football genius whose flamboyant lifestyle brought a premature end to his playing career. The Independent, 26 November: 44-45.

Preston, P. (2005). This circus of grief has nothing to do with Best. The Guardian, 29 November: 28.

Rojek, C. (2001). Celebrity. London: Reaktion Books.

Russell, D. (2006). 'We all agree, name the stand after Shankly': Cultures of commemoration in late twentieth-century English football culture. Sport in History 26 (April): 1-25.

Scally, J. (1998). Simply Red and Green: Manchester United and Ireland–A Story of a Love Affair. Edinburgh: Mainstream.

Segal, L. (1990). Slow Motion. Changing masculinities, changing men. London: Virago.

Summerbee, M. (2005). We walked down the street and the girls flocked to him, the traffic stopped. The Independent, 26 November: 76.

Thomas, J. (2002). Beneath the mourning veil. Mass-observation and the death of Diana. Mass-Observation Archive Occasional papers, No. 12. Falmer, Sussex: University of Sussex Library.

Turnock, R. (2000). Interpreting Diana. Television Audiences and the Death of a Princess. London: British Film Institute.

Walker, G. The Ibrox Stadium Disaster of 1971. Soccer and Society[5] (Summer): 169-182.

Walker, M. (2005), Yesterday in Belfast, the most poignant sadness. The Guardian Sport, 26 November: 4-5.

Walkerdine, Valerie. (1999) The crowd in the age of Diana. Ordinary investigations and the popular imagination. In A. Kear and D. L. Steinberg (Eds.) Mourning Diana. Nation, Culture and the Performance of Grief, (pp. 98-107). London: Routledge.

Whannel, G. (2002). Media sport stars. Masculinities and Moralities. London: Routledge.

THE USE OF PERFORMANCE-ENHANCING DRUGS IN EUROPEAN FOOTBALL

10

Dominic Malcolm & Ivan Waddington

INTRODUCTION

Over the last two decades a growing amount of evidence has become available about the extent of illicit drug use in sport. Although much of this evidence has been anecdotal, some has come from relatively reliable sources –testimony to parliamentary or judicial inquiries, for example. We cannot be sure of the precise level of drug use in modern sport, but most writers on the subject agree that the phenomenon has increased markedly since the Second World War, and in the last three decades in particular. Mottram has recently cited drug use as 'perhaps the biggest challenge facing sport today' (2005).

There are almost no systematic data about the extent of drug use in football.[1] We do know that the use of performance-enhancing drugs in football has a long history. In 2004 a BBC radio programme (BBC, 2004) presented wide-ranging evidence of the history of the use of performance-enhancing drugs in English football. The programme reported the Arsenal team's use of 'pep pills' prior to an FA Cup match against West Ham United in the 1924-25 season (Joy, 1952), questions raised in the House of Commons in 1939 about Wolverhampton Wanderers' use of extracts from monkey testicles (Hansard, 27th April 1939), Stanley Matthews's (2000) description of his use of amphetamines prior to an FA Cup fourth round tie in 1946, and testimony from Manchester United players Albert Scanlon and Harry Gregg of their use of amphetamines during the 1950s. There was, indeed, considerable concern over the use of drugs in football at this time. In response to a Council of Europe investigation in 1963, football was identified by the

British government as one of three sports (with cycling and athletics) with the most severe drug use problems.

Despite such historical evidence, there seems to be a relatively widely held perception that contemporary football is relatively free from drug use. For instance, the Chief Medical Officer of the Fédération Internationale de Football Association (FIFA), Jiri Dvorak, has stated that 'we do not have a problem with systematic doping at FIFA competitions ... [and] we have no reason to think that organised doping exists in the leagues' (2004: 17). FIFA president Sepp Blatter has similarly suggested that whilst football 'is not immune to the evils of drug use', drug use within the sport is confined to 'a few renegades' (2004: 3). And Gordon Taylor, Chief Executive of the Professional Footballers Association (PFA) in England, said he is "almost certain that we have a clean sheet over performance-enhancing drugs" (*The Times*, 19/10/05). Official denials are not unique to football. Since the development of anti-doping regulations in the 1960s, sport administrators have sought to protect their vested interests and depict their own athletes as clean or, at least, cleaner than those in other sports. As Yesalis et. al. note, sports federation officials, when faced with allegations of drug use in their sports, 'have often tended to deny that a major doping problem exists ... or have at least played down its magnitude' (2001: 45).

The object of this paper is to examine systematically the data relating to the use of performance-enhancing drugs in football. This is no easy task; drug use in sport is now a covert activity, and as Mottram notes, '[m]eaningful data on the prevalence of use of performance-enhancing drugs in sport are difficult to obtain' (2005: 357). Yesalis *et al.* (2001) describe four major sources of information about the prevalence of drug use among athletes: investigative journalism, including the writings and testimonials of athletes and others involved in sport; government investigations; surveys; and results from drug testing. All four sources suffer from significant methodological problems. Yesalis *et al.* suggest, for example, that those who have used drugs and who serve as informants 'may project their own behaviour onto others in an attempt to rationalize their drug use–as they may say, "Everybody does it",' and that, consequently, can lead to an overestimation of the level of drug use (2001: 45). However, they argue–almost certainly correctly— that most of the methodological difficulties are more likely to lead to an underestimation of the level of drug use. In particular, they argue that 'the responses of athletes to the questions of journalists, drug use surveys, or even government investigations may be influenced by the athlete's desire to respond to questions in a socially desirable manner, memory lapse, the illegal nature of the substances being surveyed, and a general distrust of those doing the questioning'. They also note that drug testing 'is hamstrung by significant limitations in technology', and conclude that 'all these limitations would likely result in a significant under-reporting bias' (2001: 56). While each of the sources of information on drug use in sport raises particular methodological difficulties, we are not dependent on a single source, but have several different sources of information, giving us a triangulation of sources which helps to increase the validity of our conclusions. As Goode (1997: 14) has noted in relation to the problems of estimating the extent of drug use more generally in American society:

> *As a general rule, the greater the number of* independent *sources of information that reach the same conclusion, the more confidence we can have in that conclusion. That is what we mean by triangulation: getting a factual fix on reality by using several separate and disparate sources of information. To the extent that several independent data sources say the same thing, we can say that their conclusions are more likely to be true.*

To a greater or lesser extent, data on drug use in football can be gleaned from each of the four major sources identified by Yesalis et. al. In examining these data sources, however, we made two important assumptions which should be noted here. First, we focussed primarily on the use of performance-enhancing rather than recreational drugs because across sport the former is generally perceived to be more serious than the latter. Second, analysts largely agree that drug use which is systematic and organized at an institutional level (whether by a sports team or a governing body of sport, or even by government itself), is more problematic than that which is individual and often, therefore, *ad-hoc*. Thus, in our selection of data, we have primarily been concerned with evidence of performance-enhancing rather than recreational drug use, and with the systematic administration of these substances in particular.

We will examine each of these four data sources in turn, cross referencing the findings to provide triangulation. We conclude with some reflections on the prevalence of the use of illicit drugs in football relative to other sports. It is our contention that there are both empirical and theoretical grounds for believing, first, that a significant minority of European elite footballers are using performance-enhancing drugs and second, that some clubs have been involved in the systematic organization and delivery of doping programmes. We also argue that the use of performance-enhancing drugs is not as widespread in football as in many other sports, and that drug use is likely to be more common in some European countries than in others.

DATA ON PERFORMANCE-ENHANCING DRUG USE IN FOOTBALL

Evidence from Testing

Football was the first sport to conduct drug testing at a major event (Houlihan, 2003: 225), introducing tests for the 1966 World Cup and thus pre-empting the first testing at an Olympic Games by two years. FIFA has also been at the forefront of moves in international sport towards the use of blood tests, introducing them in 2002 to supplement urine tests at the Japan-Korea World Cup (FIFA, 2004: 79). These procedures have generated few positive results. Two players were ejected from major football tournaments for taking drugs during the 1970s: Ernest Jean Joseph of Haiti in 1974, and Willie Johnston of Scotland in 1978 (Cashmore, 1996: 143). Between 1994 and 2004, just three of the 2,400 tests carried out at 27 FIFA competitions were positive (Blatter, 2004: 3). Most famously Diego Maradona, captain of Argentina at the 1994 FIFA World Cup, tested positive for ephedrine. Amir Azmy of Egypt and Alexander Walke of Germany tested positive at the FIFA World Youth Championships in the United Arab Emirates in 2003 for nandrolone and cannabis respectively (*FIFA Magazine*, February 2004). All 216 tests on footballers at the Athens Olympics were negative (*FIFA Magazine*, November 2004, 68), though in 2005 two Mexican players were sent home from the FIFA Confederations Cup in Germany, initially on the pretext of 'disciplinary problems.' It subsequently emerged that they had failed pre-tournament drugs tests (FIFA.com, 24/6/05).[1] FIFA claimed (*FIFA Magazine*, June 2005, 68) that of 22,500 drug tests worldwide in 2004, just 92 were positive, and the majority of these positive tests derived from the use of recreational drugs such as marijuana (39 cases) and cocaine (29 cases).[2] Figures released by the World Anti-Doping Agency (WADA) indicate that of 23,478 football-related tests performed by WADA accredited laboratories in 2005, 343 produced adverse findings (WADA, 2005). Drug testing in international football, therefore, has revealed remarkably little evidence of the use of drugs in general, and the use of performance-enhancing drugs in particular. This, no doubt, is part of the reason that drug use in the game is not generally perceived to be a problem.

Drug testing programmes in domestic football leagues have similarly produced relatively few positive results for performance-enhancing drugs. Data from UK Sport, the body which administers drug tests in British football, indicate that, over the period from 1988 to 2001-2002, there were 89 positive drug tests (these data include the results of testing on behalf of the Welsh and Scottish Football Associations, as well as the English FA). The most commonly detected drugs in football were Class 1A stimulants such as pseudoephedrine and metabolites of cocaine, with 40 positive test results, and marijuana, with 29 (UK Sport, 2002). It is probably the case that the metabolites of cocaine were used recreationally, and not for performance enhancement. Since 2002 the number of positive tests per year have gradually fallen–from 14 in 2003-04 to 11 in 2004-05 and just 6 in 2005-06 (again, cocaine and marijuana cases were the most common, see www.uksport.org.uk). Included within these figures are a number of high profile footballers who have tested positive for recreational drug use, most notably Mark Bosnich and Adrian Mutu of Chelsea in 2002 and 2004 respectively, and this has reinforced the impression that a culture of recreational rather than performance-enhancing, drug use exists in English football.

However, between 1998 and 2002, footballers did produce six positive tests for anabolic agents. All of these players initially escaped or were given suspended punishments, after successfully arguing, for instance, that the substance had been ingested inadvertently. When the Rushden and Diamond's goalkeeper Billy Turley (*Guardian*, 24/12/2004) subsequently tested positive for a recreational drug his suspended two year ban (he had tested positive for the banned steroid nandrolone) was enforced. Turley remains the only British player to be punished for using a performance-enhancing drug. The only English league player to have been found guilty of taking performance-enhancing drugs since this time is Middlesborough's Portuguese international Abel Xavier, who tested positive for the anabolic steroid dianabol during a UEFA Cup tie in Greece in 2005 (*Guardian*, 24/11/2005).

A greater number of positive tests for performance-enhancing drugs have occurred in other European domestic leagues. Between April and October 1997, five players from a number of top French teams tested positive for anabolic steroids (Malcolm, 1998: 18). Similarly, in 2000-2001, nine leading players in Italy's Serie A, and a number of minor players, tested positive for nandrolone ('Testing times for football', BBC Online, 9/5/2001), as did two further Serie A players, Mohamed Kallon

(Inter Milan) and Saadi Al-Gaddafi (Perugia) in 2003. A number of the positive tests in 2000-01 involved leading Dutch international footballers (notably Jaap Stam and Edgar Davids), and with the Dutch captain Frank de Boer also testing positive for nandrolone whilst playing for Spanish team Barcelona, there were suggestions that a common link might have been the Dutch national squad ('Dutch launch drug probe', BBC Online 9/5/2001). But 31 first division players in Portugal also tested positive during a five month period in 2001, suggesting that the use of nandrolone at this time was becoming more widespread (Campbell, 2002).

Notwithstanding the relatively high number of positive tests in Portugal, the data from drug testing in football worldwide do suggest that the use of performance-enhancing drugs in football is still relatively rare. However, there is a widespread recognition among informed observers that the number of positive test results is a very poor indication of the extent of drug use in sport. More detailed investigations of the phenomenon, such as government enquiries, suggest that those who do test positive represent merely the tip of a much larger iceberg. The Dubin Commission in Canada, for instance, concluded that 'many, many more athletes than those actually testing positive have taken advantage of banned substances and practices' and that 'positive test results represent only a small proportion of actual drug users' (Dubin, 1990: 349-350). It therefore seems possible that this pattern of positive drug tests merely scratches the surface of a more widespread phenomenon, as other sources of information on the prevalence of drug taking in football seem to suggest.

Testimonials of Those Involved in Football

A number of allegations of doping made by players and managers also suggest that the number of positive drug tests is a poor indicator of the extent of drug use in football. In 1999, Dr. Wilfried Schiesslir (club doctor with German Bundesliga club Nuremburg) and Robert Louis Dreyfus (head of Adidas and president of Olympique Marseilles) called for the liberalization of anti-doping laws in football because the 'current system of doping control is flawed' (*Observer*, 17/10/1999). In 2002, Dr. Michel D'Hooghe, chairman of FIFA's medical commission, argued that players across Europe were using erythropoietin (EPO), human growth hormone and anabolic steroids. He further claimed that 'high profile stars' had started to employ their own medical specialists and that doctors known to have been active in administering performance-enhancing drugs in cycling and endurance skiing were 'suddenly appear(ing) around football clubs all over Europe' (*Observer*, 31/3/2002). Players such as Emmanuel Petit, Marc Overmars and Gianluca Vialli have made similar, non-specific, allegations that leading players in the game were using performance-enhancing drugs to cope with the increasing number of games and the related physical demands on players. In 1999, for instance, Petit said that, 'If the present number of games continues, something is going to give. We will all have to take drugs to survive. Some footballers already do. I know that' (cited in Campbell, 2002).

Perhaps more interesting, however, is the testimony of Arsenal manager Arsene Wenger. Speaking in 2004 Wenger claimed that some players joining Arsenal had displayed symptoms of EPO use. He said, 'We have had some players come to us at Arsenal from other clubs abroad and their red blood cell count has been abnormally high. That kind of thing makes you wonder.' He went on to exonerate the players, stating that 'There are clubs who dope players without players knowing. The club might say that they were being injected with vitamins and the player would not know that it was something different' (*Independent*, 8/10/2004; *Guardian*, 9/10/2004). Wenger's comments are based on tangible evidence derived from Arsenal's own blood testing programme. The evidence upon which Wenger based his suggestion that such players had been subject to club-administered doping regimes, is less clear.

That such organized and systematic doping occurs in European football is, however, indicated by the testimony of a number of retired players. For example, two former Marseilles players have publicly stated that the club provided players with performance-enhancing drugs. In his autobiography (published in 2002) Marcel Desailly wrote that club chairman Bernard Tapie had instructed the squad to take pills before big matches and that whilst some team mates, such as Didier Deschamp, refused, Desailly himself took the tablets 'several' times. Desailly was not sure what these pills were, but he recalled that the box of tablets contained the warning that: 'This medicine, above a certain dose, can be considered as a doping substance for high-level sportsmen' (Campbell, 2002). Four years later midfielder Jean-Jacques Edelie made further allegations in his autobiography. Edelie confessed that he agreed to take an illicit substance prior to the 1993 Champions League Final. Moreover, he argued that performance-enhancing drug use occurred in all but one of the clubs for which he had played, and that at Marseilles, 'we all (except Rudi Voller) took a series of injections and I felt different during the game, as my physique responded differently under strain' ('Marseille doping scandal rocks Milan', channel4.com, 21/1/2006). Only one Marseilles player (Christophe Dugarry) tested positive for a banned substance, and then some years later (*Guardian*, 30/6/99), though he was subsequently acquitted of a doping offence due to a technicality when the French FA ruled that the doctor who conducted the test was not on their list of authorized testers (*Observer*, 17/10/99).

In contrast to the Marseilles evidence, allegations of a systematic doping programme at Spartak Moscow football club arose directly from the positive test of a player. Yegor Titov tested positive for bromantan (a stimulant and masking agent) whilst playing for Russia against Wales in November 2003. The Russian media subsequently claimed that this drug had been administered as part of a systematic doping programme at Spartak, citing the sudden withdrawal of Spartak players on the eve of Russia's match against Ireland in September 2003 as suspicious. Two former Spartak players, Vladislav Vashchyuk and Maxim Demenko, also provided testimony of their participation in this doping programme. Demenko recalled that 'Small white pills were given to first team players before each game', and Vashchyuk said that doctors often used a drip to administer banned drugs. Following the election of a new Russian Football Union president, it also emerged that Spartak had sacked their team doctor after the 2003 positive test, and that another Spartak doctor had been disciplined by the national governing body (Mosnews, 2005).

Evidence from testimonials, therefore, suggests that organized doping programmes have existed at a number of leading clubs in a number of different European countries. These specific testimonials were not volunteered by players who were found guilty of doping offences, but came from those who were neither accused nor convicted of taking performance-enhancing drugs. Indeed, the players have largely projected themselves as 'victims' in these scenarios, either given insufficient information or misled by doctors and football club administrators, a scenario similar to that portrayed by Wenger. Clearly, some have stood to benefit commercially from such revelations (e.g. through increased sales of an autobiography), but this notwithstanding, these testimonials point to a relatively coherent and consistent picture: in some European countries, leading football clubs have administered systematic doping programmes.

Government and Judicial Investigations

Across sport, the most penetrating investigations of doping have come from government inquiries and quasi-legal investigations. It is widely acknowledged, for instance, that the Dubin Commission of Inquiry established in Canada following the positive drug test of Ben Johnson at the 1988 Olympic Games (Dubin, 1990), and the inquiry headed by Australian Senator Black (Australian Parliament, 1989), have furnished us with the greatest understanding of the use of performance-enhancing drugs in sport. Though neither looked at drug use in football there have been two inquiries–one in Germany and one in Italy–that are relevant here.

Post-unification inquiries into the state sponsored doping programmes operated in East Germany provide perhaps the most comprehensive and compelling evidence of doping in sport. These inquiries have shown that elite athletes were systematically doped by the East German state and tested in the GDR prior to competition to ensure that athletes representing their country could evade official drug testing. As in other sports, the East German national football teams were 'required to use drugs in order to compete successfully against other nations' (Spitzer, 2006: 112). Research has, for instance, revealed records of drugs tests which demonstrated that two thirds of whole teams were using amphetamines to enhance performance (Spitzer 2000: 351). The use of performance-enhancing drugs within the national leagues was officially forbidden by the East German state, in an attempt to promote greater playing equality between clubs. Despite these regulations, evidence suggests that individual clubs did not comply with state orders, and used the knowledge developed at the national level within their own club-based systematic doping programmes. It is quite clear therefore that football was no different from any other sport in communist East Germany, and that systematic doping programmes existed at both club and international levels prior to 1989.

The events surrounding the Italian inquiries into drug use in football are rather more complicated. Because they involved leading players at a leading club, and because Italy is part of the democratic West, where systematic doping programmes have been less common, the findings were more sensationalized. Though events unfolded in an unpredictable manner, the data were derived from a range of sources, providing triangulation and more confidence in their validity.

Events were triggered by an interview with the then AS Roma manager, Zdenek Zeman, published in *L'Espresso Magazine* in July 1998 (Grayson and Ioannidis, 2001: 247). Zeman stated that the use of performance-enhancing drugs was rife in Serie A, and suggested that football needed to 'come out of the pharmacy'. In particular he referred to two Juventus players, Gianluca Vialli and Alessandro Del Piero, whose muscular development had 'surprised him'. Given the implication of illegal drug use, Vialli and Del Piero started legal proceedings against Zeman. Debate in the Italian and international press generated pressure sufficient to lead the Public Attorney of Turin, Raffaele Guarinielo, to start an investigation. Guarinielo interviewed first Zeman and then Sandro Donati, a member of the Italian National Olympic Committee's (CONI) medical commission, leading to two significant findings.

On the basis of the interview with Zeman, Guarinielo ordered a raid on the Juventus premises which revealed that the club held 281 different pharmaceutical substances. The majority of these substances were not on the IOC's list of banned substances, though at least five anti-inflammatory drugs containing banned substances were found (*The Times*, 1/12/2004). It was, however, the sheer quantity of pharmaceuticals found that raised suspicions; as Gianmartino Benzi, medical advisor to Guarinielo, noted, 'the club was equipped like a small hospital' (*The Independent*, 1/12/2004). As a witness at the subsequent trial suggested, 'either the players were always sick or they took drugs without justification ... to improve performance ('Justice of the pieces', SI.com, 7/12/2005).

Donati (2001) claims that his accusations of irregular testing procedures led Guarinielo to order that the IOC accredited Acqua Acetosa laboratory in Rome be searched. The laboratory was closed after police discovered documents hidden in air vents in the building. It was later revealed that some documents relating to drug tests in football had disappeared (*Times*, 27/11/2004) and that, according to the Milan newspaper, *Corriere Della Sera*, a Udinese player had tested positive following a match against Roma in 1997, but laboratory technicians had been told not to publicize the result (Grayson and Ioannidis, 2001: 247). The president of CONI resigned and the director of the laboratory was sacked when it came to light that some of the doping controls conducted on footballers did not include tests for the detection of anabolic steroids or other hormones. Further documents revealed that some 24 Parma players had abnormally high haematocrit levels, indicative of the probable use of EPO. Government raids on doping laboratories around Italy discovered 'a trail of abuse involving officers who had falsified documents and were guilty of fraud in relation to doping' (Donati, 2001). The Acqua Acetosa laboratory remained closed until September 2000, and it is probably no coincidence that so many players during the following season tested positive for nandrolone.

The steady accumulation of evidence led Gauriniello to bring charges against two Juventus club officials in January 2002. The initial charge was that Juventus managing director Antonio Giraudo and club doctor Riccardo Agricola were involved in supplying pharmaceutical products to several of the club's players between July 1994 and September 1998, a period in which Juventus won three Italian titles and the European Cup. The substances in question were legal, but administered in such a manner as to produce the same effects as illicit substances ('Juventus Doping Trial Opens', BBC Online, 31/1/2002).

The trial lasted almost two years, during which time some of the world's leading players, including Zinedine Zidane, Roberto Baggio, Del Piero and Vialli, were called as witnesses. The players stated that they had taken legal substances—for instance, Zidane revealed that he had used creatine—but the testimony of two court-appointed independent witnesses proved crucial. Eugenio Muller, a pharmacologist, stated that there could be 'no therapeutic justification' for the club's administration of prescription-only drugs (*Independent*, 1/12/2004). Three drugs were cited in particular: Samyr, an anti-depressant, was taken by 23 players; Neoton, a drug containing creatine used for heart conditions, by 14 players; and Voltaren, a pain killer and anti-inflammatory drug, by 32 players. In the case of Voltaren in particular, the drug was not used to treat isolated or occasional injuries; rather, according to Muller, its use was, 'planned, continuous and substantial' (*Independent*, 1/12/2004).

Juventus lawyers protested that the use of these substances was not illegal and club president Vittorio Chiusano argued that these were 'products widely used by many other Italian footballers' ('Juventus doping trial opens', BBC Online, 31/1/2002). Post-trial revelations suggest that he was probably correct, but new charges introduced during the trial relating to the use of EPO proved more damning. Club records produced in court indicated that Juventus' own blood testing programme revealed particularly high hematocrit levels from a number of players, amongst them leading internationals Didier Deschamp, Del Piero and Angelo Di Livio. On two occasions Deschamp recorded increases of 20 percent in the space of a few months (Donati, 2001). Deschamp's red blood cell count of 51.2 percent (45-47 percent is considered normal) would have been sufficient for cycling's international governing body (the UCI) to withdraw a cyclist from racing (*The Times*, 1/12/2004). Reviewing these records, a leading haematologist, Giuseppe d'Onofrio, said that it was 'very probable' that Deschamps was among seven players who had taken small doses of EPO. Moreover, d'Onofrio was 'practically certain' that two other players—Antonio Conte and Alessio Tacchinardi—had used EPO to overcome bouts of anaemia (*Independent*, 1/12/2004) and other reports have suggested that the judge listed as many as 20 players involved in the 'chronic use' of EPO (*Independent on Sunday*, 27/3/2005).

The court found this evidence compelling, and in November 2004, Agricola was given a 22 month suspended jail sentence for supplying performance-enhancing drugs, barred from practising medicine for 22 months and fined 2000 Euros. Giraudo was cleared of all charges and a third defendant, Giovanni Rossano, a pharmacist accused of supplying drugs on false prescriptions, agreed a plea bargain and was fined 5000 Euros. In the aftermath of the trial, a number of commentators questioned the consistency of the sentencing which implied that Agricola was acting independently ('Justice of the pieces: conviction of Juventus doctor in doping case leaves team off hook', SI.Com, 7/12/2004); it is unlikely, for example, that Agricola alone had funded the purchase of 281 different drugs.

Evidence from Surveys

Though government and judicial inquiries into drug use in football have been few in number, where they have been undertaken, legally scrutinized evidence has been produced which indicates that organized and systematic doping programmes have occurred in elite European football. However, by their very nature, inquiries tend to provide us with depth rather than breadth of understanding and can therefore only point us towards the existence of relatively small pockets of drug taking in football. What is interesting about the Juventus trial is not simply that it provides almost incontrovertible evidence of a club-administered doping programme, but that the doping which it revealed is almost identical to that described in various player and manager testimonials. There are, therefore, good grounds for believing that such practices are more widespread.

An alternative way of assessing how widespread the use of performance-enhancing drugs is in sport is through the use of athlete surveys. A number of such surveys have been undertaken in different sports and different countries (Scarpino, 1990; Anshel, 1991. See also Waddington, 2005) but there has been, to date, just one comprehensive survey of drug use in professional football, conducted by ourselves and colleagues in 2003. With the aid and support of the English Professional Footballers Association (PFA), reply-paid postal questionnaires were sent to the home addresses of all 2,863 members of the Association. 706 questionnaires were returned, giving a response rate of just under 25 percent. Such surveys are not without their methodological problems, for it is clear that athletes have a great deal, potentially, to lose from participation in a survey which requires the truthful reporting of covert and illegitimate activities. As Mottram (2005: 370) notes, elite athletes are generally reluctant to discuss drug use in their sport and thus low response rates are to be expected. Encouragingly, there was an even spread of responses from players of different kinds (i.e. players were evenly distributed across the top 4 divisions of English football, represented a cross-section of ages, and were spread between regular first team and 'squad' players), suggesting that a representative sample was obtained. In an attempt to improve response rates the survey asked not about players' personal use of drugs but, less threateningly, asked them to estimate the prevalence of drug use in the sport and whether they personally knew players who used drugs. Although such surveys cannot be expected to give a precise indication of the extent of drug use in sport, it is important to bear in mind that the results will almost certainly underestimate, rather than overestimate, the real level of drug use.

One-half of all players (49 percent) felt that there was no use of illicit performance-enhancing drugs in professional football. About a third of players (34 percent) felt that performance-enhancing drugs were being used by some players, though the great majority felt that their use was rare. Twenty-three percent of players felt that performance-enhancing drugs were used by under 2 percent of players; 8 percent felt that between 3-5 percent of players used such drugs and less than 1 percent felt that performance-enhancing drugs were being used by 10 percent or more of their fellow professionals. Seventeen percent of players had no opinion as to whether or not performance-enhancing drugs were being used.

Almost 6 percent of respondents (39 players in total) indicated that they personally knew players who used performance-enhancing drugs. Those who personally knew players who used performance-enhancing drugs were spread across all four divisions, with 18 percent playing for Premier League clubs, 24 percent for clubs in Division One of the Nationwide League, 36 percent for Second Division clubs and 21 percent for clubs in Division Three. Of the players who indicated that they knew players who used performance-enhancing drugs, most (68 percent) indicated that the drug using players were at a previous club, though one in five indicated that the drug using players were at their current club, and 12 percent indicated that they knew drug using players at *both* their current and previous clubs. In all, 4 Premier League players indicated that they knew players at their current club who used performance-enhancing drugs, while 2 First Division players, 4 Second Division players and 4 Third Division players also indicated they knew players at their current club who used performance-enhancing drugs.

The research also found that the use of recreational drugs is considerably more widespread than the use of performance-enhancing drugs. Only 29 percent of players felt that recreational drugs were not used by professional footballers. Almost 28 percent of respondents felt that recreational drugs were used by fewer than 2 percent of players, 13 percent felt that between 3-5 percent of players used recreational drugs, 9 percent felt they were used by 6-10 percent of players while 4 percent felt that recreational drugs were used by more than 10 percent of players. 18 percent of players had no opinion about how widely they were used.

Nearly one-half of all players (45 percent) indicated that they personally knew players who used recreational drugs. Among Premier League players, 31 percent personally knew players who used such drugs, compared with 45 percent of players in the First Division of the Nationwide League, 44 percent of Second Division players and 52 percent of Third Division players. Of those who knew players who use recreational drugs, 15 percent indicated that the players who used such drugs were at their present club, 63 percent indicated the drug-using players were at a previous club, while 23 percent knew players at *both* their current and previous clubs who used recreational drugs. In all, 16 Premier League players indicated that they knew players at their current club who used recreational drugs, while 23 First Division players, 21 Second Division players and 39 Third Division players also indicated they knew players at their current club who used recreational drugs.

These data provide clear evidence that performance-enhancing drugs are used in English professional football, though their use appears to be quite rare; by contrast, the use of recreational drugs is more common. That player estimates of the proportion of footballers using performance-enhancing drugs are relatively low, and that players with personal knowledge of performance-enhancing drug users are spread across the divisions, suggest that in English football the doping of players as part of systematic, club-run programmes is not widespread. Rather, those using performance-enhancing drugs normally act independently of their employers.

DISCUSSION

In this final section we wish to address three questions which arise from our examination of the data relating to the use of performance-enhancing drugs in European football. First, how does doping in football compare with that in other sports? Second, are there grounds for believing that performance-enhancing drug use in football varies from country to country? And third, why is the scale of drug use in football indicated by the testing programmes much lower than that indicated by other sources?

The Prevalence of Doping in Football Relative to Other Elite Sports

The data reviewed above, which are taken from several sources, suggest that drug use appears to be less prevalent in football than in a number of other sports. For example, of the 23,478 drug tests conducted in football internationally in 2005, just 1.46 percent proved positive compared to an average of 2.12 percent for international sports in general (WADA, 2005). Moreover, a survey of 1,300 elite British athletes across nine sports (including football), conducted by the *Independent* in 1998, found that 54 percent of all athletes believed that up to 30 percent of competitors in their sport were using performance-enhancing drugs; 5 percent believed that between 30 percent and 60 percent were using drugs; and 4 percent believed that over 60 percent of competitors were using drugs. In this survey, 20 percent of those from the sports of weightlifting and powerlifting admitted using anabolic agents, and 15 percent of those from rugby league admitted using testosterone. In contrast to the finding that almost one-half of all PFA members felt that there was no use of illicit performance-enhancing drugs in professional football, no weightlifters or rugby league players, and just 3 percent of track and field athletes responding to the *Independent* survey, made a comparable claim. Indeed, in a more recent *Independent* survey, 84 percent of footballers in England expressed the view that the sport had no problem at all with the use of performance-enhancing drugs (12/4/2006).

This kind of cross-sport comparison seems to indicate that the use of performance-enhancing drugs in football, at least English football, is rather more limited than it is in other sports. One explanation for this disparity is the high skill-level required by football compared to other sports. All sports require a combination of physical strength and power and technical skill, and those sports which place a premium on the former rather than the latter are the sports in which the performance gains from the use of drugs are likely to be greatest (Malcolm, 1998: 19). Thus, participants in those sports which are based largely on physical strength and power–weightlifting, cycling, and athletics, for instance–are most likely to use performance-enhancing drugs, whilst those sports which are primarily skill-based, such as football, are likely to have lower rates of performance-enhancing drug use. Such an argument has been advanced by Sepp Blatter, who has suggested that 'footballers have absolutely nothing to gain from taking drugs because–in contrast to other sports– they need a vast array of qualities and skills to succeed in the game, such as strength, endurance, speed, intelligence, tactical understanding and ball control' (2004: 3).

Whilst such structural properties of different sports are clearly important factors influencing whether or not participants are likely to use performance-enhancing substances, and the types of substances they use, the balance between strength and skill requirements in a sport is not static, but varies over time (as evidenced by Emmanuel Petit's comments cited earlier). It is not the case, as Blatter claims, that 'footballers have absolutely nothing to gain' from taking drugs. In addition to the data on the use of performance-enhancing drugs discussed above, there is growing evidence to suggest that footballers use significant quantities and varieties of legal pharmaceutical products in search of improved performance. For instance, the survey of members of the English PFA found that 58 percent of players used vitamin pills, 37 percent used creatine and 24 percent used protein powders (Waddington et al., 2005). The comments of FIFA's Chief Medical Officer, Jiri Dvorak, confirm this impression. Dvorak has stated that FIFA's Sports Medical Committee is aware that creatine is 'widely used' by footballers in Italy,

France, Portugal and Spain (2004: 18) (interestingly the English league was not mentioned in this list) and has further commented that he has been struck by 'how much medication is used at FIFA tournaments' (2004: 19).

In the wake of the Italian judicial inquiry, two further 'scandals' provided further support for the claim that it is not uncommon for footballers actively to seek to improve performance through the use of pharmaceutical substances. In April 2005, film footage was broadcast which showed Parma footballer Fabio Cannavaro using a drip on the eve of the 1999 UEFA Cup final. It was later claimed that the drip contained Neoton (*International Herald and Tribune*, 30/4/2005), a drug cited in the Juventus trial, and that the film had been made 'as a joke' by team mates (*Deccan Herald*, 30/4/2005). Juan Sebastion Veron indicated that the club made the substance available to all the players and he further suggested that 'All the teams (in Italy) use it' (Reuters, 2005). Secondly, in 2005 Florentine public prosecutor Luigi Bocciolini opened an investigation into the deaths of three former Fiorentina players whose deaths were suspected of being linked to their use of drugs as players. The suspicion stemmed from Guariniello's investigation, which revealed a high incidence of cancer, leukaemia and disease of the nervous system amongst players who had appeared for top Italian clubs. Former Fiorentina player Nello Saltutti told Guariniello that before every match 'they gave us medicines, telling us they were vitamins' (*Guardian*, 3/3/2005). One such drug was Micoren, banned by the IOC in 2000. Despite warnings that prolonged use of Micoren could have negative consequences for the arteries, Saltutti claimed to have used it approximately 300 times during a 500 match career. In 2003, at the age of 56, he died of a heart attack.

Although a clear distinction should be drawn between these events and the illegal use of drugs to enhance sporting performance, drug use demonstrates a perceived need amongst footballers to enhance physical performance, and a willingness on their part to use medical substances to obtain that goal. Moreover, the evidence quite consistently points toward the use of products (both legal and illegal) which build stamina and improve cardiovascular fitness. It might be concluded, therefore, that whilst the physical requirements of football mean that drug taking to enhance performance may not be as widespread as it is in sports such as cycling and weightlifting, footballers still have use for such substances. Moreover, recent developments in the way that the game is played–in particular, the increasing pace of the game and the increased number of games players at top clubs are expected to play in a season—suggest that the demands for these substances might well be increasing and thus that patterns of drug use in football may converge with those in more strength- and power-based sports in future.

The Use of Performance-Enhancing Drugs in Football in Different European Countries

Our second question relates to the extent of the use of performance-enhancing drugs in football in different European countries. The evidence reviewed here suggests that in contrast to Italy, in particular, the use of performance-enhancing drugs and the administration of systematic doping programmes are much less common in England. Can such a contention be justified?

Waddington argues that the increased use of performance-enhancing drugs in sport is the product of two social processes: the medicalization of social life in general and of sport in particular, and the increasing competitiveness of sport, its de-amateurization, politicization and commercialization (2000: 127-128). However, the degree to which these two processes have converged appears to vary from sport to sport and from nation to nation. One notable aspect of the development of sports medicine has been the relative slowness with which it became established in England (Waddington, 1996). Moreover, research conducted into the contemporary provision of sports medicine in English professional football has indicated that football club doctors are usually family doctors, recruited on the basis of family or personal connections with the club. This research similarly pointed towards an 'old boy's network' of recruitment amongst physiotherapists at football clubs. Significantly, few of the medical staff working in professional football clubs have specialist qualifications in sports medicine or much experience of practising medicine in other sports contexts, and very few indicated that sports medicine was their major work interest (Waddington et. al., 2001; Waddington, 2002). Whether judged in terms of club doctors' methods of appointment, qualifications and experience, or their generally modest salaries, the medical care of players has been viewed as a low priority in English football. It might be argued therefore that, by comparison with the situation in some other European countries, English football has been relatively untouched by the broader medicalization process and this has had the unintended consequence of limiting the extent of the application of sports medicine in general, and the use of drugs in particular, to the search for improved performance.

An important caveat to this argument, however, is to note the international nature of football, and the increasing heterogeneity of English football in particular. The English football league is the most cosmopolitan in the world (Maguire and Pearton, 2000) and particularly notable has been the influence not just of overseas players, but also overseas managers in recent times. If, as some evidence indicates, drug use is more prevalent and more organized in some continental countries, then the recruitment by English clubs of players and managers from clubs in those countries may have some unintended consequences. In particular, it may lead to the increased use not only of the legitimate principles of sports in the search for improved performance, but also to the increased use of illegal doping practices.

Doping Control in Football

Finally, why is it that the scale of drug use in football as indicated by testing programmes is much lower than that indicated by other sources? First, it should be re-emphasized that few people believe that drugs tests show the true extent of doping in any sport. For instance, though we now know that illegal drug use was widespread during the 1998 Tour de France, not one rider tested positive for performance-enhancing drugs during the event (Waddington, 2000: ch. 9). But while general criticisms can be made of the ability of doping control programmes to reveal the prevalence of drug use, particular criticisms can be made of the doping control programmes in football. The criticism falls into the following categories: failures in testing procedure, attempts by clubs to circumvent drugs testing, and the inability of football administrators properly to enforce doping controls.

As revealed in the Juventus inquiry, during the 1990s there appear to have been specific instances of malpractice by testers which served to obscure the extent of drug use (e.g. by testing for a limited range of substances), or to cover up those positive tests which did occur. It is interesting to note that the re-opening of the Rome Acqua Acetosa laboratory in 2000 coincided with an unparalleled number of positive tests in Italian football in the following season (largely for the banned steroid nandrolone). Italian football now conducts an extensive doping control programme entailing three times as many tests as in English football (*Times*, 19/10/2005), including the testing of two players from each side after every Serie A match (*Observer*, 31/3/2002). As stringent as this testing programme appears, it is not mandatory for players to take these tests. The regulators state that a refusal will make a player ineligible for the national side, but when Lazio midfielder Rino Gattuso failed to take a urine test in March 2005, he was selected to play for the national side against Scotland just a week later (*Independent on Sunday*, 27/3/2005).

Testing procedures in English football are similarly problematic. Though the Football Association claims that football is the most tested sport—there were 1516 tests carried out between April 2004 and March 2005 (*Guardian*, 18/6/2005)—such is the scale of the professional game in England, and such is the distribution of tests throughout different levels of the game, that the testing programme appears to have only a limited deterrent effect. For instance, tests are rarely conducted after professional football matches, with only eight of the 380 Premiership matches in 2000-01 subject to doping controls (*Observer*, 31/3/2002). Indeed, the survey of PFA members indicated that only about a third of professional footballers are likely to be tested during the course of a season, and that a substantial majority (60 percent) felt that they were unlikely to be tested in the next 12 months. This compares very badly with other sports in the UK. For instance, a Sports Council survey (1996) found that 77 percent of elite track and field athletes had been tested by the Sports Council and 37 percent had been tested by other agencies in the previous year. Former Liverpool manager Gerard Houllier has suggested that any club can expect to be visited only two or three times a year by testers, and has called for tests to be more frequent.[3]

Concerns have also been expressed about the rigour of the testing procedures in English football. In October 2003 England and Manchester United defender Rio Ferdinand failed to present himself to doping control officers at the club's training ground. Ferdinand claimed that, due to the stress of moving house, he had forgotten that he had been required to provide a sample. Ferdinand was subsequently suspended from football for eight months for his failure to undergo the drugs test (failure to comply with testing is deemed an offence equivalent to testing positive for a performance-enhancing drug), but, more interestingly for present purposes, the inquiry into this incident revealed how lax procedures had been. What was clear from the Ferdinand case was that at that time there was no requirement for testers to accompany footballers until they provided a sample (*Guardian*, 19/10/2004).

Rather, testers were forced to act through club medical officers (*Independent on Sunday*, 30/11/2003) who then presented players for testing. Such an arrangement is unusual in sport, for it presents the opportunity for players, in collaboration with the club's medical staff, to avoid testing positive (e.g. through the administration of a masking drug). Thus, whilst doping control in English football may appear relatively comprehensive, the sampling and testing procedures have been such that users of performance-enhancing drugs could have evaded testing positive.

A further point of concern is the extent to which clubs perform their own testing programmes. Evidence presented in the Juventus inquiry demonstrated that the club had an internal drug testing programme (SI.com, 7/12/2004) and, following Ferdinand Couto's positive test for nanadrolone in 2001, his club, Lazio, stated that they regularly performed drug tests on their entire squad (BBC Sport online, 21/4/2001). Internally administered testing programmes appear to be even more widespread amongst English clubs. It has been alleged that 'almost all of England's top clubs require players to give samples several times a season' and that 'all test results are kept secret' (Campbell, 2003). The objection to clubs performing their own drug tests is that this information may enable them to shelter some players from official doping controls (as the East German state did prior to 1989), and indeed, two English clubs, Chelsea (*Guardian*, 9/9/2005) and Arsenal (*Observer*, 23/3/2003), have been sanctioned by the FA for their illegal testing of players.

Finally, it should be noted that various governing bodies of football have been criticized for their commitment to, and their enforcement of, doping controls. In particular, FIFA has clashed with the World Anti-Doping Agency which was formally established on 10 November 1999 with the mission 'to promote, coordinate, and monitor at the international level the fight against doping in sport in all its forms'. Most analysts have seen WADA as a significant development in anti-doping policy. Houlihan (2002: 172) sees it as 'play(ing) an important part in raising the level of confidence in drug testing procedures', but throughout its history FIFA, alongside cycling's UCI, has been WADA's 'sternest critic' (*Guardian*, 4/3/2003). FIFA has continually resisted WADA's attempts to standardize doping procedures and penalties across sports and across national boundaries on the grounds that the imposition of a mandatory two year suspension for performance-enhancing drugs would be 'problematic from a legal perspective because ... it does not take into account the extent of the offender's guilt' (FIFA.com, 22/11/2005). FIFA has therefore insisted on 'individual case management and flexibility when imposing sanctions' (*FIFA Magazine*, Sept. 2004, 68). Bodies like the IOC object, arguing that such clauses mean that standardized minimum penalties cannot be enforced. Indeed, IOC president Jacques Rogge criticized lenient penalties in football after Edgar Davids was given a four month suspension for testing positive for nandrolone ('IOC warns football over drugs bans', BBC Sport online, 27/12/2001). Rogge stated that any sport that did not sign up to the WADA code would be dropped from the Olympic programme (4/3/2003), but at FIFA's centennial congress in Paris in May 2004, three months before the Athens Olympic Games, FIFA and WADA signed a 'cooperative agreement' in which WADA agreed to fully respect FIFA's stipulations of individual case management and flexibility when imposing sanctions, whilst FIFA accepted WADA's right to appeal to the Court of Arbitration for Sport over any football related doping cases. The consequences of allowing FIFA such freedom were illustrated during the Euro 2004 tournament. Croatian Ivica Olic tested positive for a banned substance but was cleared of any doping offence on the grounds that a doctor had provided him with this medication for therapeutic purposes. Under the strict liability rules favoured by WADA and applied in almost all other sports, this defence would not have been accepted (*Guardian*, 21/6/2004).

Inconsistencies between FIFA and other international governing bodies of sport are further compounded by FIFA's inability to gain compliance from national football federations. Sepp Blatter rebuked English FA chairman Geoff Thompson over his handling of the aforementioned Rio Ferdinand case in 2003 (*Guardian*, 17/12/2003) and since then, FIFA has taken harder action against the national associations of France, Italy and the Netherlands, who have been fined between £4500 and £6000 for failing to adhere to FIFA's minimum stipulation for punishing doping infringements (FIFA.com, 28/9/2004; *Guardian*, 19/10/2004). Not only is FIFA out of step with the majority of the world sporting community over punishments for the illegal use of performance-enhancing drugs, but the considerable autonomy wielded by national governing bodies of football provides greater inconsistencies within football itself.

CONCLUSION

By drawing together and triangulating disparate bodies of evidence, we can conclude that the use of performance-enhancing drugs in football is a problem that has not been fully recognized by the game's administrators. In particular, it appears that a number of elite European football clubs have administered their own systematic doping programmes. Whilst there are considerable methodological difficulties with each of the data sources drawn upon here, their reasonably consistent results lead us to believe that we can have a relatively high level of confidence in the accuracy of our depiction of this phenomenon. Moreover, it should be reiterated that as Yesalis et. al. note, any methodological difficulties with these sources are more likely to lead to an underestimate, rather than an overestimate, of drug use in the sport.

We should, however, be circumspect in our claims, for there are both empirical and theoretical grounds to think that the use of performance-enhancing drugs in football is not as widespread as it is in other sports. This claim can only really be judged when significant modifications have been made to the anti-doping programmes operated in football in various international contexts and when, therefore, we have more confidence in their effectiveness as both a deterrent and as a measure of revealing performance-enhancing drug use.

NOTES

1. However, there is a study of drug use by amateur footballers in Cameroon (Ama et. al., 2003).
2. The Mexican FA, its president, the national team doctor, and the chair of the Mexican FA's medical committee were all disciplined for their conduct in relation to this matter (FIFA.com, 27/7/05).
3. Cocaine is a stimulant and therefore technically a performance-enhancing drug. However it is more widely used as a recreational drug, both within and outside of sport.
4. Whilst officials in athletics have long called for the publication of the names of athletes who test negative, Gordon Taylor, chief executive of the PFA is reported to be resistant to such a policy. Journalists have suggested that football administrators fear that the publication of these details would draw attention to how few Premiership players are tested (Guardian, 25/2/2004).

REFERENCES

Anshel, M. H. (1991). A survey of elite athletes on the perceived causes of using banned drugs in sport. *Journal of Sport Behaviour,* 14(4): 283-307.

Australian Parliament. (1989). Drugs in Sport: an Interim Report of the Senate Standing Committee on Environment, Recreation and the Arts. Commonwealth of Australia.

Blatter, S. (2004). Delight and despair. FIFA Magazine, March 2004, p. 3.

Campbell, D. (2002). Is football in denial over drugs? Observer.co.uk, 31/3/2002.

Campbell, D. (2003). Premiership football clubs secretly testing players. The Observer, 23/3/2003.

Cashmore, E. (1996). Making Sense of Sports. London: Routledge, 2nd edition.

Donati, S. (2001). Anti-doping: the fraud behind the stage. Sports Intelligence Unit, Vingsted, Denmark. Reproduced, *www.ergogenics.org/donati.html.*

Dubin, The Hon. C. L. (1990). Commission of Inquiry into the Use of Drugs and Banned Practices Intended to Increase Athletic Performance. Ottawa, Canadian Government Publishing Centre.

Dvorak, J. (2004). There is nothing to gain from using drugs. FIFA Magazine, March 2004, pp.16-19.

FIFA (2004). Activity Report. April 2002-March 2004: 54th Ordinary FIFA Congress, Paris. Zurich: FIFA.

Goode, E. (1997). Between politics and reason: the drug legalization debate. New York: St. Martin's Press.

Grayson, E. and Ioannidis, G. (2001). Drugs, health and sporting values, in John O'Leary (ed.) Drugs and Doping in Sport: Socio-Legal Perspectives. London: Cavendish Publishing, pp. 255-268.

Houlihan, B. (2002). Dying to wing: Doping in sport and the development of anti-doping policy. Strasbourg: Council of Europe Publishing, 2nd edition.

Houlihan, B. (2003). Doping in sport: more problems than solutions?, in Barrie Houlihan (ed.), Sport and Society: a Student Introduction. London: Sage, pp. 218-234.

Joy, B. (1952). Forward Arsenal: the Arsenal Story, 1888-1952. London, Phoen House.

Maguire, J. and Pearton, B. (2000). Global sport and the migration patterns of France '98 World Cup Finals players: Some preliminary observations, in Jon Garland, Dominic Malcolm and Michael Rowe (eds) The Future of Football: Challenges for the Twenty-First Century. London: Frank Cass, pp. 175-189.

Malcolm, D. (1998). White lines, grass and the level playing field, in Singer & Friedlander Review of 1997-98 Season. London: Singer and Friedlander, pp. 17-19.

Matthews, S. (2000). The Way It Was: My Autobiography. London: Headline.

Mosnews. (2005). New Russian Soccer Chief to Probe Spartak Doping Claims. *http://www.mosnews.com/news.2005/05/03/spartakdoping.shtml.*

Mottram, D. R. (ed.). (2005). Drugs in Sport. London: Routledge, 4th Edition.

Reuters. (2005). Veron in Cannavaro video. Reproduced, *http://www.ergogenics.org/neoton.html.*

Scarpino, V, Arrigo, A, Benzi, G. (1990). Evaluation of prevalence of doping among Italian athletes. Lancet, 336: 1048-1050.

Spitzer, G. (2000). Doping in der GDR: Ein historischer Ûberblick zu einer konspirativen Praxis. Klön: Bundesinstitut für Sportwissenschaft.

Spitzer, G. (2006). Sport and the systematic infliction of pain: A case study of state-sponsored mandatory doping in East Germany, in Sigmund Loland, Berit Skirstad and Ivan Waddington (eds), Pain and Injury in Sport: Social and Ethical Analysis. London: Routledge, pp. 109-126.

Sports Council. (1996). Doping Control in the UK: A Survey of the Views of Elite Competitors 1995. Sports Council, London.

UK Sport. (2002). Anti-Doping Report 2001/2002. UK Sport, London.

WADA. (2005). Adverse Analytical Findings Reported by Accredited Laboratories: Overview of results. *http://www.wada-ama.org/rtecontent/document/ LABSTATS_2005.pdf.* 13th June 2006.

Waddington, I. (2002). Jobs for the boys? A study of the employment of club doctors and physiotherapists in English professional football. Soccer and Society, 2002, 3(3): 51-64.

Waddington, I., Roderick, M. and Naik, R. (2001). Methods of appointment and qualifications of club doctors and physiotherapists in English professional football: some problems and issues. *British Journal of Sports Medicine,* 35 (1): 48-53.

Waddington, I. (2000). Sport, health and drugs: a critical sociological perspective. London: E&FN Spon.

Waddington, I. (2005). Changing patterns of drug use in British sport from the 1960s. Sport in History, 25(3): 472-496.

Waddington, I., Malcolm, D., Roderick, M. and Naik, R. (2005). Drug use in English Professional Football. British Journal of Sports Medicine, 2005, 39: e18.

Yesalis, C. E. III, Kopstein, A. N., and Bahrke, M. S. (2001). Difficulties in estimating the prevalence of drug use among athletes, in Wayne Wilson and Edward Derse, (eds), Doping in Elite Sport: The Politics of Drugs in the Olympic Movement. Human Kinetics, Champaign, IL, pp. 43-62.

INDEX